750+
BLOCKBUSTER
PROBLEMS in
BIOLOGY
for NEET

Corporate Office

DISHA PUBLICATION

45, 2nd Floor, Maharishi Dayanand Marg,
Corner Market, Malviya Nagar, New Delhi - 110017
Tel : 49842349 / 49842350

Typeset by Disha DTP Team

www.dishapublication.com
Books & ebooks for School & Competitive Exams

www.mylearninggraph.com
Etests for Competitive Exams

Write to us at feedback_disha@aiets.co.in

Contents

The Living World

1. Which of the classification is considered as a modern phylogenetic system?
   - (a) Linnaeus
   - (b) Bentham and Hooker
   - (c) Hutchinson
   - (d) Engler and Prantl

2. System of classification used by Linnaeus was
   - (a) Natural system
   - (b) Artificial system
   - (c) Phylogenetic system
   - (d) Asexual system

3. The characteristic which define a family are more general than those which define a
   - (a) Genus
   - (b) Class
   - (c) Phylum
   - (d) Cohort

4. The particular purpose of classification of living organisms is to
   - (a) name the living organisms
   - (b) explain the origin of living organisms
   - (c) trace the evolution of living organisms
   - (d) Facilitate identification of unknown organisms

5. Pick up the correct match

Column I (Fathers)		Column II (Branches)
I.	Aristotle	A. Eugenics
II.	Galton	B. Green Revolution
III.	Gregor Mendel	C. Zoology
IV.	Borlaug	D. Genetics

   - (a) I-A, II-B, III-C, IV-D
   - (b) II-A, IV-B, I-C, III-D
   - (c) III-A, I-B, II-C, IV-D
   - (d) IV-A, III-B, II-C, I-D

6. The branch of biology which deals with the study of identification, nomenclature and classification of organisms is
   - (a) Exobilogy
   - (b) Ecology
   - (c) Taxonomy
   - (d) Toxicology

7. Binomial nomenclature means writing the name of a plant into two names. These two names refer to
   - (a) class and order
   - (b) family and genus
   - (c) genus and species
   - (d) order and genus

8. In five kingdom system of classification, how many kingdoms contain eukaryotes?
   - (a) four kingdoms
   - (b) one kingdom
   - (c) two kingdoms
   - (d) three kingdoms

9. Which one of the taxonomic aids can give comprehensive account of complete compiled information of any one genus or family at a particular time?

(a) Taxonomic key   (b) Flora

(c) Herbarium   (d) Monograph

(e) Dictionary

10. Which one of the following organisms is scientifically correctly named, correctly printed according to the International Rules of Nomenclature and correctly described?

(a) *Musca domestica* - The common house lizard, a reptile.

(b) *Plasmodium falciparum* – A protozoan pathogen causing the most serious type of malaria.

(c) *Felis tigris* - The Indian tiger, well protected in Gir forests.

(d) *E.coli* - Full name *Entamoeba coli*, a commonly occurring bacterium in human intestine.

11. Scientific name of Mango plant is *Mangifera indica* (Linn.) Santapau. In the above name Santapau refers to

(a) Variety of Mango

(b) A taxonomist who proposed the present nomenclature in honour of Linnaeus

(c) A scientist who for the first time described Mango plant

(d) A scientist who changed the name proposed by Linnaeus and proposed present name

12. Match the following and choose the correct combination from the options given.

Column I (Common Name)	Column II (Taxonomic Category Family)
(A) Man	(1) Poaceae
(B) *Datura*	(2) Anacardiaceae
(C) Mango	(3) Solanaceae
(D) Wheat	(4) Hominidae

(a) A-4, B-3, C-2, D-1

(b) A-4, B-3, C-1, D-2

(c) A-1, B-2, C-3, D-4

(d) A-1, B-3, C-2, D-4

(e) A-3, B-4, C-1, D-2

ANSWER KEY

1	2	3	4	5	6	7	8	9	10
(d)	(b)	(a)	(d)	(b)	(c)	(c)	(a)	(d)	(c)

11	12
(d)	(a)

Biological Classification

1.

Column-I		Column-II	
A.	Phycomycetes	I.	Sac fungi
B.	Ascomycetes	II.	Algal fungi
C.	Basidiomycetes	III.	Fungi imperfecti
D.	Deuteromycetes	IV.	Club fungi

The correct combination is –

(a) A – II, B – I, C – IV, D – III

(b) A – II, B – IV, C – I, D – III

(c) A – IV, B – I, C – II, D – III

(d) A – IV, B – III, C – II, D – I

2. Which is the correct option for the all given characteristics of fungi ?

I. It includes unicellular as well as multicellular fungi.

II. In multicellular forms hyphae are branched and septate.

III. Conidiophore produces conidia (spores) exogenously in chain.

IV. Sexual spores are ascopores produced endogenously in chain.

V. Fruiting body is called ascocarp.

(a) Phycomycetes

(b) Sac fungi

(c) Club fungi

(d) Fungi imperfecti

3. Choose the correct statements that correctly apply to kingdom Fungi.

(a) Some fungi form beneficial interrelationships with plants

(b) Certain fungi are natural sources of antibiotics

(c) The fungal life cycle typically includes a spore stage

(d) All

4. The chemical compounds produced by the host plants to protect themselves against fungal infection is

(a) phytotoxin

(b) pathogen

(c) phytoalexins

(d) hormone

5. Which of the following is not correctly matched?

(a) Root knot disease - *Meloidogyne javanica*

(b) Smut of bajra - *Tolysporium penicillariae*

(c) Covered smut of barley - *Ustilago nuda*

(d) Late blight of potato - *Phytophthora infestans*

6. A few organisms are known to grow and multiply at temperatures of 100–105ºC. They belong to

(a) marine archaebacteria

(b) thermophilic sulphur bacteria

(c) blue-green algae (cyanobacteria)

(d) thermophilic, subaerial fungi

7. Match the items in column I with those in column II and choose the correct option

	Column-I		Column-II
(A)	Ascus	1.	*Spirulina*
(B)	Basidium	2.	*Penicillium*
(C)	Protista	3.	*Agaricus*
(D)	Cyanobacteria	4.	*Euglera*
(E)	Animalia	5.	Sponges

(a) A – 2, B – 3, C – 4, D – 5 E – 1

(b) A – 1, B – 2, C – 3, D – 5 E – 4

(c) A – 2, B – 5, C – 3, D – 1 E – 4

(d) A – 1, B – 2, C – 3, D – 4 E – 5

(e) A – 2, B – 3, C – 4, D – 1 E – 5

8. Which one is the wrong pairing for the disease and its causal organism?

(a) Black rust of wheat - *Puccinia graminis*

(b) Loose smut of wheat - *Ustilago nuda*

(c) Root-knot of vegetables - *Meloidogyne sp*

(d) Late blight of potato - *Alternaria solani*

9. Slimy mass of protoplasm with many nuclei and an *Amoeba*-like thalloid body is a characteristic feature of

(a) ascomycetes

(b) actinomycetes

(c) phycomycetes

(d) basidiomycetes

(e) myxomycetes

10. Which one of the following pairs is wrongly matched while the remaining three are correct?

(a) *Penicillium* - Conidia

(b) Water *hyacinth* - Runner

(c) *Bryophyllum* - Leaf buds

(d) *Agave* - Bulbils

11. Consider the following four statements whether they are correct or wrong?

(A) The sporophyte in liverworts is more elaborate than that in mosses

(B) Salvinia is heterosporous

(C) The life cycle in all seed-bearing plants is diplontic

(D) In Pinus male and female cones are borne on different trees

(a) Statements (A) and (C)

(b) Statements (A) and (D)

(c) Statements (B) and (C)

(d) Statements (A) and (B)

12. Match column I with column II and choose the right option

	Column-I		Column-II
A.	*Rhizopus*	1.	ascomycetes
B.	*Penicillium*	2.	basidiomycetes
C.	*Ustilago*	3.	deuteromycetes
D.	*Alternaria*	4.	phycomycetes

(a) A – 4, B – 3, C – 1, D – 2

(b) A – 2, B – 3, C – 4, D – 1

(c) A – 4, B – 1, C – 2, D – 3

(d) A – 3, B – 4, C – 2, D – 1

(e) A – 2, B – 1, C – 4, D – 3

13. Match column I with column II and select the correct option.

	Column-I (Kingdom)		Column-II (Class)
A.	Morels	1.	Deuteromycetes
B.	Smut	2.	Ascomycetes
C.	Bread mould	3.	Basidiomycetes
D.	Imperfect fungi	4.	Phycomycetes

(a) A – 3, B – 4, C – 1, D – 2

(b) A – 2, B – 3, C – 4, D – 1

(c) A – 4, B – 1, C – 2, D – 3

(d) A – 3, B – 4, C – 2, D – 1

(e) A – 2, B – 1, C – 4, D – 3

14. The most abundant prokaryotes helpful to humans in making curd from milk and in production of antibiotics are the ones categorised as

(a) Cyanobacteria

(b) Archaebacteria

(c) Chemosynthetic autotrophs

(d) Heterotrophic bacteria

15. Movements by pseudopodia of *Amoeba* are due to change in

(a) pressure   (b) atmosphere

(c) temperature   (d) viscosity

16. The most abundant prokaryotes helpful to humans in making curd from milk and in production of antibiotics are the ones categorised as :

(a) Cyanobacteria

(b) Archaebacteria

(c) Chemosynthetic autotrophs

(d) Heterotrophic bacteria

17. Match the following and choose the correct combination from the options given.

Column I (Group)		Column II (Example)
A.	Eubacteria	1. *Trichoderma*
B.	Dinoflagellates	2. *Albugo*
C.	Phycomycetes	3. *Gonyaulax*
D.	Deuteromycetes	4. *Anabaena*

(a) A – 1; B – 2; C – 3; D – 4

(b) A – 2; B – 3; C – 4; D – 1

(c) A – 4; B – 3; C – 2; D – 1

(d) A – 3; B – 4; C – 1; D – 2

(e) A – 4; B – 3; C – 1; D – 2

18. Match column I with Column II and choose the correct option.

Column I		Column II
(A)	Ernst Mayr	1. Discovered viroids
(B)	Whittaker	2. Gave the name virus
(C)	Pasteur	3. Proposed Five Kingdom classification
(D)	Diener	4. Darwin of the 20th century

(a) A-4, B-3, C-2, D-1   (b) A-3, B-4, C-2, D-1

(c) A-2, B-3, C-4, D-1   (d) A-1, B-2, C-3, D-4

(e) A-4, B-3, C-1, D-2

19. Match the following and choose the correct combination from the options given.

(Column I) (Fungus Name)		Column II (Commonly called)
(A)	*Puccinia*	1. Yeast
(B)	*Ustilago*	2. Mushroom
(C)	*Agaricus*	3. Smut fungus
(D)	*Saccharomyces*	4. Rust fungus

(a) A-1, B-2, C-3, D-4   (b) A-2, B-3, C-4, D-1

(c) A-3, B-4, C-1, D-2   (d) A-4, B-3, C-2, D-1

(e) A-4, B-3, C-1, D-2

20. The imperfect fungi which are decomposer of litter and help in mineral cycling belong to:

(a) Basidiomycetes   (b) Phycomycetes

(c) Ascomycetes   (d) Deuteromycetes

21. The structures that help some bacteria to attach to rocks and / or host tissues are:

(a) Fimbriae   (b) Mesosomes

(c) Holdfast   (d) Rhizoids

22. Match the following

Column-I (Group)		Column-II (Example)
A.	Bacillariophyceae	I. *Paramoecium*
B.	Dinoflagellates	II. *Euglena*
C.	Euglenoids	III. *Gonyaulax*
D.	Protozoans	IV. Diatoms

	A	B	C	D
(a)	I	III	II	IV
(b)	I	IV	III	II
(c)	IV	II	III	I
(d)	IV	III	II	I

23. Match Column I with Column II.

Column-I		Column-II
(Spores)		**(Organisms)**
(A) Ascospores	p.	Diatoms
(B) Endospores	q.	*Agaricus*
(C) Auxospores	r.	Bacteria
(D) Basidiospores	s.	Yeast
	t.	*Nephrolepis*

(a) A – s, B – r, C – p, D – q

(b) A – s, B – p, C – r, D – q

(c) A – s, B – p, C – t, D – q

(d) A – s, B – t, C – p, D – q

24. Which one of the following pairs is correctly matched

(a) *Rhizobium* – Parasite in the roots of leguminous plants

(b) Mycorrhizae – Mineral uptake from soil

(c) Yeast – Production of biogas

(d) Myxomycetes – Ring worm disease

25. Match the following

Column-I		Column-II
A. M13 bacteriophage	I.	dsRNA
B. Rice dwarf virus	II.	ssRNA
C. Cauliflower mosaic virus	III.	ssDNA
D. Polio virus	IV.	dsDNA

	A	B	C	D
(a)	III	I	IV	II
(b)	II	I	III	IV
(c)	III	IV	II	I
(d)	IV	III	I	II

ANSWER KEY

1	(a)	2	(b)	3	(d)	4	(c)	5	(c)	6	(a)	7	(e)	8	(d)	9	(e)	10	(b)
11	(b)	12	(c)	13	(b)	14	(d)	15	(d)	16	(d)	17	(c)	18	(a)	19	(d)	20	(d)
21	(a)	22	(d)	23	(a)	24	(b)	25	(a)										

Plant Kingdom

3

1. Peat Moss is used as a packing material for sending flowers and live plants to distant places because
   (a) it is hygroscopic
   (b) it reduces transpiration
   (c) it serves as a disinfectant
   (d) it is easily available

2. When pollen of a flower is transferred to the stigma of another flower of the same plant, this pollination is referred to as
   (a) xenogamy   (b) geitonogamy
   (c) autogamy   (d) allogamy

3. An important difference between the zoospores and aplanospores is that
   (a) zoospores are uninucleate while aplanospores are binucleate
   (b) zoospores are large while aplanospores are smaller
   (c) zoospores are motile while aplanospores are non-motile
   (d) None of the above

4. Which of the following correctly explains why rhodophyta exhibit a red colour ?
   (a) Since most rhodophyta grow at great depths, the chlorophyll can only absorb light in the red area of the spectrum.
   (b) The wavelengths of light that are absorbed by chlorophyll are passed to phycoerythrin (a red pigment).
   (c) Phycoerythrin absorbs all the light waves.
   (d) Light reaching the greatest depth in water is in the blue-green region of the spectrum. This light is absorbed by phycoerythrin.

5. Which is the right option ?

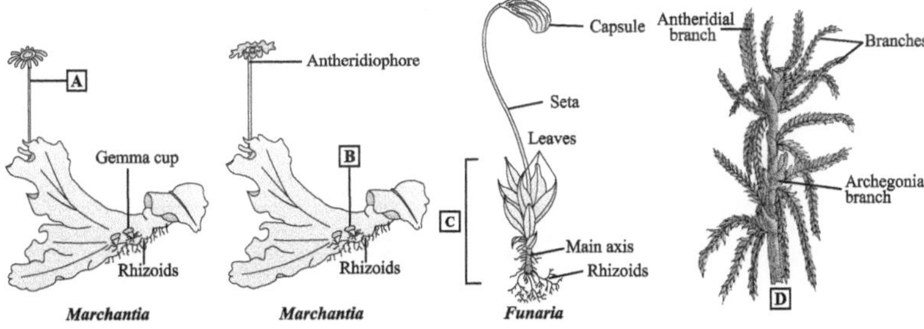

	A	**B**	**C**	**D**
(a)	Gemma cup	Archegoniophore	Sporophyte	*Sphagnum*
(b)	Archegoniophore	Gemma cup	Gametophyte	*Sphagnum*
(c)	Archegonia	Antheridia	Gemma cup	*Sphagnum*
(d)	Antheridia	Archegonia	Gemma cup	*Sphagnum*

6. Identify the dicot and monocot characters respectively.

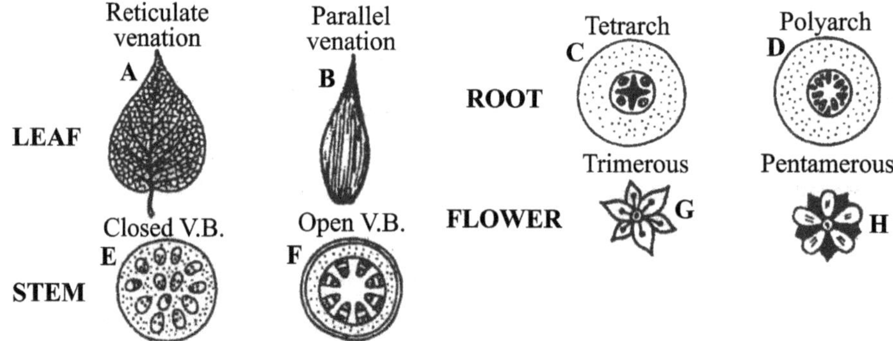

  (a) A, C, F, H; and B, D, E, G

  (b) A, D, F, H; and B, C, E, G

  (c) A, C, E, G; and B, D, F, H

  (d) B, C, F, H; and A, D, E, G

7. Identify the plants which are given below and choose the correct option.

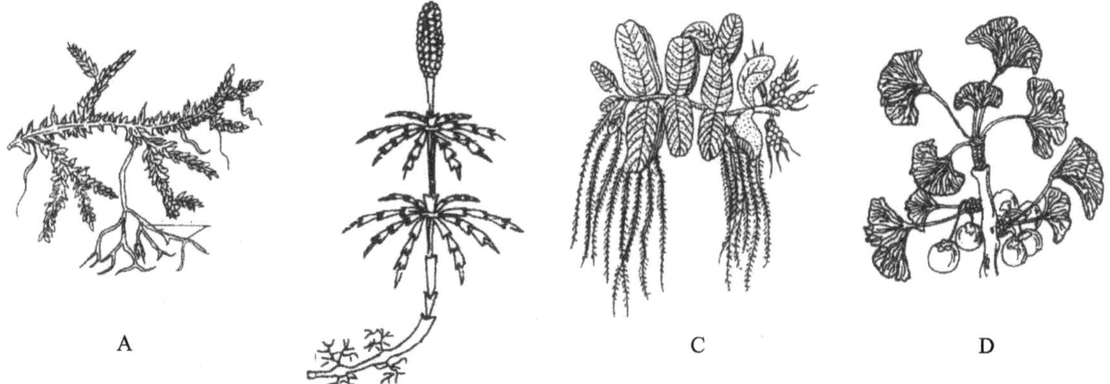

	A	**B**	**C**	**D**
(a)	*Equisetum*	*Ginkgo*	*Selaginella*	*Lycopodium*
(b)	*Selaginella*	*Equisetum*	*Salvinia*	*Ginkgo*
(c)	*Funaria*	*Adiantum*	*Salvinia*	*Riccia*
(d)	*Chara*	*Marchantia*	*Fucus*	*Pinus*

8. What structures A and B respectively indicate in the life cycle of bryophytes, pteridophytes and gymnosperms?

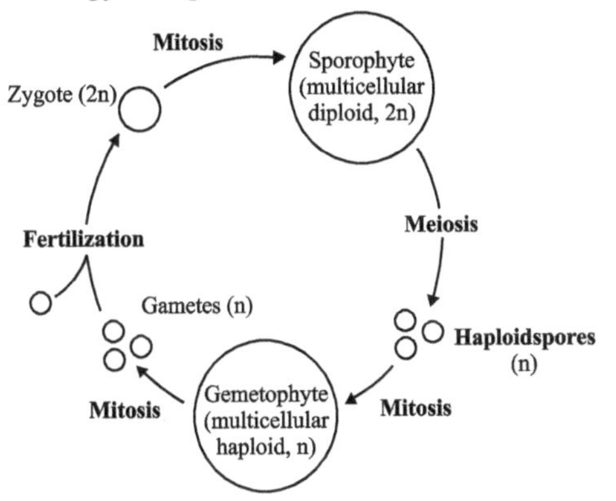

	A		B
(a)	Bryophytes	:	sporangium, capsule
	Pteridophytes	:	strobili, sporangia
	Gymnosperms	:	flowers, cones
(b)	Bryophytes	:	capsule, protonema (gametophores)
	Pteridophytes	:	sporangia, cones, sporophyll
	Gymnosperms	:	fertile fronds, megasporangia and microsporangia
(c)	Bryophytes	:	protonema, gametophores
	Pteridophytes	:	strobili, sporangia
	Gymnosperms	:	flowers, cones
(d)	Bryophytes	:	strobili, capsule
	Peteridophytes	:	cones, sporangia
	Gymnosperms	:	flowers, cones

9. Which is the correct combination ?

	Column-I		Column-II
(A)	Agar	(I)	Single cell protein, use as food supplements by space travellers
(B)	Algin	(II)	Red algae
(C)	Carrageen	(III)	Brown algae
(D)	*Chlorella and Spirullina*	(IV)	*Gelidium, Gracilaria*

(a) A → I; B → II; C → III; D → IV
(b) A → IV; B → III; C → II; D → I
(c) A → II; B → I; C → III; D → IV
(d) A → III; B → II; C → I; D → IV

10. Match the following

	Column-I (Classes)		Column-II (Examples)
(A)	Psilotopsida	(I)	*Dryopteris, Pteris, Adiantum*
(B)	Lycopsida	(II)	*Equisetum*
(C)	Sphenopsida	(III)	*Selaginella*
(D)	Pteropsida	(IV)	*Lycopodium*
		(V)	*Psilotum*

(a) A → V; B → III; C → II; D → I
(b) A → I; B → II; C → III; D → IV
(c) A → IV; B → III; C → II; D → I
(d) A → III; IV; B → V; C → I; D → II

11.

	Column-I		Column-II
(A)	Haplontic life cycle	(I)	Bryophytes, Pteridophytes, *Ectocarpus, Polysiphonia,* kelps
(B)	Diplontic life cycle	(II)	Seed bearing plants (Gymnosperm and Angiosperm), *Fucus*
(C)	Haplo-diplontic life cycle	(III)	Many algae (*Volvox, Spyrogyra,* and some species of *Chlamydomonas*)

Which is the correct combination ?

(a) A → III; B → II; C → I
(b) A → I; B → II; C → III
(c) A → II; B → I; C → III
(d) A → III; B → I; C → II

12. Which one of the following is the correct about *Pinus* ?
    (a) Monoecious – Male (microsporangiate) and female (megasporangiate) cones are produced on same plant.
    (b) Monoecious – Male and female sporophylls borne on same strobilus.
    (c) Dioecious – Male and female cones are produced on different plants.
    (d) Monoecious – Micro and megasporocarp develop on same plant.

13. A well developed archegonium with neck consisting of 4-6 rows of neck canal cells, is a characteristic of
    (a) gymnosperms only
    (b) bryophytes and pteridophytes
    (c) pteridophytes and gymnosperms
    (d) gymnosperms and angiosperms

14. A research student collected certain alga and found that its cells contained both chlorophyll *a* and chlorophyll *b* as well as phycoerythrin. The alga belongs to
    (a) rhodophyceae
    (b) bacillariophyceae
    (c) chlorophyceae
    (d) phaeophyceae

15. "Chilgoza", a gymnosperm seed, that is eaten as a "dry fruit" is produced by
    (a) *Pinus roxburghii*
    (b) *Pinus gerardiana*
    (c) *Ginkgo biloba*
    (d) *Cedrus deodara*

16. In the vast marine ecosystem, certain sea develop red colouration. This red colour is due to the presence of large population of which one of the following organisms?
    (a) *Trichodesmium erythrium*
    (b) *Physarium*
    (c) Dinoflagellates
    (d) Diatoms and members of red algae

17. Like angiospermic parasite such as *Cuscuta*, there are some parasitic forms of rhodophyta, which are colourless, heterotrophic and grow on other members of rhodophyta. Select which one is a parasitic form of red algae:
    (a) *Gelidium*
    (b) *Harveyella*
    (c) *Choridras*
    (d) Both (a) and (b)

18. People recovering from long illness are often advised to include the alga *Spirulina* in their diet because it
    (a) makes the food easy to digest.
    (b) is rich in proteins.
    (c) has antibiotic properties.
    (d) restores the intestinal microflora.

19. Match items in Column I with those in Column II:

Column -I		Column -II
(I) Peritrichous flagellation	(J)	*Ginkgo*
(II) Living fossil	(K)	*Macrocystis*
(III) Rhizophore	(L)	*Escherichia coli*
(IV) Smallest flowering plant	(M)	*Selaginella*
(V) Largest perennial alga	(N)	*Wolffia*

    Select the correct answer from the following:
    (a) I-L; II-J; III-M; IV-N; V-K;
    (b) I-K; II-J; III-L; IV-M; V-N
    (c) I-N; II-L; III-K; IV-N; V-J;
    (d) I-J; II-K; III-N; IV-L; V-K

20. Which one of the following is common to multicellular fungi, filamentous algae and protonema of mosses
    (a) Diplontic life cycle
    (b) Members of kingdom plantae
    (c) Mode of Nutrition
    (d) Multiplication by fragmentation

21. In gymnosperms, the pollen chamber represents
    - (a) a cell in the pollen grain in which the sperms are formed
    - (b) a cavity in the ovule in which pollen grains are stored after pollination
    - (c) an opening in the mega gametophyte through which the pollen tube approaches the egg
    - (d) the microsporangium in which pollen grains develop

22. The first plants to appear after a forest fire are the ferns, this is because of the survival of their
    - (a) spores
    - (b) leaves
    - (c) fronds
    - (d) rhizomes

ANSWER KEY																			
1	(a)	2	(b)	3	(c)	4	(b)	5	(b)	6	(a)	7	(b)	8	(b)	9	(b)	10	(a)
11	(a)	12	(a)	13	(b)	14	(a)	15	(b)	16	(a)	17	(b)	18	(b)	19	(a)	20	(d)
21.	(d)	22	(d)																

Animal Kingdom

1. The members of following phylum represent cellular level of organization
   (a) Cnidaria
   (b) Porifera
   (c) Protozoa
   (d) Both (a) and (b)

2. Given below are four statements regarding Aschelminthes
   A. They are bilaterally symmetrical and triploblastic
   B. They are dioecious
   C. All are plants or animals' parasites
   D. They are acoelomate
   Mark the option that has both the correct statements
   (a) A, B
   (b) A, C
   (c) B, C
   (d) B, D

3. Following organism is triploblastic, bilaterally symmetrical and marine, and respires through gills
   (a) *Echinus*
   (b) *Hirudinaria*
   (c) *Balanoglossus*
   (d) *Physalia*

4. Which set has the two members of the same phylum ?
   (a) Cuttle fish and jelly fish
   (b) Tape worm and earthworm
   (c) Dog fish and dolphin
   (d) Sea mouse and sea lion

5. Crocodile and penguin are similar to Whale and Dogfish in which one of the following features?
   (a) Possess a solid single stranded central nervous system
   (b) Lay eggs and guard them till they hatch
   (c) Possess bony skeleton
   (d) Have gill slits at some stage

6. Deuterostomate and enterocoelomate invertebrate is
   (a) *Pila*
   (b) *Ascaris*
   (c) Aphrodite
   (d) *Asterias*

7. Sponge structure corresponding to mouth of other animals is
   (a) Incurrent canal
   (b) Ostium
   (c) Osculum
   (d) Excurrent canal

8. Elasmobranchs generally lack
   (a) Gill slits
   (b) Operculum
   (c) Notochord
   (d) Placoid scales

9. An arthropod belonging to onychophora which possesses nephridia is
   (a) *Limulus*   (b) *Peripatus*
   (c) *Daphnia*   (d) *Lepisma*

10. Characteristic free swimming larva of coelenterates is
    (a) Onchosphere   (b) Hydrula
    (c) Planula   (d) Amphiblastula

11. Which one of the following is a matching pair of an animal and certain phenomenon it exhibits
    (a) *Pheretima* – Sexual dimorphism
    (b) *Musca* – Complete metamorphosis
    (c) *Caraucius* – Mimicry
    (d) *Taenia* - Polymorphism

12. Match the following column I with column Ii and choose the correct combination from the options given

Column I		Column II
A.	earthworm	I.	*Gizzard*
B.	cockroach	II.	*Caecum*
C.	frog	III.	*Clitellum*
D.	rat	IV.	*Cloaca*

    (a) A-I, B-II, C-IV, D-III
    (b) A-III, B-I, C-IV, D-II
    (c) A-II, B-I, C-III, D-IV
    (d) A-III, B-I, C-II, D-IV

13. Which one of the following features is common in silverfish, scorpion, dragonfly and prawn?
    (a) Three pairs of legs and segmented body
    (b) Chitinous cuticle and two pairs of antennae
    (c) Jointed appendages and chitinous exoskeleton
    (d) Cephalothorax and tracheae

14. Match item in column A with those given in column B

Column A		Column B
A.	limbless reptile	1.	lamprey
B.	jawless vertebrate	2.	salamander
C.	amphibian	3.	snake
D.	cartilaginous fish	4.	shark
E.	flightless bird	5.	ostrich

    (a) A-1, B-2, C-3, D-4, E-5
    (b) A-2, B-1, C-3, D-4, E-5
    (c) A-3, B-1, C-2, D-4, E-5
    (d) A-4, B-2, C-3, D-1, E-5

15. Match the following :

List I		List II
A.	*Echidna*	1.	Ophidia
B.	*Echinus*	2.	Teleostei
C.	*Echeneis*	3.	Platyhelminthes
D.	*Echis*	4.	Echinoidea
E.	*Echinococcus*	5.	Prototheria

    (a) A-5, B-1, C-2, D-4, E-3
    (b) A-5, B-1, C-3, D-4, E-2
    (c) A-5, B-4, C-2, D-3, E-1
    (d) A-5, B-4, C-2, D-1, E-3

16. A lizard- like member of reptilia is sitting on a tree with its tail coiled around a twig. This animal could be
    (a) *Hemidactylus* showing sexual dimorphism
    (b) Varanus showing mimicry
    (c) garden lizard (*Calotes*) showing camouflage
    (d) *Chamaeleon* showing protective colouration

17. Match the followings

	Set-I		Set-II
1.	*Latimeria*	(i)	Discontinuous Distribution
2.	*Zygaena*	(ii)	Remora
3.	*Echeneis*	(iii)	Aestivation
4.	*Protopterus*	(iv)	Ureotelic
5.	Dipnoi	(v)	Rhipidistia

(a) 1 - (iv), 2 - (v), 3 - (ii), 4 - (i), 5 - (iii)

(b) 1 - (v), 2 - (iv), 3 - (ii), 4 - (i), 5 - (iii)

(c) 1 - (v), 2 - (iv), 3 - (ii), 4 - (iii), 5 - (i)

(d) 1 - (v), 2 - (iv), 3 - (iii), 4 - (ii), 5 - (i)

18. Match the following

1.	*Euplectella*	(i)	Phytomastigophora
2.	*Echinoderis*	(ii)	Echinoidea
3.	*Echinus*	(iii)	Ophidia
4.	*Echis*	(iv)	Echinodera
5.	*Euglena*	(v)	Hexactinellida

(a) 1 - (v), 2- (iv), 3 - (ii), 4 - (i), 5 - (iii)

(b) 1 - (iv), 2- (v), 3 - (ii), 4 - (iii), 5 - (i)

(c) 1 - (v), 2- (iv), 3 - (i), 4 - (ii), 5 - (iii)

(d) 1 - (v), 2- (iv), 3 - (ii), 4 - (iii), 5 - (i)

19. Which one of the following phyla is correctly matched with its two general characteristics ?

(a) Mollusca   -   Normally oviparous and development through a trochophore or veliger larva

(b) Arthropoda   -   Body divided into head, throax and abdomen and respiration by tracheae

(c) Chordata   -   Notochord at some stage and separate anal and urinary openings to the outside.

(d) Echinodermata   -   Pentamerous radial symmetry and mostly internal fertilization

20. The figure shows four animals (A), (B), (C) and (D).

Select the correct answer with respect to a common characteristics of two of these animals.

(A) 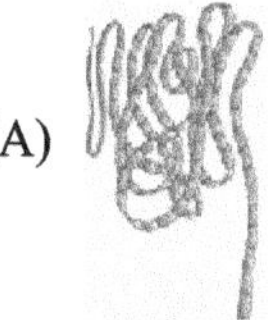

(B) 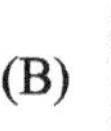 

(C)  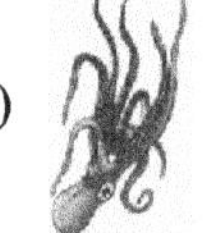

(D) 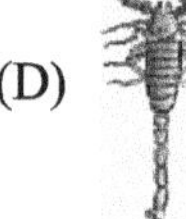

(a) (A) and (D) have cnidoblasts for self-defence

(b) (C) and (D) have a true coelom

(c) (A) and (D) respire mainly through body wall

(d) (B) and (C) show radial symmetry

21. Which of the following animal has '*Tube within Tube*' body plan

(a) Round worm

(b) Liver fluke

(c) Jelly fish

(d) None of these

22. 'Pigeon milk' is secreted in the
    (a) Uropygeal gland of pigeon
    (b) Crop gland of female pigeon
    (c) Crop glands of male and female pigeon
    (d) Mammary glands of the pigeon

23. **Ampullae of Lorenzini** in dog fish are
    (a) Thermoreceptors
    (b) Rheoreceptors
    (c) Balancing structures
    (d) Auditory Structures

24. Birds have :
    (a) Amphiplatyon centrum and monocondylic skull
    (b) Hetroceoelus centrum and monocondylic skull
    (c) Hetrocoelus centrum and Dicondylic skull
    (d) Amphiplatyon centrum and Dicondylic skull

25. Two chief features of mammals which distinguish them from other vertebrates are :
    (a) Hairy skin and oviparity
    (b) Hairy skin and mammary glands
    (c) Mammary glands and teeth
    (d) Pinna and teeth

ANSWER KEY																			
1	(b)	**2**	(a)	**3**	(c)	**4**	(c)	**5**	(d)	**6**	(d)	**7**	(b)	**8**	(b)	**9**	(b)	**10**	(c)
11	(b)	**12**	(b)	**13**	(c)	**14**	(c)	**15**	(d)	**16**	(d)	**17**	(c)	**18**	(d)	**19**	(a)	**20**	(b)
21	(a)	**22**	(c)	**23**	(a)	**24**	(b)	**25**	(b)										

Morphology of Flowering Plants

5

1. Most plants are green in colour because

   (a) the atmosphere filters out all the colours of the visible light spectrum except green.

   (b) green light is the most effective wavelength region of the visible spectrum in sunlight for photosynthesis.

   (c) chlorophyll is least effective in absorbing green light.

   (d) green light allows maximum photosynthesis.

2. In a cereal grain the single cotyledon of embryo is represented by

   (a) scutellum   (b) plumule

   (c) coleoptile   (d) coleorhiza

3. Choose the correct option for A, B and C.

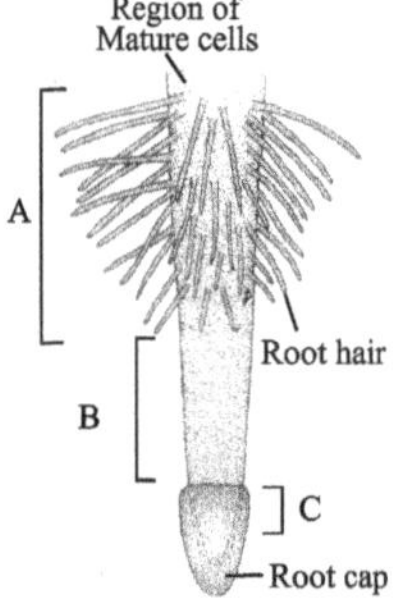

   (a) A - zone of elongation, B - zone of meiosis, C - zone of mitosis

   (b) A - zone of maturation, B - zone of meristematic activity, C - zone of elongation

   (c) A - zone of mitosis, B - zone of elongation, C - zone of root cap

   (d) A - region of maturation, B - region of elongation, C - meristematic activity

4. Which one of the following option is incorrect?

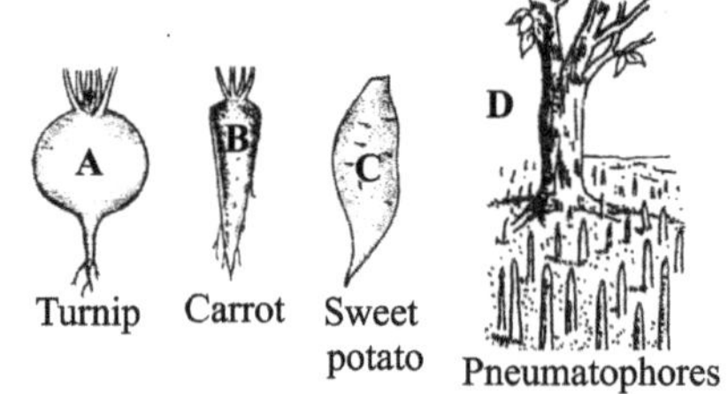

   (a) Tap roots of carrot, turnip and adventitious root of sweet potato, get swollen and store food.

   (b) Pneumatophores help to get oxygen for respiration.

   (c) Pneumatophore is found in the plants that grow in sandy soil.

   (d) A, B and C are underground roots but D grows vertically upwards.

5. Which of the following option is correct?

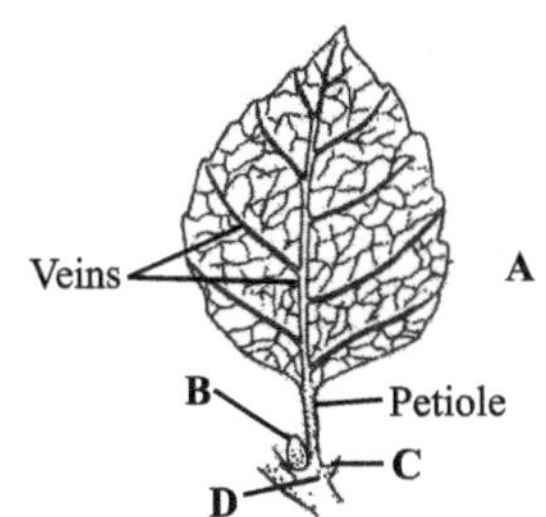

	A	B	C	D
(a)	Lamina	Axillary bud	Stipule	Leaf base
(b)	Lamina	Stipule	Axillary bud	Leaf base
(c)	Lamina	Axillary bud	Stipule	Pedicel
(d)	Leaflet	Axillary bud	Stipule	Leaf base

6. Choose the correct option for A and B.

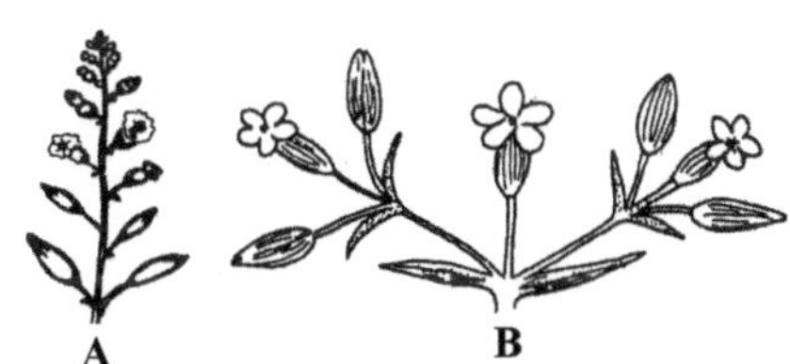

(a) A-Cymose, B-Racemose

(b) A-Racemose, B-Cymose

(c) A- Racemose, B - Racemose

(d) A- Cymose, B - Cymose

7. Chosse the correct combinations.

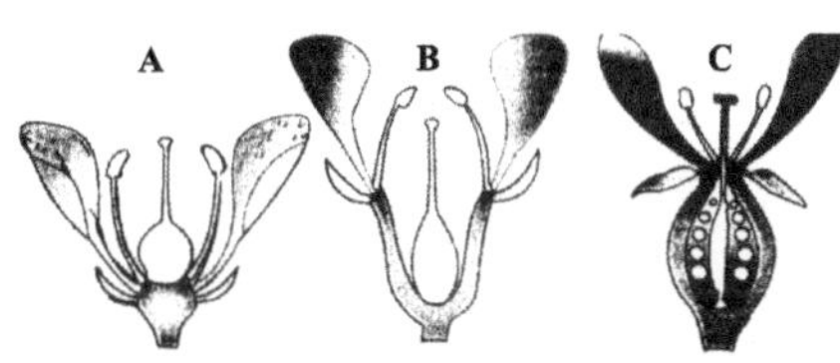

I. Hypogynous flower

II. Perigynous flower

III. Epigynous flower

(a) A-I, B-II, C-III

(b) A-I, B-III, C-II

(c) A-III, B-II, C-I

(d) A-III, B-I, C-II

8. Which is the correct combination?

Column I	Column II	Column III
A. Mariginal	I. 	p. Sunflower, Marigold
B. Axile	II. 	q. Dianthus, Primrose
C. Parietal	III. 	r. Mustard, Argemone
D. Free Central	IV. 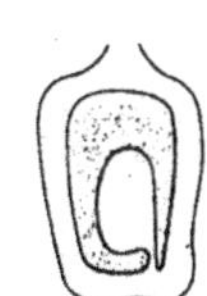	s. China rose, Tomato, Lemon
E. Basal	V. 	t. Pea

(a)   A- V, t; B -II, s; C -I, r; D -III, q; E -IV, p

(b)   A - I, t; B - II, s; C - III, r; D - IV, p; E - V, q

(c)   A - V, p; B - II, s; C - I, q; D - III, r; E - IV, t

(d)   A - V, p; B - III, q; C - II, s; D - I, t; E - IV, r

9.   Choose the correct option for A and B.

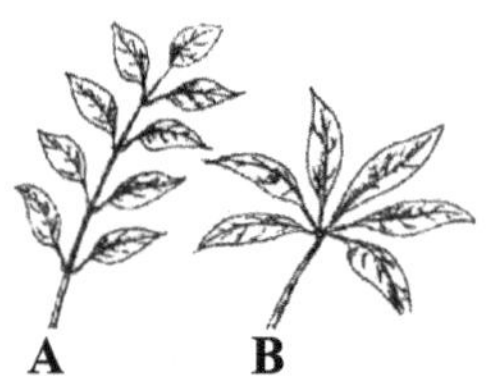

(a)   A - Pinnately compound leaf, B - Palmately compound leaf

(b)   A - Palmately compound leaf, B - Pinnately compound leaf

(c)   A- Pinnately compound leaf, B - Pinnately compound leaf

(d)   A - Palmately compound leaf, B - Palmately compound leaf

10.   Choose the correct option.

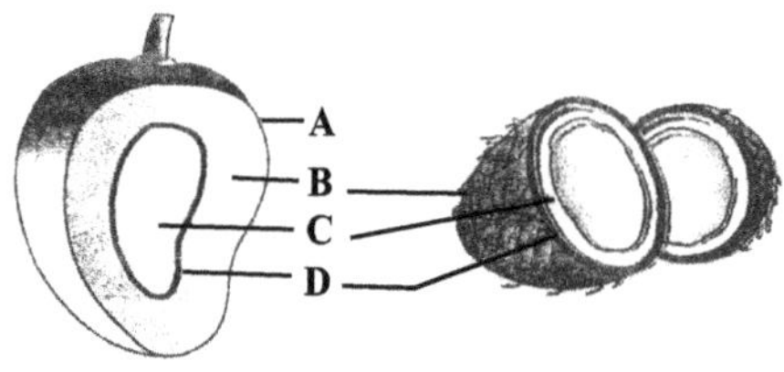

(a)   Epicarp, Mesocarp, Seed, Endocarp

(b)   Epicarp, Mesocarp, Ovule, Endocarp

(c)   Epicarp, Mesocarp, Ovary, Endocarp

(d)   Epicarp, Mesocarp, Embryo, Endocarp

11.   Which one is correct option for the species belong to given families respectively?

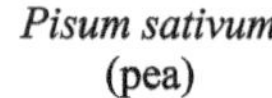

Pisum sativum   *Solanum nigrum*   *Allium cepa*
(pea)   (makoi)   (onion)

(a)   Liliaceae, Compositae, Malvaceae

(b)   Fabaceae, Solanaceae, Liliaceae

(c)   Compositae, Malvaceae, Liliaceae

(d)   Solanaceae, Fabaceae, Liliaceae

12.   Matching the following and choose the correct option

Column I		Column II	
A.	Bud in the axil of leaf	I.	Pitcher plant and Venus fly trap
B.	Outer layer of seed coat	II.	Cacti
C.	Spines (modified leaves)	III.	Testa
D.	Leaves modiied to catch insects	IV.	Simple leaf
E.	Fleshy leaves with stored food	V.	Garlic and onion

	A	B	C	D	E
(a)	I	II	III	IV	V
(b)	V	IV	III	II	I
(c)	IV	III	II	I	V
(d)	IV	II	III	I	V

13.   Choose the correct combinations.

Column I		Column II	
A.	Gamosepalous	I.	Flower of lily
B.	Polysepalous	II.	Sterile anther
C.	Gamopetalous	III.	Free petals
D.	Polypetalous	IV.	Free sepals
E.	Epiphyllous	V.	Fused petals
F.	Staminode	VI.	Fused sepals

	A	B	C	D	E	F
(a)	IV	V	III	I	VI	II
(b)	IV	V	III	I	II	VI
(c)	VI	IV	V	III	I	II
(d)	VI	IV	V	III	II	I

14. Matching the following and choose the correct option.

Column I		Column II
A. Coleorrhiza	I.	Grapes
B. Food storing tissue	II.	Mango
C. Parthenocarpic fruit	III.	Maize
D. Single seeded fruit developing from monocarpellary superior ovary	IV.	Radicle
E. Membranous seed coat	V.	Endosperm

(a) A - III, B-I, C -IV, D - II, E - V

(b) A - IV, B-II, C - V, D - I, E - III

(c) A - V, B-I, C - III, D - IV, E - II

(d) A - IV, B - V, C - I, D - II, E - III

15. Which is the correct combinations ?

Column I (Members of Fabaceae)		Column II (Economic importance)
A. Gram, sem, moong, soyabean	I.	Medicine
B. Soyabean, groundnut	II.	Ornamental
C. Indigofera	III.	Fodder
D. Sunhemp	IV.	Fibres
E. *Sesbania, Trifolium*	V.	Dye
F. Lupin, Sweet potato	VI.	Edible oil
E. *Mulaaithi*	VII.	Pulses

(a) A - I, B - II, C - III, D - IV, E - V, F - VI, G - VII

(b) A-VII, B - VI, C - V, D -IV, E - III, F - II, G-I

(c) A - II, B - IV, C - VI, D - I, E - III, F - V, G - VII

(d) A - I, B - III, C - V, D - VII, E - II, F - IV, G - VI

16. Which plant will lose its economic value if its fruits are produced by induced parthenocarpy?

(a) grape

(b) pomegranate

(c) banana

(d) orange

17. If a fruit is developed from bicarpellary, bilocular with one ovule in each locule and pendulously attached and the wall of the ovary possess vittae, the fruit is designated as

(a) caryopsis

(b) cypsela

(c) cremocarp

(d) capsule

18. Edible part of banana is

(a) epicarp

(b) mesocarp and less developed endocarp

(c) endocarp and less developed mesocarp

(d) epicarp and mesocarp

19. Match the following and choose the correct option

List I		List II
I. Acicular	(A)	grass
II. Linear	(B)	*nerium*
III. lanceolate	(C)	banana
IV. oblong	(D)	pine

(a) I-D, II-A, III-B, IV-C

(b) I-D, II-A, III-C, IV-B

(c) I-D, II-B, III-C, IV-A

(d) I-D, II-C, III-B,IV-A

20. In *Cuscuta* the nodes give rise to special roots which penetrate the host tissue upto

(a) cortex

(b) phloem

(c) epidermis

(d) pericycle

21. Match column I with II and choose the right option

	I		II
1.	*Artemisia*	A.	Fibre
2.	*Astragalus*	B.	Insecticide
3.	*Phormium*	C.	Rat poison
4.	*Chrysanthemum*	D.	Medicine
5.	*Withania*	E.	Vermifuge
		F.	Gum

(a) 1 - D, 2 - C, 3 - F, 4 - B, 5 - E

(b) 1 - B, 2 - E, 3 - D, 4 - C, 5 - A

(c) 1 - C, 2 - E, 3 - A, 4 - F, 5 - D

(d) 1 - E, 2 - F, 3 - A, 4 - B, 5 - D

22. Select the characters which are not applicable to the family solanaceae?

(i) epipetalous and syngenesious anthers

(ii) bicarpellary and syncarpous ovary

(iii) oblique ovary with axile placentation

(iv) stamens six, arranged in two whorls

(v) bicarpellary, syncarpous and inferior ovary

(a) (ii) and (iii) only

(b) (i), (iv) and (v) only

(c) (ii), (iv) and (v) only

(4) (i) and (iii) only

23. Which one of the following floral formulae represents the mustard plant?

(a) $\oplus \, \updownarrow \, K_{2+2} \, C_4 A_{2+4} \, \overline{G}_{(2)}$

(b) $\oplus \, \updownarrow \, P_{3+3} \, C_4 A_{3+3} \, \underline{G}_{(3)}$

(c) $\oplus \, \updownarrow \, K_{(5)} \overset{\frown}{C}_{(5)} A_{(5)} \, \underline{G}_{(2)}$

(d) $\oplus \, \updownarrow \, K_{2+2} \, C_4 \, A_{2+4} \, \underline{G}_{(2)}$

24. Typical floral formula of Ranunculaceae is

(a) $\oplus \, \female \nearrow K_5 C_5 A \propto G_{\propto}$

(b) $\oplus \, \female \nearrow K_{(5)} C_{(6)} A_{9+1} \propto G_1$

(c) $\oplus \, \female \nearrow K_{(5)} C_{(6)} A_{(\propto)} G_{(5-8)}$

(d) $\oplus \, \female \nearrow K_{2+2} C_4 A_{4+2} G_{(2)}$

25. Match the following and choose the correct combination from the options given below:

Column I (Placentation Type)		Column II (Represented in)
A. Basal	1.	*Dianthus*
B. Free central	2.	Pea
C. Parietal	3.	Lemon
D. Axile	4.	Marigold
E. Marginal	5.	*Argemone*

(a) A – 1, B – 2, C – 3, D – 4, E – 5

(b) A – 2, B – 3, C – 4, D – 5, E – 1

(c) A – 4, B – 1, C – 5, D – 3, E – 2

(d) A – 4, B – 3, C – 5, D – 1, E – 2

26. Match the following and select the correct combination from the options given below.

Column I (Stem Modifications)		Column II (Found in)
A. Underground stem	1.	*Euphorbia*
B. Stem tendril	2.	*Opuntia*
C. Stem thorns	3.	Potato
D. Flattened stem	4.	*Citrus*
E. Fleshy cylindrical stem	5.	Cucumber

(a)   A – 1, B – 2, C – 3, D – 5, E – 4

(b)   A – 2, B – 3, C – 4, D – 5, E – 1

(c)   A – 3, B – 4, C – 5, D – 1, E – 2

(d)   A – 3, B – 5, C – 4, D – 2, E – 1

27.   Which one of the following is correct explanation for the floral formulas % $\male\female$ $K_{(5)}$ $C_{1+2+(b)}$ $A_{(9)+1}$ $\underline{G}_I$?

(a)   Zygomorphic, bisexual, sepals five and gamosepalous, petals five and papilionaceous, anthers ten and monadelphous ovary superior and monocarpellary.

(b)   Zygomorphic, unisexual, sepals five and gamosepalous, petals five and polypetalous, anthers nine united and one free, ovary superior and monocarpellary.

(c)   Zygomorphic, bisexual, sepals five and gamosepalous, petals five and papilionaceous, anthers ten and diadelphous, ovary superior and monocarpellary.

(d)   Zygomorphic, bisexual, sepals five and united, petals five and united, anthers ten and diadelphous, ovary superior and monocarpellary.

28.   Matching the following and choose the correct option

Column – I		Column – II
A.	Tubercular Storage roots	I. *Tinospora*
B.	Pneumatophores	II. *Heritiera*
C.	Haustoria	III. *Asparagus*
D.	Prop-roots	IV. *Viscum*
E.	Assimilatory roots	V. *Screwpine*

(a)   A–II, B–III, C–IV, D–V, E–I

(b)   A–III, B–IV, C–V, D–I, E–II

(c)   A–III, B–I, C–II, D–V, E–IV

(d)   A–III, B–II, C–IV, D–V, E–I

29.   Parts of two plants were observed. Structure-A develops aerially and produces roots when comes in contact with the soil. Structure-B develops from underground part of the stem, grows obliquely, becomes aerial and produces roots on its lower surface. Identify A and B.

(a)   Sucker, stolon

(b)   Stolon, runner

(c)   Stolon, sucker

(d)   Runner, stolon

30.   Chosse the correct combinations

List-I		List-II
(A)	Entire leaf modified into a spine	(i) *Clematis*
(B)	Leaf except stipules modified into a tendril	(ii) *Citrus*
(C)	Stipules modified into a tendril	(iii) *Euphorbia*
(D)	First leaf of axillary bud modified into a spine	(iv) *Lathyrus*

	A	B	C	D
(a)	(iii)	(iv)	(i)	(ii)
(b)	(iii)	(i)	(iv)	(ii)
(c)	(ii)	(iii)	(i)	(iv)
(d)	(iv)	(ii)	(i)	(iii)

31.   Select the correct option

List I		List II
A.	Spike	I. *Bougainvillea*
B.	Capitulum	II. *Coleus*
C.	Dichasial cyme	III. *Adhatoda*
D.	Multiparous cyme	IV. *Zinnia*
E.	Verticillaster	V. *Asclepias*

    (a) A – III, B – IV, C – I, D – V, E – II

    (b) A – III, B – I, C – IV, D – V, E – II

    (c) A – II, B – IV, C – I, D – V, E – III

    (d) A – IV, B – II, C – V, D – I, E – III

32. Given inflorescence is a

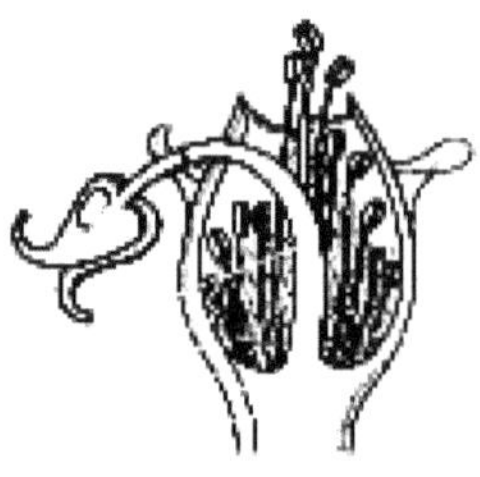

    (a) cyathium

    (b) dichasial cyme

    (c) umbel

    (d) verticillaster

33. In which aestivation in which members of a whorl lie close but do not overlap

    (a) vexillary

    (b) valvate

    (c) imbricate

    (d) twisted

34. The correct sequence of types of corolla in the following figures is

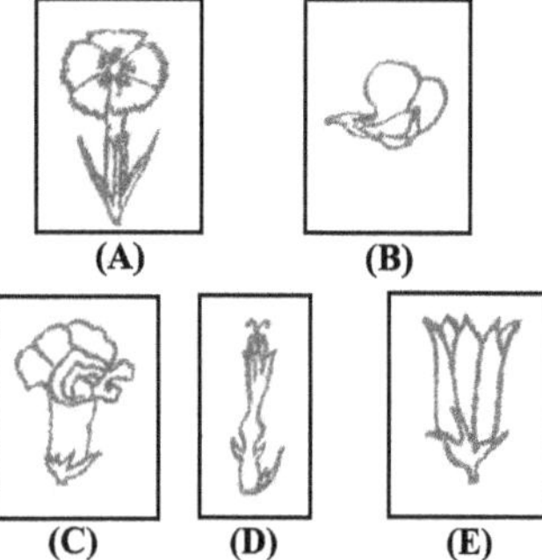

    (a) A – Caryophyllaceous, B – papilionaceous, C – bilabiate, D – tubular, E – bell- shaped

    (b) A – papilionaceous, B – bilabiate, C – tubular, D – bell-shaped, E – caryophyllaceous

    (c) A – bilabiate, B – papilionaceous, C – caryophyllaceous, D – bell-shaped, E – tubular

    (d) A – caryophyllaceous, B – bilabiate, C – papilionaceous, D – tubular, E – bell-shaped

35. Which one of the following sets of characters denote that plant possess all advanced morphological characters?

    (a) Dioecious condition, gamopetalous corolla and multiple fruit.

    (b) Actinomorphic flowers, free stamens and endospermic seeds.

    (c) Perennial life span, dichlamydous flower and simple fruit.

    (d) Simple leaves, monoecious condition and apocarpous pistil.

36. Two dry fruits (A & B) were observed. Both developed from unilocular ovaries of monocarpellary gynoecia. In fruit A, pericarp and seed coat are free. It liberated the seeds only after the disintegration of the pericrap. Fruit B dehisced dorsiventrally liberating the seeds. In the following, the former in the pair represents A and latter B. To which types of fruits A and B respectively belong?

    (a) achene and legume

    (b) nut and follicle

    (c) cypsella and silliqua

    (d) pyxidium and septicidal capsule

37. The correct floral formula of Liliaceae is

    (a) $Br \oplus \male\female P_{3+3} A_{3+3} \underline{G}_{(3)}$

    (b) $Br \oplus \male\female P_{3+3} A_{3+3} \underline{G}_{(3)}$

    (c) $\dagger \oplus \male\female P_{3+3} A_{3+3} \underline{G}_{(3)}$

    (d) $\dagger \oplus \male\female P_{3+3} A_{3+3} \underline{G}_{(6)}$

38. Match the following

	List-I		List-II
(A)	Spongy aril	(I)	*Jussiaea*
(B)	Multiple epidermis	(II)	*Pistia*
(C)	Respiratory roots	(III)	*Nerium*
(D)	Root pockets	(IV)	*Sagittaria*
		(V)	*Nymphaea*

	A	B	C	D
(a)	I	III	II	V
(b)	II	I	IV	III
(c)	IV	II	III	I
(d)	V	III	I	II

ANSWER KEY																			
1	(c)	**2**	(a)	**3**	(d)	**4**	(c)	**5**	(a)	**6**	(b)	**7**	(a)	**8**	(a)	**9**	(a)	**10**	(a)
11	(b)	**12**	(c)	**13**	(c)	**14**	(d)	**15**	(b)	**16**	(b)	**17**	(c)	**18**	(b)	**19**	(a)	**20**	(b)
21	(d)	**22**	(b)	**23**	(d)	**24**	(a)	**25**	(c)	**26**	(d)	**27**	(c)	**28**	(d)	**29**	(d)	**30**	(a)
31	(a)	**32**	(a)	**33**	(b)	**34**	(a)	**35**	(a)	**36**	(a)	**37**	(b)	**38**	(d)				

Anatomy of Flowering Plants

1. The cork cambium, cork and secondary cortex are collectively called

   (a) phelloderm   (b) phellogen

   (c) periderm   (d) phellem

2. Identified A, B and C of root apex.

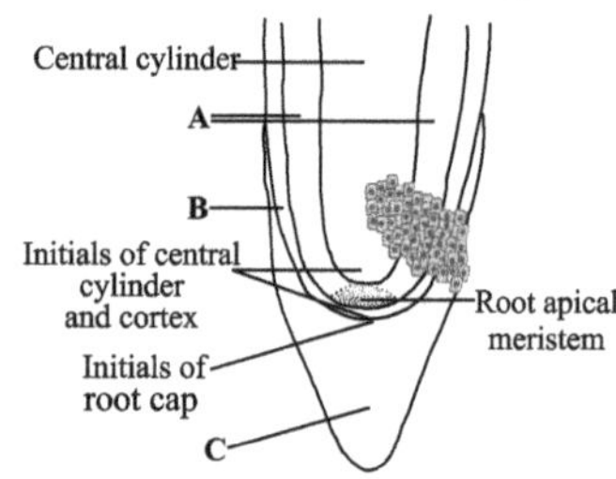

   (a) A – Vascular structure, B – Protoderm, C – Root cap

   (b) A – Cortex, B – Endodermis, C – Root cap

   (c) A – Cortex, B – Protoderm, C – Root cap

   (d) A – Tunica, B – Protoderm, C – Root cap

3. Choose the correct option –

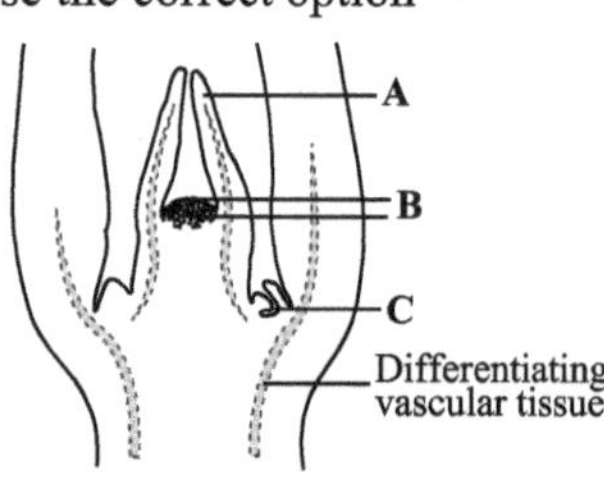

   (a) A – Leaf primordium, B – Shoot apical meristem, C – Axillary bud

   (b) A – Leaf primordium, B – Shoot apical meristem, C – Apical bud

   (c) A – Root hair primordium, B – Root apical meristem, C – Axillary bud

   (d) A – Root hair primordium, B – Root apical meristem, C – Terminal bud

4. Identify the types of simple tissue indicated by A, B, C and D.

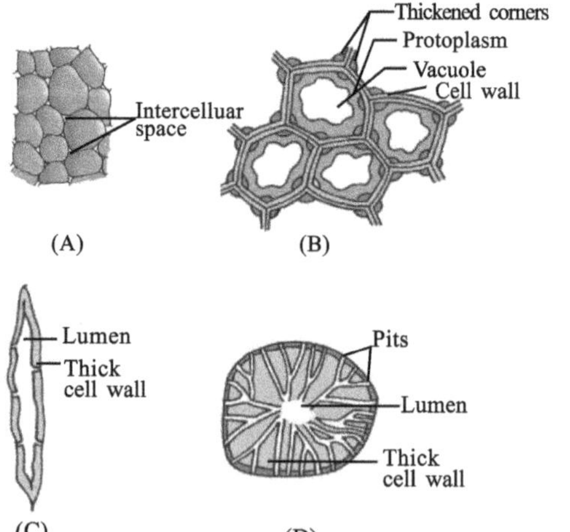

(a) A – Parenchyma, B – Collenchyma, C – fibre (Sclerenchyma), D – Sclereid (Sclerenchyma)

(b) A – Collenchyma, B – Parenchyma, C – fibre (Sclerenchyma), D – Sclereid (Sclerenchyma)

(c) A – Parenchyma, B – Collenchyma, C – Sclereid (Sclerenchyma), D – fibre (Sclerenchyma)

(d) A – Collenchyma, B – Parenchyma, C – Sclereid (Sclerenchyma), D – fibre (Sclerenchyma)

5. Choose the correct option for A and B –

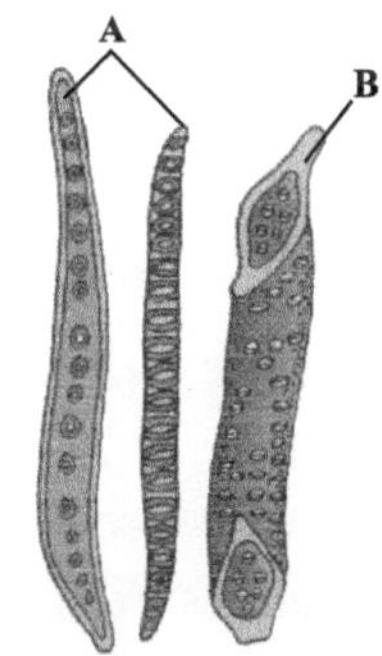

(a) A – Tracheid, B – Vessel

(b) A – Vessel, B – Tracheid

(c) A – Fibre, B – Tracheid

(d) A – Fibre, B – Sclereid

6. Which is the correct option for A, B and C ?

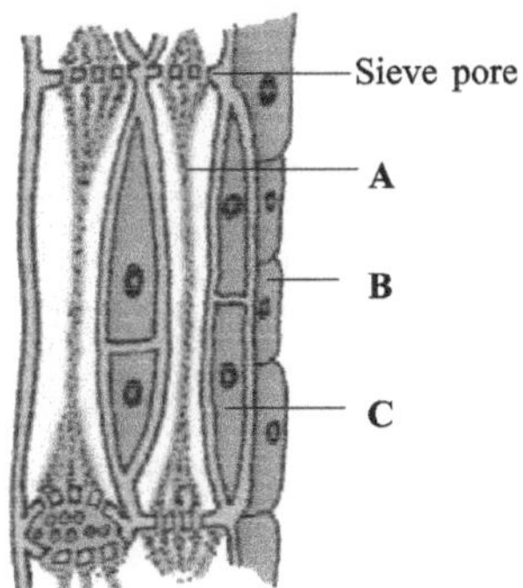

(a) A – Sieve tube, B – Phloem parenchyma, C – Companion cell

(b) A – Vessel, B – Phloem parenchyma, C – Companion cell

(c) A – Sieve tube, B – Phloem parenchyma, C – Phloem fibre

(d) A – Sieve tube, B – Companion cell, C – Phloem parenchyma

7. Which one of the following option is true about bulliform/motor cell ?

(a) It is seen in grasses.

(b) It is large-sized, thin-walled colourless, vacoulate cells on the adaxial surface.

(c) It helps in rolling of leaf to minimise water loss when it is flaccid.

(d) All

8. Which one of the following statement is false ?

(I) Epidermal cell has small amount of cytoplasm and a large vacuole.

(II) Waxy cuticle layer is absent in roots.

(III) Root hairs are unicellular, while stem hairs / trichomes are multicellular.

(IV) Trichomes may be branched or unbranched, soft or stiff and prevent transpiration.

(V) Guard cells are dumbell shaped in dicots and bean-shaped in monocots (*e.g.* grass).

(a) I   (b) IV

(c) III   (d) V

9. Which option is true about heart wood/ duramen?

(i) It does not help in water and mineral conduction.

(ii) It is dark coloured but soft.

(iii) It has tracheary elements filled with tannins, resins, gums, oil, etc.

(iv) It is a peripheral part.

(v) Sensitive to microbes and insects, hence least durable.

(a) I, III   (b) II, III

(c) IV, V   (d) III, IV

10. Identify types of vascular bundles.

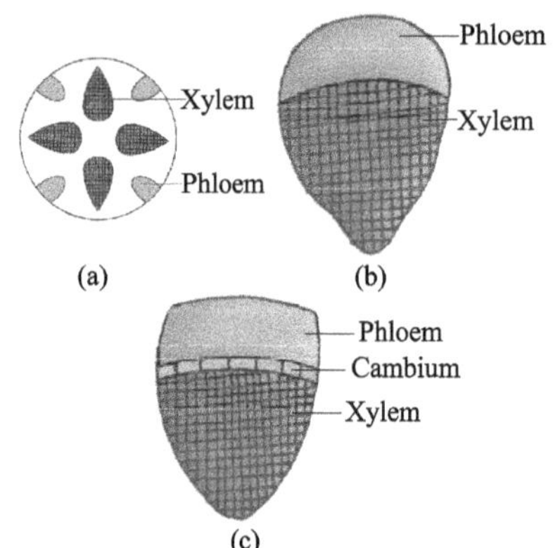

(a) Radial; Conjoint closed; Conjoint open

(b) Conjoint closed; Conjoint open; Radial

(c) Conjoint open; Conjoint closed; Radial

(d) Bicollateral; Concentric; Radial

11.

Column-I	Column-II
A. Spring wood or early wood	I. Lighter in colour
B. Autumn wood or late wood	II. Density high
	III. Density low
	IV. Darker in colour
	V. Larger number of xylem elements
	VI. Vessels with wider cavity
	VII. Lesser number of xylem elements
	VIII. Vessels with small cavity

Which of the following combination is correct?

(a) A – II, IV, VII, VIII; B – I, III, V, VI

(b) A – I, II, VII, VIII; B – III, IV, V, VI

(c) A – I, III, V, VI; B – II, IV, VII, VIII

(d) A – I, III, VII, VIII; B – II, IV, V, VI

12. Which of the following meristems is responsible for extrastelar secondary growth in dicotyledonous stem?

(a) Intrafascicular cambium

(b) Interfascicular cambium

(c) Intercalary meristem

(d) Phellogen

13. A leaf primordium grows into the adult leaf lamina by means of

(a) apical meristem

(b) lateral meristem

(c) marginal meristems

(d) at first by apical meristem and later largely by marginal meristems

14. Transition of radial vascular bundle in root to conjoint vascular bundle in stem occurs in which zone?

(a) Epicotyl   (b) Hypocotyl

(c) Meristem   (d) At base of stem

15. Girdling experiment cannot be performed in sugarcane because

(a) vascular bundles are scattered

(b) vascular bundles are in a ring

(c) it is unbranched

(d) it is delicate cannot withstand injury

16. Passage cells are thin walled cells found in

(a) phloem elements that serve as entry points for substance to transport to other plant parts

(b) testa of seeds to enable emergence of growing embryonic axis during seed germination

(c) central region of style through which the pollen tube grows towards the ovary

(d) endodermis of roots facilitating rapid transport of water from cortex to pericycle

17. Anatomically fairly old dicotyledonous root is distinguished from the dicotyledonous stem by

(a) absence of secondary phloem

(b) presence of cortex

(c) position of protoxylem

(d) absence of secondary xylem

18. The annular and spirally thickened conducting elements generally develop in the protoxylem when the root or stem is:
    (a) elongating   (b) widening
    (c) differentiating   (d) maturing

19. Consider the following statements and choose the correct option.
    (A) The thread-like cytoplasmic strands, running from one cell to other is known as plasmodesmata.
    (B) Xylem and phloem constitute the vascular bundle of the stem.
    (C) The first form xylem elements are described as metaxylem.
    (D) Radial vascular bundles are mainly found in the leaves.
    (a) (A) is true, but (B), (C) and (D) are wrong
    (b) (B) is true, but (A), (C) and (D) are wrong
    (c) (C) is true, but (A), (B) and (D) are wrong
    (d) (D) is true, but (A), (B) and (C) are wrong
    (e) (A) and (B) are true, but (C) and (D) are wrong

20. In woody trees, the exchange of gases between the outer atmosphere and the internal tissue of the stem takes place through
    (a) aerenchyma
    (b) stomata
    (c) pneumatophores
    (d) lenticels
    (e) trichomes

21. In the sieve elements, which one of the following is the most likely function of P-proteins?
    (a) Deposition of callose on sieve plates
    (b) Providing energy for active translocation
    (c) Autolytic enzymes
    (d) Sealing off mechanism on wounding

22. Match Column I with Column II and choose the correct option.

Column I		Column II
(A) Bulliform cells	1.	Initiation of lateral roots
(B) Pericycle	2.	Root
(C) Endarch xylem	3.	Grasses
(D) Exarch xylem	4.	Dicot leaf
(E) Bundle sheath cells	5.	Stem

    (a) A-3, B-5, C-4, D-1, E-2
    (b) A-2, B-5, C-1, D-3, E-4
    (c) A-2, B-4, C-1, D-3, E-5
    (d) A-3, B-1, C-5, D-2, E-4
    (e) A-5, B-4, C-2, D-1, E-3

23. In one tissue, the cells are isodiametric, walls are thin and made up of cellulose and the other consists of long, narrow cells with thick and lignified cell walls. They are
    (a) Parenchyma and sclerenchyma
    (b) Parenchyma and sclerenchyma
    (c) Sclerenmchyma and collenchyma
    (d) Collenchyma and parenchyma
    (e) Sclerenchyma and parenchyma

24. Which of the following statement(s) is/are true?
    (A) Uneven thickening of cell wall is characteristic of sclerenchyma.
    (B) Periblem forms cortex of the stem and the root.
    (C) Tracheids are the chief water transporting elements in gymnosperms.
    (D) Companion cell is devoid of nucleus at maturity.
    (E) The Commercial cork is obtained from *Quercus suber.*
    (a) A and D only
    (b) B and E only
    (c) C and D only
    (d) B, C and E only

25. Match the followings and choose the right combination

    A. Endodermis   (i) Companion cells

    B. Stomata   (ii) Lenticels

    C. Sieve tube   (iii) Palisade cells

    D. Periderm   (iv) Passage cells

    E. Mesophyll   (v) Accessory cells

    (a) A – (iv), B – (v), C – (ii), D – (i), E – (iii)

    (b) A – (v), B – (iii), C – (i), D – (ii), E – (iv)

    (c) A – (iv), B – (v), C – (i), D – (ii), E – (iii)

    (d) A – (ii), B – (v), C – (iii), D – (iv), E – (i)

26. Match the followings and choose the correct option.

    A. Meristem   (i) Photosynthesis, storage

    B. Parenchyma   (ii) Mechanical support

    C. Collenchyma   (iii) Actively dividing cells

    D. Sclerenchyma   (iv) Stomata

    E. Epidermal tissue   (v) Sclereids

    (a) A – (i), B – (iii), C – (v), D – (ii), E–(iv)

    (b) A – (iii), B – (i), C – (ii), D – (v), E – (iv)

    (c) A – (ii), B – (iv), C – (v), D – (i), E – (iii)

    (d) A – (v), B – (iv), C – (iii), D – (ii), E – (i)

27. Match the following and choose the correct combination

    A. Xylem vessels   (i) Store food materials

    B. Xylem tracheids   (ii) Obliterated lumen

    C. Xylem fibre   (iii) Perforated plates

    D. Xylem parenchyma   (iv) Chisel-like ends

    (a) A – (iv), B – (iii), C – (ii), D – (i)

    (b) A – (iii), B – (ii), C – (i), D – (iv)

    (c) A – (iii), B – (iv), C – (ii), D – (i)

    (d) A – (i), B – (ii), C – (iii), D – (iv)

28. The following diagrams show the types of secondary thickenings in the xylem vessels. Identify the types labelled from A to F. Choose the correct option from those given

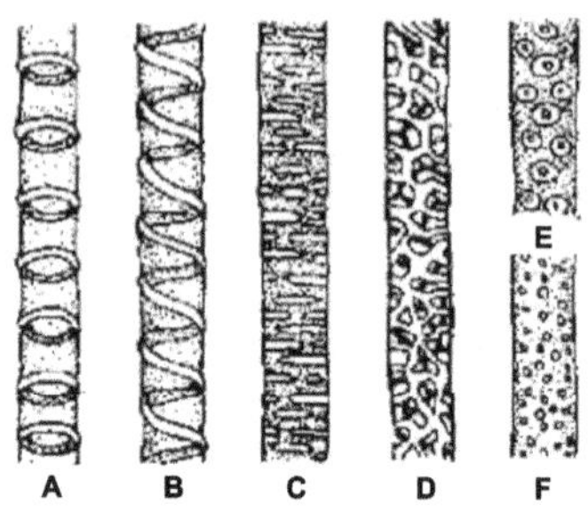

    (a) A – spiral, B – annular, C – reticulate, D – scalariform, E – pitted with border, F – pitted, simple

    (b) A – annular, B – spiral, C – scalariform, D – reticulate, E – pitted with border, F – pitted, simple

    (c) A – annular, B – spiral, C – scalariform, D – reticulate, E – pitted, simple, F – pitted with border

    (d) A – spiral, B – annular, C – scalariform, D – reticulate, E – pitted with border, F – pitted, simple

29. The distinct cavities (lacunae) found in a mature vascular bundle of maize stem are formed due to

    (a) disruption of protoxylem as well as lysis of adjacent xylem parenchyma.

    (b) disruption of protoxylem alone.

    (c) lysis of xylem parenchyma.

    (d) dissolution of common wall between a few metaxylem elements and their consequent coalition.

30. Match the following and choose the correct option

    A. Cuticle   (i) guard cells

    B. Bulliform cells   (ii) outer layer

    C. Stomata   (iii) waxy layer

    D. Epidermis   (iv) empty colourless cell

    (a) A – (iii), B – (iv), C – (i), D – (ii)

    (b) A – (i), B – (ii), C – (iii), D – (iv)

    (c) A – (iii), B – (ii), C – (iv), D – (i)

    (d) A – (iii), B – (ii), C – (i), D – (iv)

31. Match the names of the structures listed under column-I with the functions given under column-II, choose the answer which gives the correct combination of the alphabets of the two columns :

Column-I (Structure)		Column-II (Function)
A.	Stomata	(i) Protection of stem
B.	Bark	(ii) Plant movement
C.	Cambium	(iii) Secondary growth
D.	Hydathode	(iv) Transpiration
		(v) Guttation

(a) A – (v), B – (iii), C – (i), D – (iv)
(b) A – (i), B – (iv), C – (v), D – (iii)
(c) A – (ii), B – (iv), C – (i), D – (iii)
(d) A – (iv), B – (i), C – (iii), D – (v)

ANSWER KEY

1	(c)	2	(c)	3	(a)	4	(a)	5.	(a)	6	(a)	7	(d)	8	(d)	9	(a)	10	(a)
11	(c)	12	(d)	13	(d)	14	(b)	15.	(a)	16	(d)	17	(c)	18	(d)	19	(e)	20	(d)
21	(d)	22	(d)	23	(b)	24	(d)	25.	(c)	26	(b)	27	(c)	28.	(b)	29	(b)	30	(a)
31	(d)																		

Structural Organisation in Animals

1. Out of the four basic types of tissues, which is not the one ?
   (a) Muscular tissue
   (b) Skeletal tissue
   (c) Neural tissue
   (d) Epithelial tissue

2. In all connective tissues except the following, the cells secretes the fibres of collagen or elastin protein
   (a) Bone
   (b) Cartilage
   (c) Areolar connective tissue
   (d) Fluid connective tissue

3. The epithelium of following structure provides protection against chemical and mechanical stresses
   (a) Skin   (b) Pharynx
   (c) Buccal cavity   (d) All of these

4. Consider the following three statements and mark the right options
   A. The plasma without clotting factors is called semen
   B. Thymus is called the graveyard of RBCs
   C. Thrombocytes are the cell fragments produced from megakaryocytes
   (a) Only A is correct
   (b) Both A and C are correct
   (c) Both B and C are correct
   (d) Only C is correct

5. Read the following statements and mark the right option
   A. A healthy person has 12 to 16 g. of haemoglobin per 100 ml of blood
   B. The number of platelets in a normal individual is 1.5 lac to 3.5 lac per mm^3 of blood
   C. Eosinophils are involved in allergic reactions
   (a) Only B is correct
   (b) Only B and C are correct
   (c) Only A and C are correct
   (d) All A, B and C are correct

6. The haemoglobin content per 100 ml of blood of a normal healthy human adult is
   (a) 5 - 11 g
   (b) 25 - 30 g
   (c) 17 - 20 g
   (d) 12 - 16 g

7. Read the following statements and mark the right option

A. The numebr of segments in the body of earthworm is 100-120

B. Prostomium is the first segment and contains mouth

C. Clitellum is present in segments numbered 14 to 16.

(a) A and B are correct

(b) B and C are correct

(c) A and C are correct

(d) All, A, B and C are correct

8. Which one of the following cellular components of the blood is responsible for the production of antibodies?

(a) Thrombocyte   (b) Lymphocyte

(c) Monocyte   (d) Erythrocyte

9. Which of the following statements is correct for node of Ranvier of nerve?

(a) Covered by myelin sheath

(b) Neurilemma is discontinuous

(c) Myelin sheath is discontinuous

(d) Both neurilemma and myelin sheath are discontinuous

10. In female *Pheretima posthuma* pharyngeal nephridia are present in

(a) 3, 4, 5   (b) 7, 8, 9

(c) 4, 5, 6   (d) 5, 6, 7

11. Match the items in colum A with column B and choose the correct answers given below

Column A		Column B
1.	neuron	A.	ossein
2.	bone matrix	B.	nissl bodies
3.	RBC of man	C.	antibodies
4.	lymphocytes	D.	non-nucleated.

(a) 1 - D, 2 - B, 3 - C, 4 - A

(b) 1 - D, 2 - A, 3 - C, 4 - B

(c) 1 - D, 2 - B, 3 - A, 4 - C

(d) 1 - B, 2 - A, 3 - D, 4 - C

12. Choose the odd pair out in the following

(a) areolar connective tissue - collagen

(b) epithelium -keratin

(c) neuron - melanin

(d) muscle fibre -actin.

13. Thousands of year old mummies are still in their condition as they were before due to the non destruction of

(a) yellow elastin fibres

(b) white elastin fibres

(c) collagen fibres

(d) veins

14. The following are associated with *Pheretima*. Match them

	List I		List II
1.	Yellow cells	A.	Primardial germ cells
2.	Oval sphinctered pores	B.	Totipotent
3.	Basal cells	C.	Deamination
4.	Parietal layer	D.	The septum between 14/15

(a) 1-C, 2-D, 3-B, 4-A

(b) 1-C, 2-B, 3-D, 4-A

(c) 1-C, 2-A, 3-B, 4-D

(d) 1-D, 2-A, 3-B, 4-C

15. The gland whose secretion facilitates the attachment of two earthworms during Copulation is loacted in the segment :

(a) 14th   (b) 18th

(c) 19th   (d) 22nd

16. People living at sea level have around 5 million RBC per cubic millimeter of their blood whereas those living at an altitude of 54 00 metres have around 8 million. This is because at high altitude

(a) atmospheric O_2 level is less and hence more RBCs are needed to absorb the required amount of O_2 to survive

                                                                 BIOLOGY

(b) there is more UV radiation which enhances RBC - production

(c) people eat more nutritive food, therefore more RBCs are formed

(d) people get pollution - free air to breathe and more oxygen is available

17. Match the following simple epithelia tissues in column I with their occurrence in column II and choose the correct combination from the options given.

Column I		Column II
A. squamous	1.	intestinal glands
B. cuboidal	2.	trachea
C. columnar	3.	ovary
D. ciliated	4.	blood vessels
E. pseudo stratified	5.	bronchioles

(a) A–1,. B–2, C–4, D–3, E–5
(b) A–5,. B–4, C–2, D–1, E–3
(c) A–4,. B–5, C–1, D–2, E–3
(d) A–4,. B–3, C–1, D–5, E–2

18. Match the following

A. neutrophil	1.	single large necleus
B. eosinophil	2.	2 to 3 tobed nucleus
C. basophil	3.	kindney shaped nucleus
D. lymphocyte	4.	2 to 7 lobed nucleus
E. monocyte	5.	bilobed nucleus

(a) A–4,. B–1, C–3, D–5, e–2
(b) A–2,. B–5, C–1, D–4, e–3
(c) A–4,. B–5, C–2, D–1, e–3
(d) A–2,. B–4, C–5, D–3, e–1

19. Arrangement of tarsus, femur, trochanter, tibia and coxa in cockroach leg is

(a) Tibia, trochanter, femur, tarsus and coxa
(b) Trochanter, coxa, tibia, femur and tarsus
(c) Coxa, femur, trochanter, tibia and tarsus
(d) Coax, trochanter, femur, tibia and tarsus
(e) Trochanter, coxa, femur, tarsus and tibia

ANSWER KEY																			
1	(b)	**2**	(d)	**3**	(d)	**4**	(d)	**5**	(d)	**6**	(d)	**7**	(c)	**8**	(b)	**9**	(c)	**10**	(c)
11	(d)	**12**	(c)	**13**	(a)	**14**	(a)	**15**	(c)	**16**	(a)	**17**	(d)	**18**	(c)	**19**	(d)		

Cell : The Unit of Life

8

1. Three of the following statements regarding cell organelles are correct while one is wrong. Which one is wrong ?
   (a) Lysosomes are double membraned vesicles budded off from Golgi apparatus and contain digestive enzymes.
   (b) Endoplasmic reticulum consists of a network of membranous tubules and helps in transport, synthesis and secretion.
   (c) Leucoplasts are bound by two membranes, lack pigment but contain their own DNA and protein synthesizing machinery.
   (d) Sphearosomes are single membrane bound and associated with synthesis and storage of lipids.

2. The section view of a mitochondrion showing the different parts.

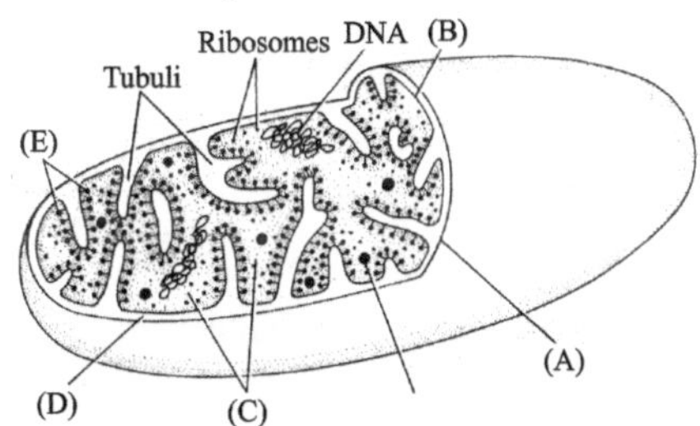

   Identify A to E.
   (a) A - Outer membrane, B - Inner membrane, C - Matrix, D - Inter- membrane space, E - Crista
   (b) A - Outer membrane, B - Inner membrane, C - Inter-membrane space, D - Matrix, E - Crista
   (c) A - Outer membrane, B - Inner membrane, C - Matrix, D - Crista, E - Inter - membrane space
   (d) A - Outer membrane, B - Inner membrane, C- Crista, D - Matrix, E - Inter-membrane space

3. Match the components A, B, C, D and E in the diagram (cell membrane) below from the list (i) to (vii)

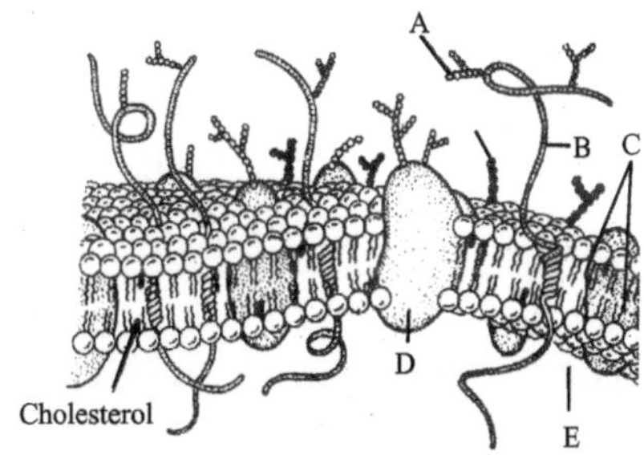

(i)   Sugar   (ii)   Protein

(iii) Lipid bilayer   (iv) Integral protein

(v)   Cytoplasm   (vi) Cell wall

(vii) External protein

(a)   A - (i), B - (ii), C - (iii), D - (iv), E - (v)

(b)   A - (ii), B - (i), C - (iii), D - (iv), E - (v)

(c)   A - (i), B - (ii), C - (iii), D - (iv), E - (vi)

(d)   A - (i), B - (ii), C - (iii), D - (vii), E - (v)

4. The following diagram shows some of the missing structures in a plant cell (A - E). Choose the correct option.

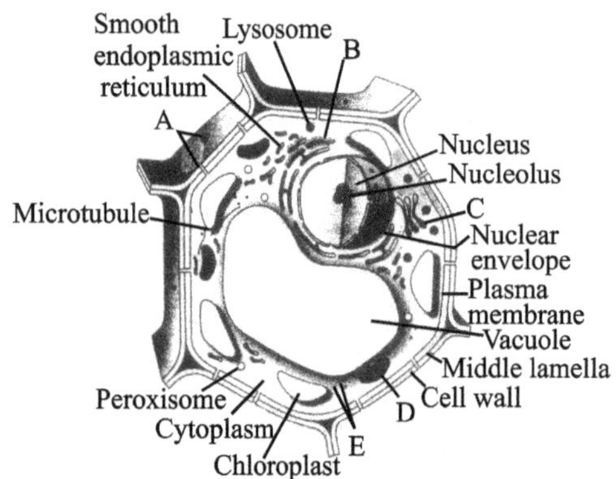

(a)   A - Plasmodesmata, B - Rough endoplasmic reticulum, C - Golgi apparatus, D - Mitochondrion, E - Ribosomes

(b)   A - Desmosome, B - Rough endoplasmic reticulum, C - Golgi apparatus, D - Mitochondrion, E - Ribosomes

(c)   A - Plasmodesmata, B - Smooth endoplasmic reticulum, C - Golgi apparatus, D - Mitochondrion, E - Ribosomes

(d)   A - Tight junction, B - Rough endoplasmic reticulum, C - Golgi apparatus, D - Mitochondrion, E - Ribosomes

5. The following diagram represents a chromosome.

Identify the structures A, B and type of chromosome (C).

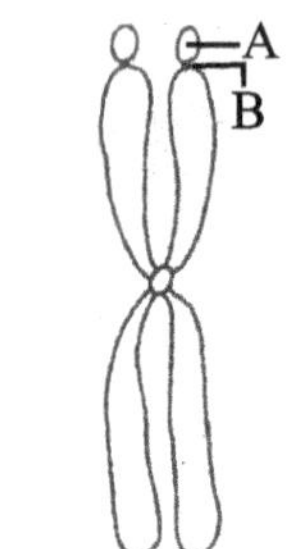

Types of Chromosome - C

(a)   A - Satellite, B - Primary constriction, C - Acrocentric

(b)   A - Satellite, B - Secondary constriction, C - Metacentric

(c)   A - Satellite, B - Centromere, C - Telocentric

(d)   A - Satellite, B - Centromere, C - Submetacentric

6. Choose the right sequence/route of the secretory product?

(a)   ER → Vesicles → cis region of GB → Trans region of GB → Vesicle → Plasma membrane

(b)   RER → GB → Lysosome → Nuclear membrane → Plasma membrane

(c)   ER → Vesicles → Trans region of GB → Cis region of GB → Vesicles → Plasma membrane

(d)   Lysosome → ER → GB → Vesicles → Cell membrane

7. Which one of the following combination is mismatched?

(a)   Glycocalyx - may be capsule or slime layer

(b)   Pili - Reproduction

(c)   Cell wall - Protective, determines shape, prevents from bursting

(d)   Flagella, Pili and Fimbriae - Surface structures of bacterial cell

8. Which of the following statement regarding mitochondrial membrane is not correct ?
    (a) The enzymes of the electron transfer chain are embedded in the outer membrane
    (b) The inner membrane is highly convoluted forming a series of infoldings
    (c) The outer membrane resembles a sieve
    (d) The outer membrane is permeable to all kinds of molecules

9. The dry weight of macromolecules like DNA, RNA and proteins can be determined using
    (a) fluorescent microscopy
    (b) dark field microscopy
    (c) phase contrast microscopy
    (d) differential interference contrast microscopy

10. Analyse the following pairs and identify the correct options given
    A. Chromoplasts - Contains pigments other than chlorophyll
    B. Leucoplasts - Devoid of any pigments
    C. Amyloplasts - Store proteins
    D. Alueroplasts - Store oils and fats
    E. Elaioplasts - Store carbohydrates
    (a) B and C are correct
    (b) C and D are correct
    (c) D and E are correct
    (d) A and B are correct

11. Select the alternative giving correct identification and function of the organelle 'A' in the diagram

    (a) Endoplasmic reticulum-synthesis of lipids
    (b) Mitochondria-produce cellular energy in the form of ATP
    (c) Golgi body-provides packaging material
    (d) Lysosomes - secrete hydrolytic enzymes

12. Match the following and choose the correct combination from the options given.

Column I (Cell type)		Column II (Size)
(A) Viruses	(1)	1-2 μm
(B) PPLO	(2)	10-20 μm
(C) Eukaryotic cell	(3)	About 0.1 μm
(D) Bacterium	(4)	0.02 - 0.2 μm

    (a) A-1, B-2, C-3, D-4   (b) A-4, B-3, C-2, D-1
    (c) A-1, B-3, C-2, D-4   (d) A-4, B-2, C-3, D-1

13. Select the matched ones.
    (1) Amyloplasts - store proteins
    (2) Mitochondrion - 'powerhouse' of the cell
    (3) Stroma - chlorophyll pigment
    (4) Axoneme - 9 + 2 array
    (a) (1) and (3) only
    (b) (2), (3) and (4) only
    (c) (3) and (4) only
    (d) (2) and (4) only

14. Match the following and select the correct answer:
    (A) Centriole   (i) Infoldings in mitochondria
    (B) Chlorophyll   (ii) Thylakoids
    (C) Cristae   (iii) Nucleic acids
    (D) Ribozymes   (iv) Basal body cilia or fiagella

	(A)	(B)	(C)	(D)
(a)	(iv)	(ii)	(i)	(iii)
(b)	(i)	(ii)	(iv)	(iii)
(c)	(i)	(iii)	(ii)	(iv)
(d)	(iv)	(iii)	(i)	(ii)

15. The solid linear cytoskeletal elements having a diameter of 6 nm and made up of a single type of monomer are known as:

(a) Microtubules

(b) Microfilaments

(c) Intermediate filaments

(d) Lamins

16. Select the correct matching in the following pairs:

(a) Smooth ER – Synthesis of lipids

(b) Rough ER – Synthesis of glycogen

(c) Rough ER – Oxidation of fatty acids

(d) Smooth ER – Oxidation of phospholipids

17. Match the columns and identify the correct option.

Column-I		**Column-II**
(a) Thylakoids	(i)	Disc-shaped sacs in Golgi apparatus
(b) Cristae	(ii)	Condensed structure of DNA
(c) Cisternae	(iii)	Flat membranous sacs in stroma
(d) Chromatin	(iv)	Infoldings in mitochondria

    (A) (B) (C) (D)

(a) (iii) (iv) (i) (ii)

(b) (iii) (i) (iv) (ii)

(c) (iii) (iv) (ii) (i)

(d) (iv) (iii) (i) (ii)

18. Cell adhesion and cell recognition occur due to biochemicals of cell membrane named

(a) lipids

(b) proteins

(c) glycoproteins and glycolipids

(d) proteins and lipids

19. The selective permeability of the plasma membrane allows the cell to maintain a constant internal environment. This has been termed as

(a) homostasis   (b) homeostasis

(c) hemostasis   (d) homeolysis

20. Which of the following four cell structures is correctly matched with the accompanying description ?

(a) Plasma membrane — Outer layer of cellulose or chitin

(b) Mitochondria — Bacteria like elements with inner membrane forming sacs containing chlorophyll, found in plant cell and algae

(c) Chloroplasts — Bacteria like elements with inner membrane highly folded

(d) Golgi apparatus — Stacks of flattened vesicles

21. Match the items in column I with column II and choose the correct option.

	Column I		**Column II**
A.	Sap vacuole	1.	Contain digestive enzyme
B.	Contractile vacuole	2.	Store metabolic gases
C.	Food vacuole	3.	Osmoregulation
D.	Air vacuole	4.	Store lipids
E.	Spherosomes	5.	Store and concentrate mineral salts and nutrients

    A B C D E

(a) 5 3 1 2 4

(b) 2 3 4 5 1

(c) 5 3 2 4 1

(d) 4 1 3 5 2

22. The chemical substances found most abundantly in the middle lamella are released into the phragmoplast by
    (a) endoplasmic reticulum
    (b) Golgi complex
    (c) spindle fragments
    (d) interzonal fibres

23. Read the following statements and identify the correct option given.
    I.   In prokaryotic cell, the nuclear membrane, chloroplast, mitochondria, microtubules and different kinds of pili are absent.
    II.   In eukaryotic cell, the nuclear membrane, chloroplast, mitochondria and pili are present.
    III.   In prokaryotic cell, the ribosome is of 70S type and in mitochondria of eukaryotic animal cell, the ribosome is of 80S type.
    (a) I and II are wrong; III is correct
    (b) I is correct; II and III are wrong
    (c) I and II are correct; III is wrong
    (d) I, II and III are wrong

24. Which of the following statements regarding cilia is not correct ?
    (a) The organised beating of cilia is controlled by fluxes of Ca^{2+} across the membrane
    (b) Cilia are hair-like cellular appendages
    (c) Microtubules of cilia are composed of tubulin
    (d) Cilia contain an outer ring of nine doublet microtubules surrounding two single microtubules

25. Choose the wrong option.
    (a) Lysosomes are double membranous vesicles budded off from Golgi apparatus and contain digestive enzymes
    (b) Endoplasmic reticulum consists of a network of membranous tubule and helps in transport, synthesis and secretion
    (c) Leucoplasts are bound by two membranes, lack pigment but contain their own DNA and protein synthesising machinery
    (d) Sphaerosomes are single membrane bound organelle which are associated with synthesis and storage of lipids

26. Which one of the following pairs is not correctly matched?
    (a) Cristae — The tubular structure formed by the folding of the inner membrane of the mitochondrion
    (b) Plasmodesmata — The membrane surrounding the vacuole in plants
    (c) Grana — Membrane bound discs in chloroplasts that contain chlorophylls and carotenoids
    (d) Middle lamella — Layer between adjacent cells walls in plants derived from cell plate

ANSWER KEY

1	(a)	2	(a)	3	(a)	4	(a)	5	(b)	6	(a)	7	(b)	8	(a)	9	(d)	10	(d)
11	(b)	12	(b)	13	(d)	14	(a)	15	(b)	16	(a)	17	(a)	18	(c)	19	(b)	20	(b)
21	(a)	22	(b)	23	(d)	24	(a)	25	(a)	26	(b)								

Biomolecules

1. Basic amino acids have more amino groups than carboxylic groups. Which of the following set has both basic amino acids?

   (a) Glutamic acid and Glycine

   (b) Histidine and Lysine

   (c) Arginine and Valine

   (d) None of these

2. Which of the following is a polysaccharide but is not the polymer of glucose.

   (a) Starch

   (b) Keratin

   (c) Chitin

   (d) Cellulose

3. In human body how much % part of total water is present as intracellular fluid

   (a) 55 %   (b) 35%

   (c) 80 %   (d) 75 %

4. Which of the following type of bond gives protein a secondary structure?

   (a) Peptide bond

   (b) Disulphide bond

   (c) Hydrogen bond

   (d) Hydrophobic and Vaander Val forces

5. With reference to double stranded DNA, The following ratio is always constant for all species

   (a) $\dfrac{A+T}{G+C}$

   (b) $\dfrac{G+C}{A+T}$

   (c) Both (a) and (b)

   (d) $\dfrac{A+G}{T+C}$

6. Which of the following classes of biomolecules are known to have catalytic properties :

   (a) Protein and lipid

   (b) Protein and RNA

   (c) Protein and carbohydrate

   (d) Carbohydrate and lipid

7. Mark the correct combination of organic compound and its test

   (a) Proteins – Biuret test and Millon's test

   (b) Lipid- Benedict test and Fehling test

   (c) Sugars – Sudan III test

   (d) All of these

8. In quaternary configuration of protein, disulphide bond may form between following amino acids
   (a) Methionine and serine
   (b) Tyrosine and valine
   (c) Methionine and crysteine
   (d) Proline and cysteine

9. The pairing of A = T, and G ≡ C is the universal phenomenon of DNA. From this we can deduce all the followings except
   (a) A+ T = G + C
   (b) Ratio of A: T is one
   (c) Guanine equals Cytosine
   (d) Nitrogenous bases in the two strands are complementary

10. Buchner discovered a complex enzyme system from yeast cells. His enzyme was :
    (a) Amylase which induces digestion of cellulose
    (b) Zymase complex which induces synthesis of vitamins
    (c) Zymase complex which induces synthesis of ethanol
    (d) Catalytic RNA like Ribozyme

11. Sulpha drugs are antibacterial and prevent the synthesis of folic acid. This type of enzymatic inhibition is
    (a) Allostearic inhibition
    (b) Competitive inhibition
    (c) Non-competitive inhibition
    (d) None of these

12. An example of competitive inhibition of an enzyme is the inhibition of
    (a) Succinic dehydrogenase by malonic acid
    (b) Cytochrome oxidase by cyanide
    (c) Hexokinase by glucose 6- phosphate
    (d) Carbonic anhydrase by carbon-di-oxide

13. The Km value of the enzyme is the value of the substrate concentration at which the reaction reaches to
    (a) Zero
    (b) 2 Vmax
    (c) ½ Vmax
    (d) ¼ Vmax

14. If a chemical does not bind with the active site and is also not the end product of the other enzymatic reaction, but still inhibits the enzymatic reaction. Such inhibition is called
    (a) Non-competitive inhibition
    (b) Allostearic inhibition
    (c) Competitive inhibition
    (d) None of these

15. The vitamin that promotes the synthesis of collagen fibres and helps in healing, is
    (a) Vitamin A
    (b) Vitamin C
    (c) Vitamin K
    (d) Vitamin E

16. Which of the following is the best evidence for the **lock and key theory** of enzymatic action
    (a) All isolated enzymes have been identified as proteins
    (b) Enzymes are formed in living organisms only
    (c) Compounds similar in structure to the substrate inhibit the reaction
    (d) Enzymes determine the direction of a reaction

17. Heart enlargement and paralysis can occur due to the deficiency of the following vitamin
    (a) Vitamin E
    (b) Vitamin B_1
    (c) Vitamin B_6
    (d) Vitamin B_{12}

18. A person comes to the doctor with complain of muscle wasting, weakness and difficulty in walking. He used polished rice in diet. What is the probable diagnosis

(a) Dry beri-beri   (b) Wet beri-beri

(c) Scurvy   (d) Pellegra

19. In an experiment it was found that adenine constitutes 31% and guanine 19%. The quantity of cytosine in this DNA is likely to be

(a) 19%   (b) 40%

(c) 31%   (d) 50%

20. Xerophthalmia in children and night blindness in adults is caused by the deficiency of

(a) Vitamin A   (b) Vitamin B

(c) Vitamin C   (d) Vitamin K

21. Which of the following is required for the development of erythrocytes?

(a) Vitamin A   (b) Vitamin B_{12}

(c) Vitamin E   (d) Vitamin K

22. A doctor advises a patient to include yellow fruits, carrots and butter in his diet. What deficiency disease to you think the patient is suffering from?

(a) Night blindness

(b) Colour blindness

(c) Kwashiorkor disease

(d) Marasmus disease

23. The given graph shows the effect of substrate concentration on the rate of reaction of the enzyme green -gram -phosphatase. What does the graph indicate ?

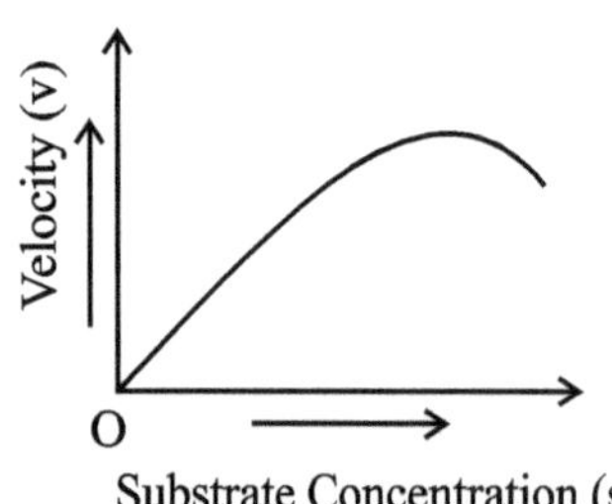

(a) The rate of enzyme reaction is direcly proportional to the substrate concentration

(b) Presence of an enzyme inhibitor in the reaction mixture

(c) Formation of an enzyme-substrate complex

(d) at higher substrate-concentration the pH increases.

24. Which group of three of the following five statements (a-e) contain is all three correct statements regarding beri-beri?

(A) a crippling disease prevalent among the native population of sub-Saharan Africa;

(B) a deficiency disease caused by lack of thiamine (vitamin B_1)

(C) a nutritional disorder in infants and young children when the diet is persistently deficient in essential protein;

(D) occurs in those countries where the staple diet is polished rice;

(E) the symptoms are pain from neuritis, paralysis, muscle wasting, progressive oedema, mental deterioration and finally heart failure;

(a) B, D and E   (b) A, B and D

(c) A, C and E   (d) B, C and E

25. Match the items in column I with items in column II and choose the correct answer

	Column I		Column II
A.	triglyceride	1.	animal hormones
B.	membrane lipid	2.	feathers and leaves
C.	steroid	3.	phospholipids
D.	wax	4.	fat stored in form of droplets

(a) a–4, b–3, c–1, d–2

(b) a–2, b–3, c–4, d–1

(c) a–3, b–4, c–1, d–2

(d) a–4, b–1, c–2, d–3

26. A sample of DNA is found to have the base composition (mole ratio) of adenine = 40, T = 22, G = 21 and cyto = 17. This
    (a) DNA is circular duplex
    (b) DNA is linear duplex
    (c) DNA is single stranded
    (d) DNA has high melting point

27. A particular enzyme molecule interacts with a specific substrate molecule is explained by
    (a) Enzyme-substrate concept
    (b) Activation energy concept
    (c) Destroyed and re-synthesized concept
    (d) Lock and key concept

ANSWER KEY																			
1	(c)	2	(c)	3	(a)	4	(d)	5	(a)	6	(a)	7	(c)	8	(a)	9	(d)	10	(d)
11	(b)	12	(a)	13	(b)	14	(b)	15	(a)	16	(c)	17	(d)	18	(a)	19	(a)	20	(a)
21	(b)	22	(a)	23	(b)	24	(a)	25	(a)	26	(c)	27	(b)						

Cell Cycle and Cell Division

1. Which one of the following is correct option for A, B and C.

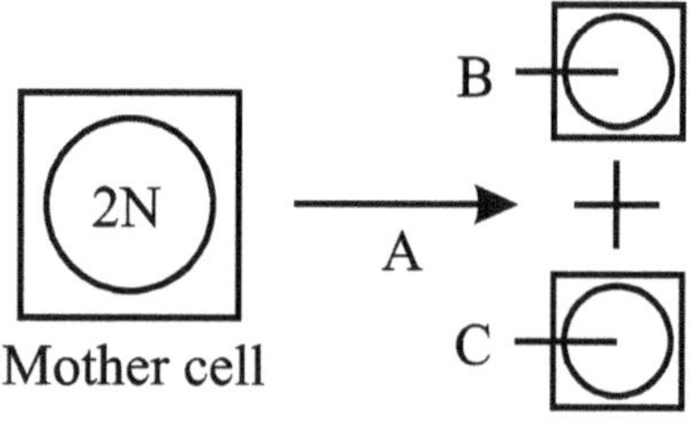

	A	B	C
(a)	Meiosis	N	N
(b)	Meiosis	2N	2N
(c)	Mitosis	N	N
(d)	Mitosis	2N	2N

2. Identify the phases from the graph given below that shows the change in DNA content during various phases (A to D) of mitotic cell cycle.

	A	B	C	D
(a)	G_2	G_1	S	M
(b)	G_2	S	G_1	M
(c)	G_1	S	G_2	M
(d)	M	G_1	S	G_2

3. In meiosis, the daughter cells differ from parent cell as well as amongst themselves due to

(a) segregation, independent assortment and crossing over

(b) segregation and crossing over

(c) independent assortment and crossing over

(d) segregation and independent assortment

4. A cell undergoing in Prophase I.

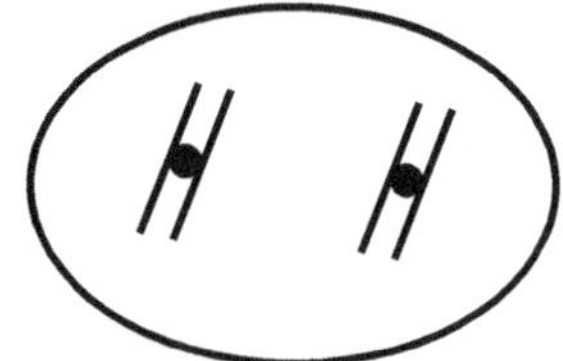

Which of the following diagram is correct for one of the cell at the end of meiosis?

(a) 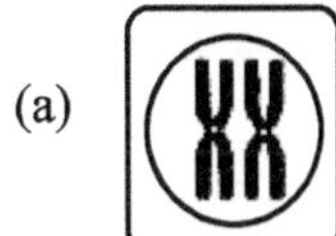

(b) 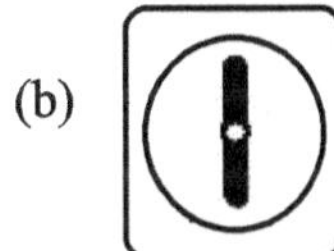

(c) 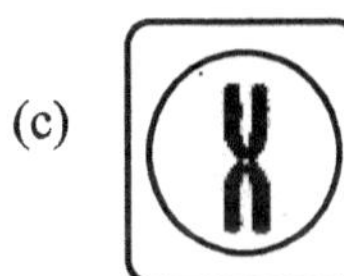

(d) 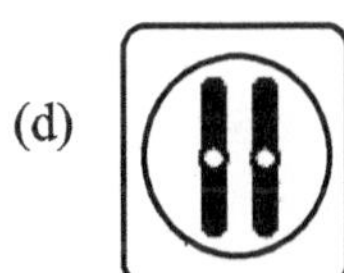

5. Match the following and choose the correct option.

	Column I		Column II
I.	Chromosomes are moved to spindle equator	(A)	Pachytene
II.	Centromere splits and chromatids apart	(B)	Zygotene
III.	Pairing between homologous chromosomes takes place	(C)	Anaphase
IV.	Crossing between homologous chromosomes	(D)	Metaphase

	I	II	III	IV
(a)	A	B	C	D
(b)	B	C	D	A
(c)	D	C	B	A
(d)	C	A	D	B

6. Which of the following events correctly indicates the stages of mitosis?

	DNA replication	Breakdown of nuclear membrane	Division of centromere
(a)	Interphase	Metaphase	Anaphase
(b)	Interphase	Prophase	Anaphase
(c)	Telophase	Interphase	Anaphase
(d)	Prophase	Metaphase	Anaphase

7. Different events that occur during different phases are given below.

(A) Centromere splits, chromatids separate and move to opposite poles and they now called chromosome

(B) Chromosomes cluster at opposite poles, decondensation of chromosome, reappearance of nuclear membrane, GB, ER and nucleolus

(C) Chromosomal replication

(D) Kinetochores attach to spindle fibres and chromosome are arranged at equatorial plate

(E) Spiration of chromosomes / condensation of chromosomal materials

Which of the following option correctly identifies each of the phases described?

	Interphase	Prophase	Metaphase	Anaphase	Telophase
(a)	C	E	D	A	B
(b)	C	D	E	A	B
(c)	C	E	D	B	A
(d)	C	A	D	E	B

8. Match the following and choose the correct option.

	Column I		Column II
I.	Terminalization of chiasmata	A.	Zygotene

II. Synapsis   B. Diplotene

III. Crossing over   C. Metaphase I

IV. Dissolution   D. Diakinesis
of Synaptonemal
complex

V. Best stage for   E. Pachytene
the study of
chiasmata

VI. Nuclear membrane and
nucleolus disappear

VII. Tetrads are arranged on
equatorial line

(a) A - II, B - V, C - VII, D - I, IV, VI, E - III

(b) A - II, B - III, C - VII, D - I, IV, VI, E - V

(c) A - II, B - VII, C - III, D - I, IV, V, E - VI

(d) A - II, B - I, C - IV, D - V, III, E - VI

9. Phragmoplast is the precursor of

(a) chloroplast

(b) chromoplast

(c) cell plate

(d) leucoplast

10. During which stages (or prophase I substages) of meiosis do you expect to find the bivalents and DNA replication respectively?

(a) Pachytene and interphase (between two meiotic divisions)

(b) Pachytene and interphase (just prior to prophase I)

(c) Pachytene and S phase (of interphase just prior to prophase I)

(d) Zygotene and S phase (of interphase prior to prophase I)

11. A bacterium divides every 35 minutes. If a culture containing 10^5 cells per ml is grown for 175 minutes, what will be the cell concentration per ml after 175 minutes?

(a) 5×10^5 cells

(b) 35×10^5 cells

(c) 32×10^5 cells

(d) 175×10^5 cells

12. During cell cycle, RNA and non-histone proteins are synthesised in

(a) S-phase

(b) G_0-phase

(c) G_2-phase

(d) M-phase

13. Which of the following stage during meiosis is concerned with DNA replication?

(a) Interphase

(b) Prophase

(c) Metaphase

(d) Anaphase

14. If we ignore the effect of crossing over, how many different haploid cells arise by meiosis in a diploid cell having 2n = 12 ?

(a) 8   (b) 16

(c) 32   (d) 64/

15. Among the following which one is longest phase in prophase of meiosis ?

(a) Leptotene

(b) Zygotene

(c) Pachytene

(d) Diplotene

16. Match List I and List II and select the correct answer using the code given below in the lists

List I (Phase of meiosis)	List II (Event that occurs)
A. Prophase I	Crossing over occurs
B. Metaphase I	Sister chromatids migrate to opposite poles
C. Anaphase I	Homologous chromosome line up at equator in pairs

(a) A, B and C are correct

(b) A and B are correct, C is false

(c) A is correct, B and C are false

(d) A and C are correct, B is false

17. Identify the meiotic stage in which the homologous chromosomes separate while the sister chromatids remain associated at their centromeres?

(a) Metaphase I

(b) Metaphase II

(c) Anaphase I

(d) Anaphase II

18. Find the correctly matched pairs and choose the correct option.

A. Leptotene - The chromosomes become invisible

B. Zygotene - Pairing of homologous chromosomes

C. Pachytene - Dissolution of the complex synaptonemal takes place

D. Diplotene - Bivalent chromosomes appear as tetrads

E. Diakinesis - Terminalization of chiasmata takes place

(a) A and B are correct

(b) B and D are correct

(c) B and E are correct

(d) B and C are correct

19. Which of the following events are not characteristic features of telophase?

A. Chromosome material condenses to form compact mitotic chromosomes.

B. Nucleolus, Golgi complex and ER reform

C. Nuclear envelope assembles around the chromosome clusters.

D. Centromeres split and chromatids separate.

E. Chromosomes cluster at opposite, spindle poles and their identity as discrete element is lost.

(a) A, B and D only

(b) A and D only

(c) B and C only

(d) C, D and E only

20. Select the correct option :

	I		II
A	"Synapsis aligns homologous chromosomes"	(i)	Anaphase-II
B	"Synthesis of RNA and protein"	(ii)	Zygotene
C	"Action of enzyme recombinase"	(iii)	G2-phase
D	"Centromeres do not separate but chromatids move towards opposite poles"	(iv)	Anaphase-I
		(v)	Pachytene

	A	B	C	D
(a)	(ii)	(iii)	(v)	(iv)
(b)	(i)	(ii)	(v)	(iv)
(c)	(ii)	(iii)	(iv)	(v)
(d)	(ii)	(i)	(iii)	(iv)

21. For viewing diakinesis which one of the following would be a suitable material

(a) Onion root tip

(b) Leaf of *Dichanthium*

(c) Rat tail

(d) Flower bud

22. If nucleus represents its large size in proportion to cytoplasm of cell, it indicates that
    (a) cell is dying
    (b) the nucleolus is in resting phase
    (c) the nucleus has entered S-phase of interphase
    (d) cell is about to die

23. The points at which crossing over has taken place between homologous chromosomes are called
    (a) protein axis
    (b) synaptonemal complexes
    (c) chiasmata
    (d) centromeres

ANSWER KEY

1	(d)	2	(c)	3	(a)	4	(b)	5	(c)	6	(b)	7	(a)	8	(a)	9	(c)	10	(d)
11	(c)	12	(c)	13	(a)	14	(d)	15	(c)	16	(c)	17	(a)	18	(c)	19	(b)	20	(a)
21	(d)	22	(c)	23	(c)															

Transport in Plants

1. A boy is studying transport of a certain type of molecules into cell. He finds that transport slows down when the cells are poisoned with a chemical that inhibits energy production. Under normal circumstances the molecules studied by the boy is probably transported by

   (a) simple diffusion

   (b) osmosis

   (c) active transport

   (d) facilitated diffusion

2. If a plant cell is immersed in water, the water continues to enter the cell until the

   (a) cell bursts.

   (b) concentration of the salts is the same inside the cell as outside.

   (c) concentration of water is the same inside the cell as outside.

   (d) diffusion pressure deficit is the same inside the cell as outside.

3. "Osmosis is the diffusion of a solution of a weaker concentration when both are separated by semipermeable membrane above". What is the error in the statement ?

   (a) The movement of solvent molecule is not specified.

   (b) There is no mention of DPD.

   (c) Behaviour of semipermeable membrane is not specified.

   (d) The exact concentration of solutions are not indicated.

4. Osmosis cannot be demostrated by a potato osmoscope using a solution of NaCl instead of sugar, because the potato tissue is

   (a) permeable to sodium ion

   (b) permeable to chloride ion

   (c) permeable to salt solution

   (d) impermeable to salt solution

5. The pathway of water from soil upto the secondary xylem is

   (a) Soil → root hair → cortex → endodermis → pericycle → protoxylem → metaxylem.

(b) Metaxylem → protoxylem → pericycle → cortex → endodermis → soil → root hair.

(c) Cortex → root hair → endodermis → pericycle → protoxylem → metaxylem.

(d) Pericycle → soil → root hair → cortex → endodermis → protoxylem → metaxylem

6. A botanist discovered a mutant plant that was unable to produce materials that form casparian strip. This plant would

(a) unable to transport water or solutes to the leaves.

(b) unable to use its sugar as a sugar sink.

(c) able to exert greater root pressure than the normal plant.

(d) unable to control amounts of water and solutes it absorbs.

7. Which of the following statements are **correct**?

I. No energy is expanded directly by the plant to translocate water.

II. The mechanisms of water transport from the soil through the plant body to the atmosphere include diffusion, bulk flow and osmosis.

III. Water moves in the root *via* the apoplast, transmembrane, and symplast pathway.

IV. The cohesion tension theory explains water transport in phloem.

(a) I, II, III, IV

(b) I, II and III

(c) III & IV

(d) Only IV

8. According to transpiration-cohesion theory water is pulled upward through the xylem. The cause of the pull is

(a) guttation

(b) root pressure

(c) transpiration

(d) condensation

9. If a cell A with D.P.D. 4 bars is connected to cell B, C, D whose O.P. and T.P. are respectively 4 and 4, 10 and 5 and 7 and 3 bars, the flow of water will be

(a) A and D to B and C

(b) A to B,C and D

(c) B to A, C and D

(d) C to A, B and D

10. Match the theories given in column I with the name of scientists listed in column II. Choose the answer which gives the correct combination of the alphabet.

	Column I		Column II
A.	Relay Pump Theory	I	Stocking
B.	Transpiration Cohesion Theory	II	Sir J. C. Bose
C.	Mass Flow Theory	III	Godlewski
D.	Pulsation Theory	IV	Dixon and Jolly
		V	Ernest Munch

(a) A – III, B – II, C – V, D – I

(b) A – II, B–I, C –V, D – III

(c) A – III, B – IV, C–V, D – II

(d) A – IV, B – III, C – I, D – II

11. A cell when dipped in 0.5 M sucrose solution has no effect but when the same cell will be dipped in 0.5 M NaCl solution, the cell will

(a) increase in size

(b) decrease in size

(c) will be turgid

(d) will get plasmolysed

12. Match the following

	Column I		Column II
(A)	Hypotonic	I	Water
(B)	Hypertonic	II	Sucrose
(C)	Solute	III	Lower tonicity
(D)	Solvent	IV	Higher tonicity

(a) A–I, B–II, C–III, D–IV

(b) A–III, B–II, C–I, D–IV

(c) A–III, B–IV, C–II, D–I

(d) A–III, B–II, C–IV, D–I

13. The following figure shows the stomatal apparatus. Identify the parts labelled as *a, b, c, d*. Choose the correct answer from the following.

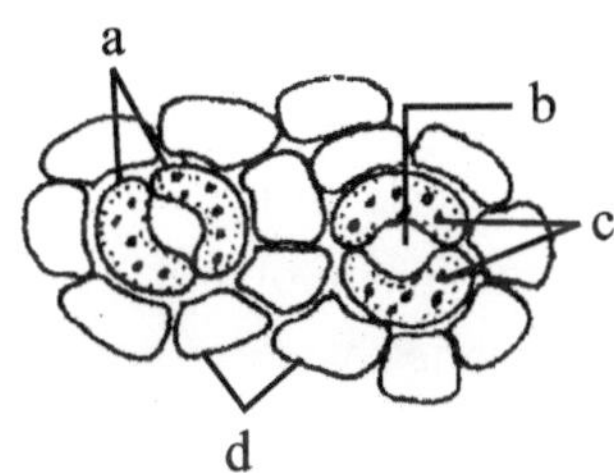

(a) *a*–subsidiary cell, *b*–chloroplasts, *c*–stoma, *d*–guard cells

(b) *a*–guard cell, *b*–stoma, *c*–chloroplast, *d*–subsidiary cells

(c) *a*–guard cell, *b*–chloroplast, *c*–stoma, *d*–subsidiary cells

(d) *a*–subsidiary cell, *b*–stoma, *c*–chloroplast, *d*–guard cell.

14. Identify the correct statements from the following.

(A) Accumulation of K^+ ions in the guard cells does not require energy.

(B) A high pH favours stomatal opening.

(C) Movement of chloride ion into guard cells as in response to the electric differential created by K^+ ions.

(D) With entry of several K^+ ions and chloride ions, water potential of guard cells increases.

The correct combination is

(a) (A) and (C) (b) (A) and (B)

(c) (B) and (C) (d) (C) and (D)

15. The value of osmotic potential (π) and pressure potential (p) of cells *a, b, c, d* are given below Cells

Cells	π	P
a	-1.0	0.5
b	-0.6	0.3
c	-1.2	0.6
d	-0.8	0.4

Identify the correct sequence that shows the path of movement of water from the following

(a) d $\longrightarrow$ c $\longrightarrow$ a $\longrightarrow$ b

(b) b $\longrightarrow$ d $\longrightarrow$ a $\longrightarrow$ c

(c) b $\longrightarrow$ c $\longrightarrow$ d $\longrightarrow$ a

(d) c $\longrightarrow$ b $\longrightarrow$ a $\longrightarrow$ d

16. Match List – I with List – II and find out the correct answer from the code given below.

List – I	**List – II**
(A) Diffusion	(i) hydrophoilic substances
(B) Osmosis	(ii) shrinkage of protoplasm
(C) Imbibition	(iii) semipermeable membrane
(D) Plasmolysis	(iv) free movement of ions and gases

(a) A – (ii), B – (i), C –(iv), D – (iii)

(b) A – (iv), B – (iii), C – (i), D – (ii)

(c) A – (iii), B – (i), C – (iv), D – (ii)

(d) A – (ii), B – (iii), C – (iv), D – (i)

17. Lenticels and hydathodes are small pores with one of the following common attribute

(a) They allow exchange of gases.

(b) Their opening and closing is not regulated.

(c) They always remain closed.

(d) They are found on the same organ of plants.

18. Dry wooden stakes, if driven into a small crack in a rock and then soaked, can develop enough pressure to split the rock. Such a pressure is built up through the phenomenon of

(a) imbibition   (b) prop roots

(c) turgor pressure   (d) buttress roots

19. Carbohydrates are commonly found as starch in plant storage organs. Which of the following five properties of starch (A-E) make it useful as a storage material?

(A) Easily translocated

(B) Chemically non-reactive

(C) Easily digested by animals

(D) Osmotically inactive

(E) Synthesized during photosynthesis

The useful properties are

(a) (B) and (C)   (b) (B) and (D)

(c) (A), (C) and (E)   (d) (A) and (E)

20. A leaf peeling of *Tradescantia* is kept in a medium having 10% NaCl. After a few minutes if we observe the peel under the microscope, we are likely to see

(a) the cells bursting out

(b) entry of water into the cell

(c) exit of water from the cell

(d) diffusion of NaCl into the cell.

21. The graph shows the relationship between ψ (water potential), ψ_s (solute potential) and ψ_p (pressure potential) for a plant cell placed in pure water.

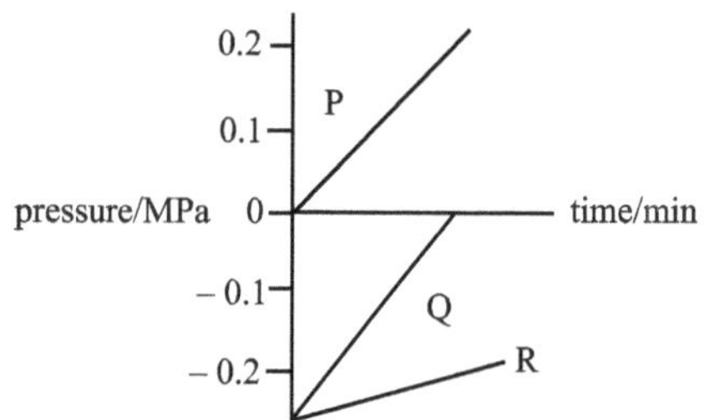

What are the correct labels for the graph?

	P	Q	R
(a)	ψ	ψ_p	ψ_s
(b)	ψ	ψ_s	ψ_p
(c)	ψ_p	ψ	ψ_s
(d)	ψ_p	ψ_s	ψ

22. Which one of the following graphs most closely represents the relationship between the rate of transpiration of a mesophytic leaf and the atmospheric humidity ?

(a)

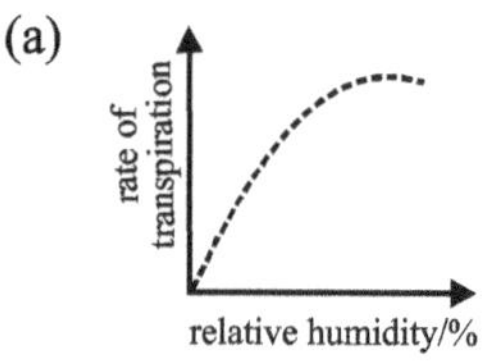

(b)

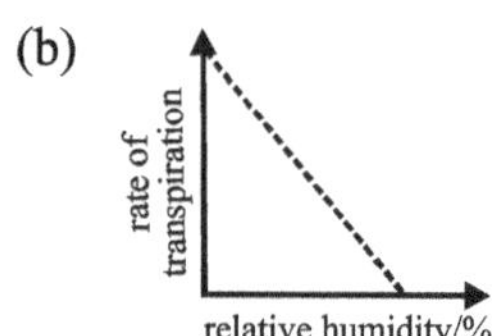

(c)

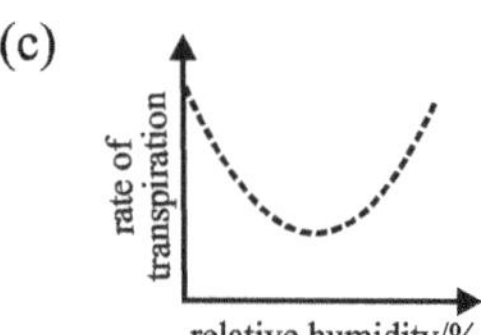

(d)

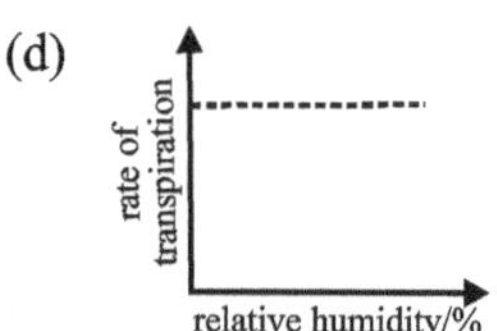

23. Imagine cutting a live twig from a tree and examining the cut surface of the twig with a magnifying glass. You locate the vascular tissue and observe a growing droplet of fluid exuding from the cut surface. This fluid is probably

(a) phloem sap

(b) xylem sap

(c) guttation fluid

(d) fluid of the transpiration stream

ANSWER KEY																			
1	(b)	2	(a)	3	(b)	4	(c)	5	(d)	6	(d)	7	(a)	8	(c)	9	(c)	10	(c)
11	(b)	12	(c)	13	(c)	14	(c)	15	(b)	16	(b)	17	(b)	18	(a)	19	(b)	20	(c)
21	(c)	22	(b)	23	(a)														

Mineral Nutrition

1. All of the following statements concerning the Actinomycetous filamentous soil bacterium *Frankia* are correct except, the *Frankia*

   (a) can induce root nodules on many plant species.

   (b) cannot fix nitrogen in the free-living state.

   (c) like *Rhizobium*, usually infects its host plant through root hair deformation and stimulates cell proliferation in the host's cortex.

   (d) forms specialized vesicles in which the nitrogenase is protected from oxygen by a chemical barrier involving triterpene hopanoids.

2. Which of the following is a component of vitamin (thiamine, biotin), Acetyl CoA, cysteine, methionine and ferrerdoxin?

   (a) Fe   (b) S

   (c) Co   (d) K

3. Which of the following statements are **correct**?

   I. Solution culture/Hydroponics contains all essential minerals except one, the usefulness of which is to be determined.

   II. Na, Si, Co and Selenium are beneficial element required by higher plants.

   III. Zn is the activator of nitrogenases while Mo is the activator of alcohol dehydrogenase.

   IV. Zn is needed for auxin synthesis.

   (a) All of these

   (b) I, II, III

   (c) I, II, IV

   (d) None of these

4. Match the column-I with column-II

	Column-I		Column-II
1.	Mg	p.	Found in some amino acids
2.	S	q.	Structural component of chlorophyll
3.	I	r.	Not important for plants
4.	Mn	s.	Required for photolysis of water

   (a) A-q, B-p, C-r, D-s

   (b) A-p, B-q, C-r, D-s

   (c) A-p, B-r, C-s, D-q

   (d) A-q, B-r, C-p, D-s

5. Match the Column-I containing minerals with the functions given in Column-II.

	Column-I		Column-II
I.	K	A.	Stomatal opening
II.	Mo	B.	Constituent of cell membrane
III.	P	C.	Photolysis of water
IV.	Mn	D.	Free ion
		E.	Component of nitrogenase and nitrate reductase

	I	II	III	IV
(a)	A, D	E	B	C
(b)	A, E	D	C	B
(c)	A, E	D	B	C
(d)	D	A	C	B, E

6. Reaction carried out by N_2 metabolising microbes include –

(i) $2HN_3 + 3O_2 \longrightarrow 2NO_2 + 2H+ + H_2O$

(ii) $2NO_2^- + O_2 \longrightarrow 2NO_3^-$

Which of the following statements about these reactions is **incorrect** ?

(a) Step (i) is carried out by *Nitrosomonas* or *Nitrococcus*.

(b) Step (ii) is carried out by *Nitrobacter*.

(c) Both steps (i) and (ii) can be called nitrification.

(d) Bacteria carrying out these steps are usually photoautotrophs.

7. The different steps in a nodule formation are given below.

I. A mature nodule establishes a direct vascular connection with the host for exchange of nutrients.

II. Root hair curls and the bacteria invade the root hair.

III. *Rhizobium* bacteria contact a susceptile root hair, divide near it

IV. The infection thread is produced carrying the bacteria and grows into the cortex of the root.

V. The bacteria get modified into rod-shaped bacteroids and cause inner cortical layer and pericycle to divide to form nodule.

The correct sequence is

(a) I, II, IV, V

(b) III, II, IV, V, I

(c) III, II, IV, I, V

(d) I, III, V, II, IV

8. Refer the figure given below and select the option which gives correct words for all the four blanks A, B, C and D.

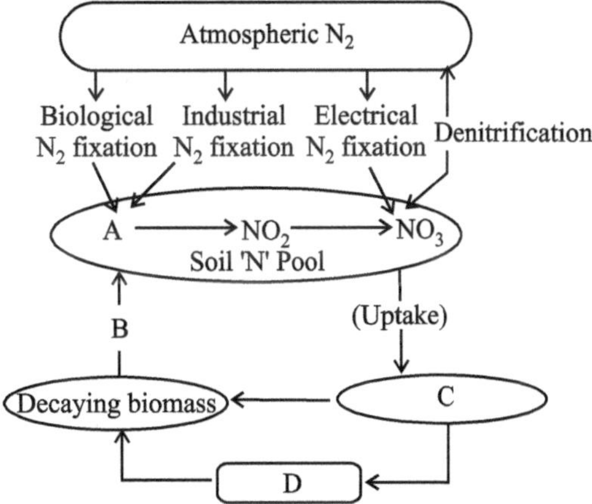

	A	B	C	D
(a)	K	Ammonification	Animal biomass	Plant biomass
(b)	NH₃	Ammonification	Plant biomass	Animal biomass
(c)	CO₂	Denitrification	Animal biomass	Plant biomass
(d)	CHO	Nitrification	Plant biomass	Animal biomass

9. Match the words of column I with the phrases in column II. Choose the answer which gives the correct combination.

	Column I		**Column II**
1.	Magnesium	(p)	Found in some amino acids
2.	Sulphur	(q)	Not important for plants
3.	Iodine	(r)	Structural component of chlorophyll
4.	Manganese	(s)	Component of sugar
		(t)	Required for enzyme activity

(a)   (1) – (r), (2) – (s), (3) – (q), (4) – (p)

(b)   (1) – (r), (2) – (p), (3) – (q), (4) – (s)

(c)   (1) – (r), (2) – (p), (3) – (q), (4) – (t)

(d)   (1) – (s), (2) – (r), (3) – (p), (4) – (t)

10. Match the following and choose the correct combination from the options given.

	Column I		**Column II**
A	Potassium	I	Constituent of ferredoxin
B	Sulphur	II	Involved in stomatal movement
C	Molybdenum	III	Needed in the synthesis of auxin
D	Zinc	IV	Component of nitrogenase

(a)   A-II, B-I, C-IV, D-III

(b)   A-I, B-II, C-III, D-IV

(c)   A-IV, B-III, C-II, D-I

(d)   A-I, B-III, C-IV, D-II

11 Which of the following option shows correct co-relation between Column-I, II and III.

Column-I	**Column-II**	**Column-III**
(1) Calcium	(I) Required for ionic-balance.	(i) Grey blot on leaves.
(2) Boron	(II) Essential for constitution of nucleic acid	(ii) Fruit-yield decreases.
(3) Phosphorus	(III) Required for absorption of calcium.	(iii) Red blots on leaves.
(4) Chlorine	(IV) Required to activate respiratory enzyme.	(iv) Fruit-size diminishes.
(5) Manganese	(V) Required for synthesis of bipolar spindle.	(v) Young root tip begin to die.

(a)   (1-I-iv), (2-II-v), (3-III-iii), (4-IV-i), (5-V-ii)

(b)   (1-V-v), (2-IV-iv), (3-III-i), (4-III-iii), (5-I-ii)

(c)   (1-IV-iii), (2-I-iv), (3-V-v), (4-III-ii), (5-II-i)

(d)   (1-V-v), (2-III-iv), (3-II-iii), (4-I-ii), (5-IV-i)

12. Study the following lists.

	List I		**List II**
(1)	Photolysis of water	(i)	Zinc
(2)	Diazotrophy	(ii)	Copper
(3)	Cytochrome 'c' oxidase	(iii)	Manganese
(4)	Biosynthesis of IAA	(iv)	Molybdenum
		(v)	Boron

Identify the correct match.

(a)   1 – (iii), 2 – (iv), 3 – (ii), 4 – (i)

(b)   1 – (v), 2 – (ii), 3 – (iii), 4 – (iv)

(c)   1 – (iii), 2 – (ii), 3 – (i), 4 – (iv)

(d)   1 – (iv), 2 – (i), 3 – (iii), 4 – (ii)

13. Leguminous plants are able to fix atmospheric nitrogen through the process of symbiotic nitrogen fixation. Which one of the following statements is not correct during this process of nitrogen fixation ?

(a) Leghaemoglobin scavanges oxygen and is pinkish in colour.

(b) Nitrogenase is insensitive to oxygen.

(c) Nodules act as sites for nitrogen fixation.

(d) The enzyme nitrogenase catalyses the conversion of atmospheric N_2 to NH_3.

14. Which one of the following is not an essential mineral element for plants while the remaining three are

(a) Iron   (b) Manganese

(c) Cadmium   (d) Phosphorus

15. Which two distinct microbial processes are responsible for the release of fixed nitrogen as dinitrogen gas (N_2) to the atmosphere?

(a) Anaerobic ammonium oxidation, and denitrification

(b) Aerobic nitrate oxidation, and nitrite reduction

(c) Decomposition of organic nitrogen, and conversion of dinitrogen to ammonium compounds

(d) Enteric fermentation in cattle, and nitrogen fixation by *Rhizobium* in root nodules of legumes

16. Consider the following statements,

(i) Sulphur is present in two amino acids-cysteine and valine.

(ii) Low level of N, K, S and Mo causes an inhibition of cell division.

(iii) The microbe that produces nitrogen fixing nodules on the roots of non-leguminous plant *"Alnus"* is *Frankia*.

(iv) Denitrification is carried by the bacteria *Nitrosomonas* and *Nitrobacter.*

Of the above statements

(a) (i) and (ii) alone are correct

(b) (i) and (iii) alone are correct

(c) (ii) and (iii) alone are correct

(d) (ii) and (iv) alone are correct

17. Ion exchange is an important process that facilitates the uptake of nutrients by plants. Which of the following statements about ion exchange is **false**?

(a) Ion exchange is most important in soils with high clay content.

(b) Clay particles have a permanent negative charge.

(c) Mineral cations bind more strongly to clay particles than do protons.

(d) Negative ions such as phosphate, nitrate, and sulfate are leached from the soil

ANSWER KEY																			
1	(b)	**2**	(b)	**3**	(c)	**4**	(a)	**5**	(a)	**6**	(d)	**7**	(b)	**8**	(b)	**9**	(c)	**10**	(a)
11	(d)	**12**	(a)	**13**	(b)	**14**	(c)	**15**	(a)	**16**	(c)	**17**	(c)						

Photosynthesis in Higher Plants

13

1. Who used prism, white light, green alga, *Cladophora* and aerobic bacteria and plotted the action spectra for photosynthesis?

   (a) Sachs   (b) Arnon

   (c) Arnold   (d) Englemann

2. Which one is the correct summary equation of photosynthesis?

   (a) $C_6H_{12}O_6 + 6O_2 \longrightarrow 6CO_2 + 6H_2O$ + energy

   (b) $C_6H_{12}O_6 + 6O_2 + 6H_2O \longrightarrow 6CO_2 + 12H_2O$ + energy

   (c) $6CO_2 + 6H_2O \xrightarrow[\text{Chlorophyll}]{\text{Light}} 6H_2O + C_6H_{12}O_6$

   (d) $6CO_2 + 12H_2O \xrightarrow[\text{Chlorophyll}]{\text{Light}} 6O_2 + C_6H_{12}O_6 + 6H_2O$

3. Which of the following statement is correct?

   (I) Light reaction occurs in stroma.

   (II) Light reaction occurs in grana and ATP + $NADPH_2$ are formed.

   (III) In stroma dark reaction occurs.

   (IV) Dark reaction is not directly light driven but is dependent on the products (ATP + $NADPH_2$) formed in light reaction.

   (a) I, II & IV are correct.

   (b) II, III & IV are correct.

   (c) All are correct.

   (d) Only II is correct.

4. The rate of photosynthesis of a freshwater plant is measured using five spectral colours. Which sequence of colours would give an increasing photosynthetic response?

   Smallest $\longrightarrow$ Largest response

   (a) Blue   Green   Yellow   Orange   Red

   (b) Green   Yellow   Orange   Red   Blue

   (c) Red   Orange   Yellow   Green   Blue

   (d) Yellow   Green   Orange   Blue   Red

5. A graph that plots the rate at which CO_2 is converted to glucose versus the wavelength of light illuminating a leaf is called

   (a) an absorption spectrum

   (b) an action spectrum

   (c) a planck constant

   (d) enzyme kinetics

6. Electrons excited by absorption of light in PSI are transferred to the primary acceptors, and therefore must be replaced. The replacements come directly from

(a) NADP   (b) ATP

(c) PSII   (d) Water

7. The following (P to U) are the main steps of chemosynthetic ATP synthesis in the light reaction. Which answer places them in correct order?

P. H^+ concentration gradient established

Q. H^+ diffuses through ATP synthetase

R. Carriers use energy from electrons to move H^+ across the membrane.

S. Electrons from PSII pass along electron transport chain.

T. Light excites electrons in PSII.

U. Energy of H^+ flow is used by ATP synthetase to make ATP.

(a) PQTSRU   (b) STPQRU

(c) TSRPQU   (d) TSRUQP

8. During light reaction, as electrons move through photosystems, protons are transported across the membrane. This happens because of

(a) the primary acceptor of e^- (located towards the outer surface of the membrane) transfers its electron not to an e^- carrier but to H carrier.

(b) the primary acceptor of e^- transfers only its e^- to e^- carrier.

(c) the primary acceptor of e^- transfers only H^+ to the next carrier.

(d) NADP - reductase is present in grana.

9. Hatch and Slack pathway (HSK pathway) is otherwise known as C_4-cycle because

(a) the first stable product is oxaloacetic acid / OAA which is a C_4-compound.

(b) the primary CO_2 acceptor is OAA, a C_4-compounds.

(c) all intermediate metabolites are C_4-compound.

(d) at one time $4CO_2$ molecules take part in carboxylation pathway.

10. The diagram below represents an experiment with isolated chloroplasts. The chloroplasts were first made acidic by soaking them in a solution at pH 4. After the thylakoid space reached pH 4, the chloroplasts were transferred to a basic solution at pH 8. The chloroplasts are then placed in the dark. Which of these compounds would you expect to be produced?

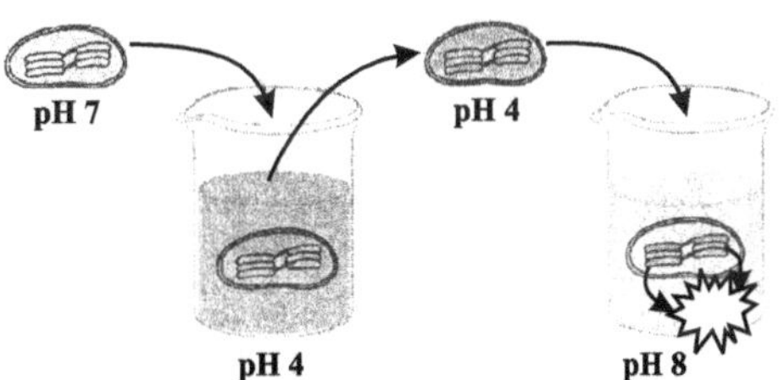

(a) ATP   (b) NAD

(c) G3P   (d) $C_6H_{12}O_6$

11. The graph below refers to an experiment involving species of alga. The relative concentrations of GP and RuPB present in the cells were monitored when the plants were in light and then in darkness

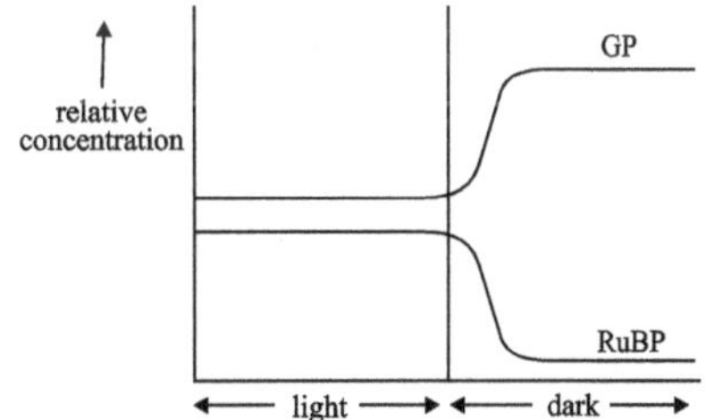

Which of the following conclusions cannot be drawn from these results?

(a) In darkness the relative concentration of GP increases.

(b) During the experiment RuBP may be converted into GP.

(c) The relative concentration of RuBP decreases on removal of CO_2.

(d) In light a steady state exists between RuBP and GP.

12. Melvin Calvin conducted two sets of experiments. In first set the *Chlorella* was fed with $^{14}CO_2$ for 3 seconds and in the second set for 60 seconds. The radioactivity of ^{14}C was found to be present in
    (a) 1-C of PGA in both the exposure.
    (b) 3–C of PGA in both the exposure.
    (c) The radioactivity of short-exposure in 1-C and long exposure in 3-C of PGA.
    (d) The radioactivity of long exposure in 1-C and of short exposure in 3-C of PGA.

13. Which fractions of the visible spectrum of solar radiations are primarily absorbed by carotenoids of the higher plants?
    (a) Violet and blue   (b) Blue and green
    (c) Green and red   (d) Red and violet

14. The chemical structure of chlorophyll *a* varies from chlorophyll *b* due to difference between
    (a) CH_3 and C_2H_5
    (b) CH_3 and $HCH = CH_2$
    (c) CH_3 and CHO
    (d) CHO and $CH = CH_2$

15. Photosynthesis in C_4 plants is relatively less limited by atmospheric CO_2 levels because
    (a) of effective pumping of CO_2 into bundle sheath cells.
    (b) RuBisCO in C_4 plants has higher affinity for CO_2.
    (c) four carbon acids are the primary initial CO_2 fixation products.
    (d) the primary fixation of CO_2 is mediated *via* PEP carboxylase.

16. Energy released during movement of electrons through the photosystems during photosynthesis is used to drive protons across the membrane against concentration gradient. As a result the protons accumulate in
    (a) thalakoid lumen

    (b) stroma
    (c) intrathylakoid space
    (d) stromal lamella

17. RuBisCO is the most abundant enzyme in the world and present in very high concentration in chloroplasts. It is required in very high concentration for photosynthesis because it
    (a) is a very slow acting enzyme.
    (b) also acts as an oxygenase.
    (c) catalyzes a reversible reaction.
    (d) is degraded very rapidly.

18. In photophosphorylation, under the circumstances when NADP is no longer available as acceptor the electrons are passed to
    (a) cytochrome-f   (b) plastocyanin
    (c) cytochrome B_6 (d) quinone

19. Which of the following with respect to early experiments of photosynthesis is wrongly matched?
    (a) Joseph Priestley   -   Showed that plants release O_2
    (b) Jan Ingenhousz   -   Showed that sunlight is essential for photosynthesis
    (c) Julius von Sachs   -   Proved that plants produce glucose when they grow.
    (d) T. W. Engelmann -   Showed that the green substance is located within special bodies in plants

20. A example of CAM plant is :
    (a) Black nightshade (*Solanum nigrum*)
    (b) Lemon grass (*Cymbopogon flexuosus*)
    (c) Sugarbeet (*Beta vulgaris*)
    (d) Snake plant (*Sanseviera trifasciata*)

21. Thomas Engelmann illuminated a filament of algae with light that passed through a prism, thus exposing different segments of the algal filament to different wavelengths of light. He added aerobic bacteria and found that these bacteria congregated in the areas illuminated by red and blue light. If you ran the same experiment without passing light through a prism, what would you predict?

    (a) There would be no difference in results.

    (b) The number of bacteria would decrease along the entire length of the filament.

    (c) The bacteria would be relatively evenly distributed along the length of the filament.

    (d) The number of bacteria would increase along the entire length of the filament.

22. The whole scheme of transfer of electrons, starting from PS-II, Uphill to the acceptor, down the e^- transport chain to PS-I, excitation of electrons, transfer to another acceptor, and finally downhill to $NADP^+$ is called

    (a) Y-scheme   (b) δ-scheme

    (c) Z-scheme   (d) None of these

23. Study the figure showing graph of light intensity on the rate of photosynthesis. Choose the correct option by matching the column I with column II

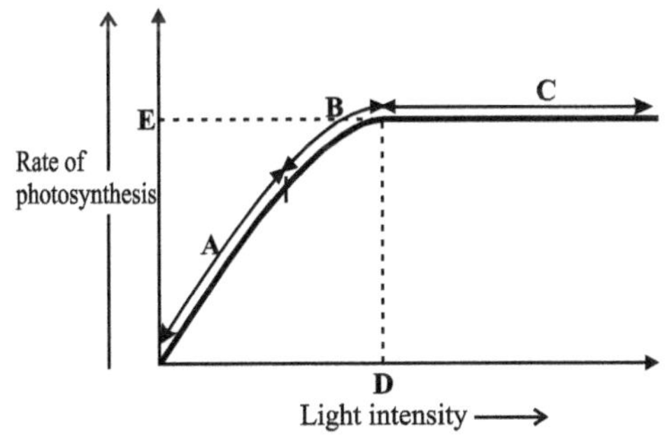

Column - I	Column - II
I. Limiting factor in region A	A. Some factor other than light intensity is becoming the limiting factor

II. B represents to	B. Light is no longer limiting factor
III. C represents to	C. Light intensity
IV. D represents to	D. Maximum rate of photosynthesis
V. E represents to	E. Saturation point for light intensity

The correct option is -

(a) I - A, II - B, III - C, IV - D, V - E

(b) I - C, II - A, III - B, IV - E, V - D

(c) I - D, II - B, III - E, IV - C, V - A

(d) I - E, II - D, III - C, IV - B, V - A

24. One plant is grown in the shade of a green house and the other is grown under a forest canopy (*i.e.* under the shade of trees). What would be the effect of these two type of shades on the rate of photosynthesis ?

    (a) The rate of photosynthesis would be equally low in both the types of shade.

    (b) The rate of photosynthesis would be greater under the forest canopy.

    (c) The rate of photosynthesis would be greater in the shade of a green house.

    (d) The shade of green house or a forest canopy would have no influence on the rate of photosynthesis because only 1% of sunlight is used in photosynthesis.

25. Assume a thylakoid is somehow punctured so that the interior of the thylakoid is no longer separated from the stroma. This damage will have the most direct effect on which of the following processes?

    (a) The splitting of water.

    (b) The absorption of light energy by chlorophyll.

    (c) The flow of electrons from photosystem II to photosystem I.

    (d) The synthesis of ATP.

26. Variegated leaves of a plant were supplied with radioactive carbon dioxide during an experiment. Leaf A was kept in the dark and leaf B was kept in the light. At the end of the experiment the radioactivity in the leaves was measured and found to be as shown on the diagram below.

What is the most likely explanation for the level of radioactivity found in the yellow zone of Y ?

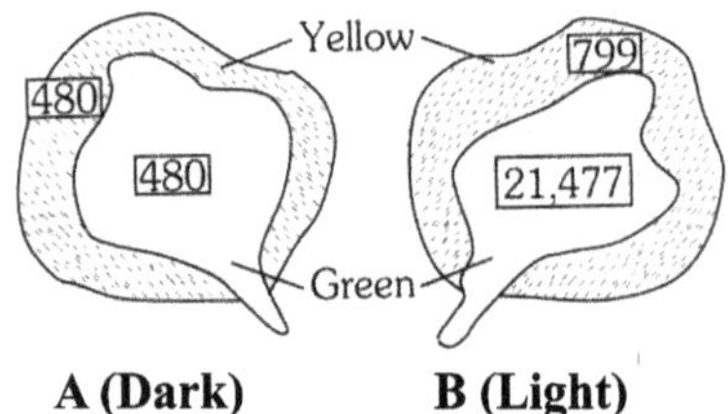

(a) Photosynthesis occurs but no storage of starch occurs in this zone.

(b) Radioactive carbon dioxide diffuses into the leaf and accumulates here.

(c) Products of photosynthesis diffuse into the yellow zone.

(d) Photosynthesis proceeds slowly in the absence of chlorophyll-*a* and *b*

27. Which one of the following expressions concerns photophosphorylation ?

(a) $AMP + Inorganic\ PO_4 \xrightarrow{Light\ energy} ATP$

(b) $ADP + AMP \xrightarrow{Light\ energy} ATP$

(c) $ADP + Inorganic\ PO_4 \xrightarrow{Light\ energy} ATP$

(d) $ADP + Inorganic\ PO_4 \rightarrow ATP$

28. Carbon dioxide labelled with ^{14}C has been used to identify the intermediate compounds in the Calvin cycle, the light independent stage in photosynthesis. Which compound would be the first to contain the ^{14}C?

(a) Glucose

(b) Starch

(c) GP (PGA)

(d) Triose phosphate

29. What advantage of CAM pathway of photosynthesis might explain why it evolved in desert plants ?

(a) The CAM pathway makes use of the enzyme Rubisco which has a higher affinity for CO_2 than PEP.

(b) Because PEP has a high affinity for CO_2, plants accumulate sufficient CO_2 in the daytime through partially opened stomata while also reducing water loss.

(c) Because the first step of the C_4 pathway occurs at night hence water loss through transpiration is reduced.

(d) None of the above

30. Which of the following terms or phrases would not be associated directly with photosystem II in plants ?

(a) Photophosphorylation

(b) The splitting of water

(c) Harvesting light energy by chlorophyll

(d) Oxygen released from water

ANSWER KEY																			
1	(d)	2	(d)	3	(b)	4	(b)	5	(b)	6	(c)	7	(c)	8	(a)	9	(a)	10	(a)
11	(c)	12	(c)	13	(a)	14	(c)	15	(d)	16	(a)	17	(a)	18	(a)	19	(d)	20	(b)
21	(c)	22	(c)	23	(b)	24	(c)	25	(d)	26	(c)	27	(c)	28	(c)	29	(c)	30	(a)

Respiration in Plants

1. Out of 36 ATP molecules produced per glucose molecule during respiration
    (a) 2 are produced outside glycolysis and 34 during respiratory chain.
    (b) 2 are produced outside mitochondria and 34 inside mitochondria.
    (c) 2 during glycolysis and 34 during Krebs cycle.
    (d) all are formed inside mitochondria.

2. The overall goal of glycolysis, Kreb's cycle and the electron transport system is the formation of
    (a) ATP in one large oxidation reaction
    (b) sugars
    (c) nucleic acids
    (d) ATP in small stepwise units

3. Which of the following represents a correct ordering of the events that occur in the catabolism of glucose in the absence of O_2?
    (a) Glycolysis; oxidative phosphorylation
    (b) Oxidative phosphorylation; TCA cycle
    (c) TCA cycle; glycolysis
    (d) Glycolysis; fermentation

4. Glycolysis occurs in the _______ and produces _______, which in the presence of O2 enters the _______.
    (a) cytosol; pyruvate; mitochondrion
    (b) cytosol; glucose; mitochondrion
    (c) mitochondrion; pyruvate; chloroplast
    (d) chloroplast; glucose; cytosol

5. During glycolysis, the conversion of one mole of 3PGAld to $C_3H_4O_3$ yield 2 moles of ATP. But the oxidation of glucose to $C_3H_4O_3$ produces a total of 4 moles of ATP. Where do the remaining 2 moles of ATP come from ?
    (a) One mole of glucose gives 2 moles of 3PGAld.
    (b) Glycolysis produces 2NADH.
    (c) Fermentation of $C_3H_4O_3$ produces 2ATP more.
    (d) 2ATP are used in the conversion of glucose to 3PGAld.

6. For bacteria to continue growing rapidly when they are shifted from an environment containing O_2 to an anaerobic environment, they must

(a) produce more ATP per mole of glucose during glycolysis.

(b) produce ATP during oxidation of glucose.

(c) increase the rate of glycolysis.

(d) increase the rate of TCA cycle.

7. Identify the correct sequence of events in Kreb's cycle.

(a) Acetyl CoA $\rightarrow$ Citrate $\rightarrow$ Pyruvate $\rightarrow$ α-ketoglutarate $\rightarrow$ Succinate $\rightarrow$ Malate $\rightarrow$ Fumarate $\rightarrow$ OAA

(b) Acetyl CoA $\rightarrow$ Citric acid $\rightarrow$ α-ketoglutaric acid $\rightarrow$ Succinic acid $\rightarrow$ Fumaric acid $\rightarrow$ Malic acid $\rightarrow$ OAA

(c) Acetyl CoA $\rightarrow$ Citric acid $\rightarrow$ Malic acid $\rightarrow$ α-ketoglutaric acid $\rightarrow$ Succinic acid $\rightarrow$ OAA

(d) None of the above

8. Inside an active mitochondrion, most electrons follow which pathway ?

(a) Glycolysis $\rightarrow$ NADH $\rightarrow$ Oxidative Phosphorylation $\rightarrow$ ATP $\rightarrow$ O_2

(b) Krebs' cycle $\rightarrow$ $FADH_2$ $\rightarrow$ ETS $\rightarrow$ ATP

(c) ETS $\rightarrow$ Krebs' cycle $\rightarrow$ ATP $\rightarrow$ O_2

(d) Krebs' cycle $\rightarrow$ NADH + H^+ $\rightarrow$ Electron transport chain $\rightarrow$ O_2

9. Refer the figure and answer the question.

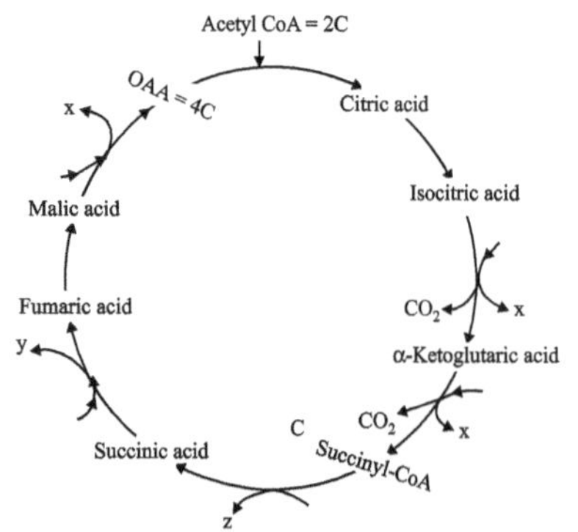

Identify X, Y and Z.

	X	Y	Z
(a)	GTP	$NADH_2$	CO_2
(b)	$FADH_2$	$NADH_2$	GTP
(c)	$NADH_2$	$FADH_2$	GTP
(d)	CO_2	$NADH_2$	ADP

10. At the end of the Krebs cycle, but before the electron transport chain, the oxidation of glucose has produced a net gain of

(a) $3CO_2$, 5 $NADH_2$, 1 $FADH_2$, 2 ATP

(b) $6CO_2$, 10 NADH2, 2 $FADH_2$, 4 ATP

(c) $6CO_2$, 10 $NADH_2$, 2 $FADH_2$, 38 ATP

(d) None of the above

11. The expressions given below shows the summary equations.

(i) Pyruvate $\xrightarrow{\text{NADH + H}^+ \quad \text{NAD}^+}$ $C_2H_5OH + CO_2$

(i) $C_6H_{12}O_6 + NAD^+ + 2ADP + 2\,iP \rightarrow$ $2C_3H_4O_3 + 2ATP + 2NADH + 2H^+$

(iii) Pyruvic acid + $4NAD^+ + FAD^+ + 2H_2O$ + ADP + Pi $\rightarrow 3CO_2 + 4NADH + 4H_+ +$ $ATP + FADH_2$

Categorise the summary equations under respective phases.

	I	II	III
1.	Krebs' cycle	Glycolysis	Fermentation
2.	Glycolysis	Krebs' cycle	Fermentation
3.	Fermentation	Krebs' cycle	Glycolysis
4.	Fermentation	Glycolysis	Krebs' cycle

12. Match the number of carbon atoms given in List - I with that of the compounds given in List - II and select the correct option.

List - I	List - II
A. 4C Compound	I. Acetyl CoA
B. 2C Compound	II. Pyruvate
C. 5C Compound	III. Citric acid
D. 3C Compound	IV. α- ketoglutaric acid
	V. Malic acid

(a) A-II, B-V, C-III, D-I

(b) A-V, B-I, C-IV, D-II

(c) A-III, B-I, C-IV, D-II

(d) A-V, B-III, C-I, D-II

13. Aerobic respiration is more advantageous to a large organism than anaerobic respiration, because aerobic respiration

(a) does not require sunlight.

(b) produces oxygen as a waste product.

(c) does not require molecular oxygen and hydrogen.

(d) releases more energy from an equal amount of nutrients.

14. Maximum usable energy per mol of glucose metabolized will be generated during

(a) aerobic respiration by germinating seeds.

(b) production of methanol by enteric bacteria.

(c) fermentation into ethanol by yeast.

(d) glycolysis in the skeletal muscle of a sprinter performing a hundred metre dash.

15. Match the sites in column I with processes in column II and choose the correct combination from the options.

	Column I		Column II
A.	Grana of chloroplast	(i)	Krebs cycle
B.	Stroma of chloroplast	(ii)	Light reaction
C.	Cytoplasm	(iii)	Dark reaction
D.	Mitochondrial matrix	(iv)	Glycolysis

(a) A – (iv), B – (iii), C – (ii), D – (i)

(b) A – (i), B – (ii), C – (iv), D – (iii)

(c) A – (ii), B – (i), C – (iii), D – (iv)

(d) A – (ii), B – (iii), C – (iv), D – (i)

16. Choose the correct combination of labelling the number of carbon compounds in the substrate molecules, involved in the citric acid cycle.

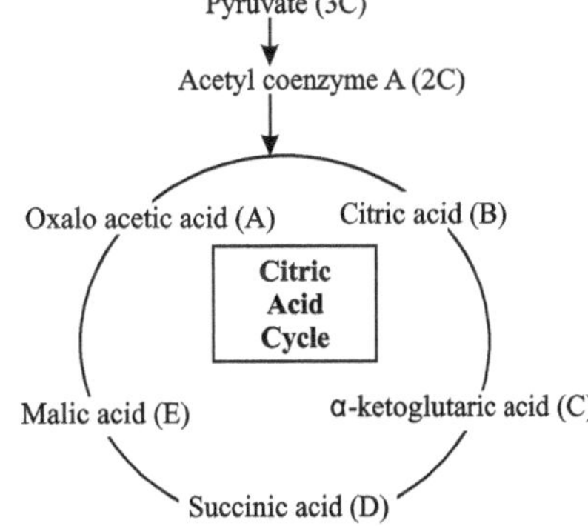

(a) (A) 4C, (B) 6C, (C) 5C, (D) 4C, (E) 4C

(b) (A) 6C, (B) 5C, (C) 4C, (D) 3C, (E) 2C

(c) (A) 2C, (B) 5C, (C) 6C, (D) 4C, (E) 4C

(d) (A) 4C, (B) 6C, (C) 4C, (D) 4C, (E) 5C

17. The three boxes in this diagram represents the three major biosynthetic pathways in aerobic respiration. Arrows represents net reactants or products.

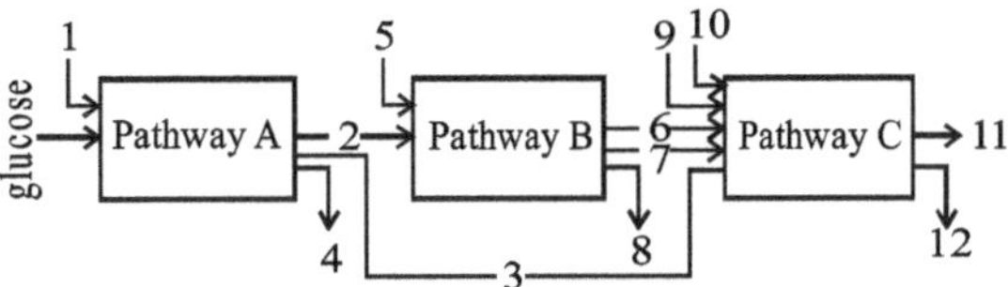

Arrows numbered 4, 8 and 12 can all be :

(a) ATP

(b) H_2O

(c) FAD^+ or FADH2

(d) NADH

18. Consider the following statements with respect to respiration.

A. Glycolysis occurs in the cytoplasm of the cell.

B. Aerobic respiration takes place within the mitochondria.

C. Electron transport system is present in the outer mitochondrial membrane.

D. $C_{51}H_{98}O_6$ is the chemical formula of Tripalmitin, a fatty acid.

E. Respiratory quotient

$$= \frac{\text{Volume of O evolved}}{\text{Volume of CO consumed}}$$

Of the above statements

(a) A, B and D alone are correct

(b) B, C and D alone are correct

(c) C, D and E alone are correct

(d) B, D and E alone are correct

(e) A, C and E alone are correct

19. Degradation of sugar and fat to acetyl CoA will not take place if the following organelle is not present in a eukaryotic cell. Identify the organelle.

(a) Golgi apparatus

(b) Mitochondrion

(c) Ribosome

(d) Nucleus

20. The given figure shows the fate of glucose during aerobic and anaerobic respiration. Identify the end products that are formed at stages indicated as A, B, C and D. Identify the correct option from those given below.

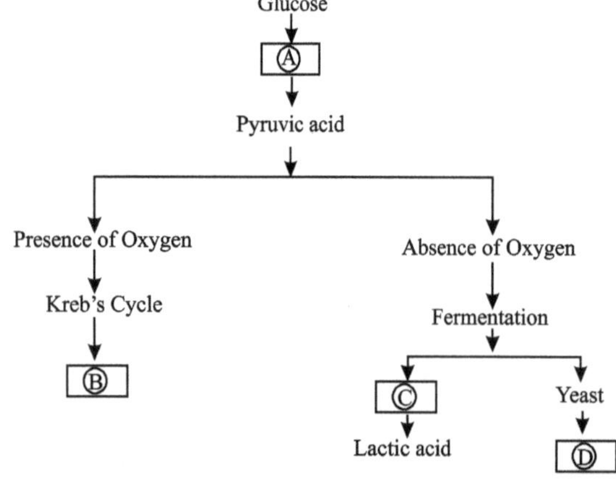

(a) A = ETS, B = pyruvic acid, C = ethyl alcohol and carbon dioxide, D = lactic acid.

(b) A = glycolysis, B = carbon dioxide and water, C = bacteria, D = ethyl alcohol and carbon dioxide.

(c) A = pyruvic acid, B = carbon dioxide and water, C = ethyl alcohol and lactic acid, D = fungi.

(d) A = ETS, B = ethyl alcohol and carbon dioxide, C = lactic acid, D = carbon dioxide and water.

21. A microbiologist discovered a new antibiotic that slowed the growth of bacteria by interfering with cellular respiration. She found that bacteria treated with the antibiotic produced about 15 ATP molecules for every glucose molecule they consumed.

Which of the following hypothesis could explain the antibiotic's effect? The treated bacteria

(a) cannot perform glycolysis.

(b) have partially crippled electron transport chains.

(c) cannot produce NADH.

(d) have to rely atleast partially on biosynthesis for their ATP.

22. Fermentation is essentially glycolysis plus an extra step in which pyruvic acid is reduced to form lactic acid or alcohol and CO_2. This last step

(a) removes poisonous oxygen from the environment.

(b) extracts a bit more energy from glucose.

(c) enables the cell to recycle NAD^+.

(d) inactivates toxic pyruvic acid.

23. The major reason that glycolysis is not as energy productive as respiration is that
    (a) NAD^+ is regenerated by alcohol or lactate production, without the high-energy electrons passing through the electron transport chain.
    (b) it is the pathway common to fermentation and respiration.
    (c) it does not take place in a specialized membrane-bound organelle.
    (d) pyruvate is more reduced than CO_2; it still contains much of the energy from glucose.

24. The diagram shows the reversible conversion of pyruvate to lactate by the enzyme lactate dehydrogenase.

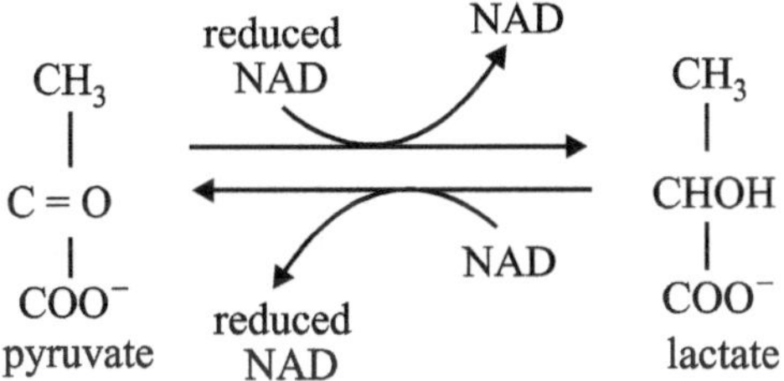

What would be the effect of inhibition of lactate dehydrogenase in a mammalian cell under anaerobic conditions?
    (a) a decrease in cell pH, due to the accumulation of lactic acid.
    (b) a decrease in glycolysis, due to the lack of NAD.
    (c) an increase in ATP production, due to increased amounts of reduced NAD.
    (d) an increase in the activity of the Krebs cycle, due to increased amounts of pyruvate.

25. Which of the following pathways outlines the order of events during aerobic cellular respiration? first → last
    (a) glucose → triose phosphate → pyruvate → Krebs cycle → CO_2 + H_2O + ATP
    (b) glucose → triose phosphate → pyruvate → Krebs cycle → CO_2 + H_2O + ADP + Pi
    (c) glucose → hexose phosphate → pyruvate → Krebs cycle → CO_2 + H_2O + ADP + Pi
    (d) glucose → hexose phosphate → pyruvate → Krebs cycle → ethanol + CO_2 + ATP

ANSWER KEY																			
1	(b)	2	(d)	3	(d)	4	(a)	5	(a)	6	(c)	7	(b)	8	(d)	9	(c)	10	(b)
11	(d)	12	(b)	13	(d)	14	(a)	15	(d)	16	(a)	17	(a)	18	(a)	19	(b)	20	(b)
21	(b)	22	(c)	23	(d)	24	(b)	25	(a)										

Plant Growth and Development

1. The method that renders the seed coat permeable to water so that embryo expansion is not physically retarded is called
   (a) vernalization
   (b) stratification
   (c) denudation
   (d) scarification

2. Identify the correct and incorrect statements from the following.
   (I) 17500 new cells are produced per hour by a single maize root apical meristem.
   (II) With the help of length, growth of pollen tube is measured.
   (III) The growth of the leaf is measured in term of volume.
   (IV) Cells in a watermelon may increase in size by upto 350000 times.
   (a) I, II, III are correct and IV is incorrect.
   (b) I, II, IV are correct and III is incorrect.
   (c) II, III are correct and I, IV are incorrect.
   (d) I, IV are correct and II, III are incorrect.

3. What will be the effect on phytochrome in a plant subjected to continuous red light?

   (a) Level of phytochrome decreases.
   (b) Phytochrome is destroyed.
   (c) Phytochrome synthesis increases.
   (d) Destruction and synthesis of phytochrome remain in equilibrium.

4. The ability of plant to follow different pathways and produce different structures in response to environment and phases of life is termed as
   (a) elasticity
   (b) growth efficiency
   (c) plasticity
   (d) heterophylly

5. Refer the functions of the growth hormones given below.
   I. Cell division
   II. Cell enlargement
   III. Pattern formation
   IV. Tropic growth
   V Flowering
   VI. Fruiting
   VII. Seed germination
   VIII.Response to wound
   IX. Response to stresses of biotic and abiotic origin

Identify the functions of growth promoters and growth inhibitors from the above.

	Functions of growth promoters	Functions of growth inhibitor
(a)	I, II, VII, IX	III, IV, V, VI, VII
(b)	VIII, IX	I, II, III, IV, V, VI, VII
(c)	I, II, III, IV, V, VI, VII	VIII, IX
(d)	I, II, III, IV, V, VI, VII, IX	VIII

6. Match the column A (Scientists) with column B (Discovery).

	Column-A		Column-B
I.	C. Darwin and F. Darwin	A.	Cytokinin
II.	Miller and Skoog	B.	ABA
III.	F.W. Went	C.	C_2H_4
IV.	Kurosawa	D.	Auxin
		E.	GA

	I	II	III	IV
(a)	D	A	C	E
(b)	D	A	E	B
(c)	C	A	B	D
(d)	E	D	A	C

8. Study the following statements.

I. "X" hormone promotes root growth and root hair formation.

II. "Y" hormone induces flowering in mango and also promotes rapid internode/petiole elongation in deep plants and hence helping leaves or upper parts of shoot above water.

III. "Z" hormone inhibits the seed germination, increase the tolerance of plant to various stresses, play import in seed development, maturation and dormancy.

Identify the correct names of hormones marked as 'X', 'Y' & 'Z'.

(a) Y = ABA; X = Auxin; Z = GA

(b) Z = GA; X = Auxin; Y = C_2H_4

(c) Y = Auxin; X = C_2H_4; Z = GA

(d) Y = C_2H_4; X = C_2H_4; Z = ABA

9. Match the plant hormones listed in column-I with their major role listed in column-II. Select the correct option from the codes given below.

	Column-A		Column-B
A.	Auxin	I.	Fruit ripening
B.	Cytokinins	II.	Phototropism
C.	Abscisic acid	III.	Antagonist to GAs
D.	Ethylene	IV.	Stomatal opening and closing
		V.	Growth of lateral buds

(a) A-IV; B-V; C-III; D-I

(b) A-II; B-IV; C-III, IV; D-I

(c) A-I; B-V; C-III, IV; D-I

(d) A-III, IV; B-V; C-II; D-I

10. A plant completing its life cycle before the onset of dry condition is said to be

(a) short day plant

(b) long day plant

(c) drought escaping

(d) all of these

11. In longitudinal section of root tip various regions of growth may be seen in sequence from top towards root cap as

(a) cell division, cell elongation, cell maturation

(b) cell maturation, cell elongation, cell division

(c) cell elongation, cell maturation, cell division

(d) cell maturation, cell division, cell elongation

12. One set of a plant was grown at 12 hours day and 12 hours night period cycles and it flowered while in the other set night phase was interrupted by flash of light and it did not produce flower. Under which one of the following categories will you place this plant?

(a) Long day

(b) Darkness neutral

(c) Day neutral

(d) Short day

13. Match the growth regulators in column-I with the processes in column-II and choose the correct combination.

	Column-I		Column-II
A.	Auxin	(i)	Colouring test in lemon
B.	Gibberellin	(ii)	Cell division test in plants
C.	Cytokinin	(iii)	Avena curvature test
D.	Ethylene	(iv)	Dwarf corn test

(a) A – (iii), B – (iv), C – (ii), D – (i)

(b) A – (i), B – (iv), C – (ii), D – (iii)

(c) A – (iv), B – (iii), C – (i), D – (ii)

(d) A – (ii), B – (i), C – (iv), D – (iii)

14. The shedding of leaves, flowers and fruits due to change in hormonal balance in plants is referred as

(a) senescence

(b) abscission

(c) photoperiodism

(d) vernalization

15. Auxin originates at the tip of the stem and controls growth elsewhere. The movement of auxin is largely

(a) acropetal and basipetal

(b) centripetal

(c) basipetal

(d) acropetal

16. 6-furfuryl amino purine, 2, 4-dichlorophenoxy acetic acid and indole-3 acetic acid are examples respectively for

(a) synthetic auxin, kinetin and natural auxin.

(b) gibberellin, natural auxin and kinetin.

(c) natural auxin, kinetin and synthetic auxin.

(d) kinetin, synthetic auxin and natural auxin.

17. Senescence as an active developmental cellular process in the growth and functioning of a flowering plant, is indicated in

(a) vessels and tracheid differentiation

(b) leaf abscission

(c) annual plants

(d) floral parts

18. Match list I and list II and select the correct option.

	List-I		List-II
A.	Auxin	I.	Herring sperm DNA
B.	Cytokinin	II.	Inhibitor of growth
C.	Gibberellin	III.	Apical dominance
D.	Ethylene	IV.	Epinasty
E.	Abscisic acid	V.	Induces amylase synthesis

(a) A-III, B-I, C-V, D-IV, E-II

(b) A-IV, B-V, C-I, D-III, E-II

(c) A-II, B-I, C-V, D-III, E-IV

(d) A-III, B-I, C-V, D-II, E-IV

19. Match the following and choose the correct combination

Column I		Column II
(A) Zeatin	1.	Flowering hormone
(B) Florigen	2.	Synthetic auxin
(C) IBA	3.	Cytokinin
(D) NAA	4.	Natural auxin

    (a) A – 3, B – 4, C – 1, D – 2

    (b) A – 2, B – 1, C – 4, D – 3

    (c) A – 1, B – 2, C – 3, D – 4

    (d) A – 3, B – 1, C – 4, D – 2

19. Match the following and choose the correct combination from the options given.

Column I		Column II
Growth Regulator		**Action**
(A) Abscisic acid	1.	Delays leaf senescence
(B) Ethylene	2.	Inhibits seed germination
(C) Cytokinin	3.	Herbicide
(D) Auxin	4.	Hastens fruit ripening

    (a) A-2, B-4, C-1, D-3

    (b) A-1, B-2, C-3, D-4

    (c) A-2, B-3, C-4, D-1

    (d) A-2, B-1, C-3, D-4

20. Dr. F. Went noted that if coleoptile tips were removed and placed on agar for one hour, the agar would produce a bending when placed on one side of freshly-cut coleoptile stumps. Of what significance is this experiment?

    (a) It made possible the isolation and exact identification of auxin.

    (b) It is the basis for quantitative determination of small amounts of growth-promoting substances.

    (c) It supports the hypothesis that IAA is auxin.

    (d) It demonstrated polar movement of auxins.

21. A few normal seedlings of tomato were kept in a dark room. After a few days they were found to have become white-coloured like albinos. Which of the following terms will you use to describe them?

    (a) Mutated

    (b) Embolised

    (c) Etiolated

    (d) Defoliated

22. A farmer noticed that some lettuce plants wilted badly and could be grown successfully only if transferred to a very humid greenhouse. What is the most likely cause of the wilting?

    (a) ABA deficiency

    (b) Inadequate stomatal density

    (c) Auxin deficiency

    (d) None of the above

23. You have installed an outdoor gas burning grill on your back patio next to your favorite camellia bush. After the first few chilly nights of using your grill you notice that your camellia, which does not normally lose its leaves, is beginning to do so. Which of the following is the best explanation for what is happening ?

    (a) The bush is getting too warm next to your grill.

    (b) Ethylene is a by-product of the gas you are burning and is causing senescence in your plant.

    (c) Abscisic acid is a by-product of the gas you are burning and is causing senescence in your plant.

    (d) The plant is a biennial and is bolting.

24. Maryland Mammoth Tobacco is a short day plant. Its critical duration of darkness is 10 hours. Under which of the following conditions will Maryland Mammoth tobacco not flower ?

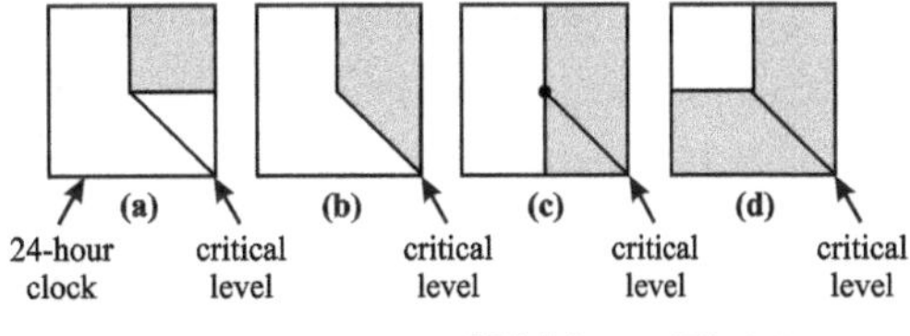

25. You are slicing a green pepper for the pizza you are making at home. As you slice into it you notice lots of tiny pepper plants emerging from the seeds of the pepper. This peeper is exhibiting_____ and may be lacking in ______ .

(a) parthenocarpy, gibberellins

(b) parthenocarpy, abscisic acid

(c) vivipary, gibberellins

(d) vivipary, abscisic acid

ANSWER KEY																			
1	(d)	2	(b)	3	(a)	4	(c)	5	(c)	6	(a)	7	(d)	8	(c)	9	(c)	10	(a)
11	(d)	12	(a)	13	(b)	14	(c)	15	(d)	16	(b)	17	(a)	18	(d)	19	(a)	20	(b)
21	(c)	22	(a)	23	(b)	24	(a)	25	(d)										

Digestion and Absorption

1. If for some reason the parietal cells of the gut epithelium become partially non-funcitonal, what is likely to happen?

   (a) The pancreatic enzymes and specially the trypsin and lipase will not work efficiently

   (b) The pH of stomach will fall abruptly

   (c) Steapsin will be more effective

   (d) Proteins will not be adequately hydrolysed by pepsin into proteoses and peptones

2. The hydrolytic action of the following enzyme produces pentose sugar

   (a) Amylase

   (b) Sucrase

   (c) Nucleotidase

   (d) None of these

3. A dental disease characterized by mottlilng of teeth due to ingredient in drinking water, namely

   (a) Fluorine

   (b) Chlorine

   (c) Boron

   (d) Mercury

4. Lathyrism due to consumption of khesari dal is characterized by

   (a) Skeletal deformation and thinning of collagen fibres

   (b) Skeletal abnormalities, diabetes mellitus and reproductive failure

   (c) Retarded growth, precocious puberty and renal dysfunction

   (d) Cardiovascular abnormalities mental retardation and delayed puberty.

5. Identify the correct set which shows the name of the enzymes from where it is secreted and substrate upon which it acts

   (a) Pepsin – Stomach wall – Caesin

   (b) Ptyalin – Intestine – Maltose

   (c) Chymotypsin – Salivary gland – Lactose

   (d) Ptyalin – Pancreas – Lipid

6. An enzyme which brings about conversion of starch into maltose is

   (a) catalase

   (b) maltase

   (c) invertase

   (d) diastase

7. If the chyme of a person who had orally consumed only starch as food is analysed before it enters the duodenum, it will show the presence of

   (a) maltose and glucose

   (b) dextrin and maltose

   (c) starch, dextrin and maltose

   (d) starch, dextrin and glucose

8. A person is passing gray white faecal matter, What is not functioning properly in the body ?

   (a) Kidney

   (b) Liver

   (c) Spleen

   (d) Pancreas

9. One of the cyanobacteria rich in vitamin B_{12} carotenoids, iron and other essential nutrients, now being used in modern medicines as nutritional supplements, is

   (a) *Nostoc*   (b) *Spirulina*

   (c) *Anacystis*   (d) *Anabaena*

10. People recoverting from long illness are often advised to include the alga *Spirulina* in their diet because is

   (a) is rich in proteins

   (b) has antibiotic properties

   (c) makes the food easy to digest

   (d) restores the intestinal microflora

11. Which one of the following four secretions is correctly matched with its source, target and nature of action ?

	Secretion	Source	Target	Action
(a)	Gastrin	Stomach lining	Oxyntic cells	Production of HCl
(b)	Inhibin	Sertoli cells	Hypo-thalamus	inhibition of secretion of ganadotropin releasing hormone
(c)	Enterokinase	Duodenum	Gall bladder	Release of bile juice
(d)	Atrial Natriuretic factor (ANF)	Sinu atrial node(SAN) M-cells of Atria	Juxta-glomerular apparatus (JGA)	Inhibition of release of renin

12. Both the crown and root of a tooth is covered by a layer of bony hard substance. It is called

   (a) enamel

   (b) dentine

   (c) bony socket

   (d) cementum

13. The main function of lacteals in the villi of human-small intestine is the absorption of

   (a) amino acids and glucose

   (b) glucose and vitamins

   (c) water and mineral salts

   (d) fatty acids and glycerol

14. The following is a scheme showing the fate of carbohydrate during digestion in the human alimentary canal. Identify the enzymes acting at stages indicated as A, B, C and D. Choose the correct option from those given.

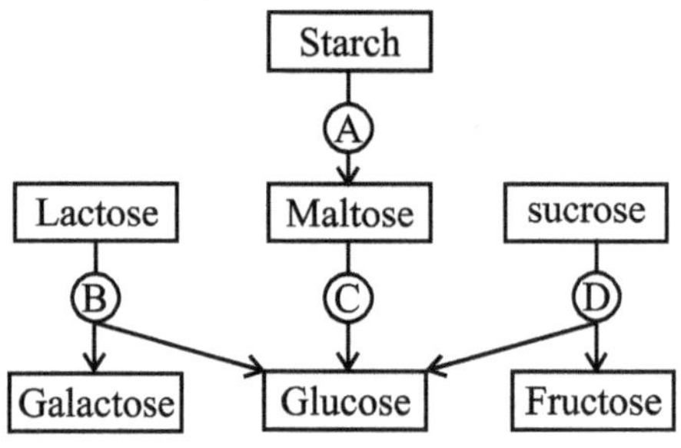

   (a) A= amylase, B = maltase, C = lactase, D = invertase

   (b) A = amylase, B = maltase, C= invertase, D= lactase

   (c) A = amylase, B = invertase, C = maltase, D= lactase

   (d) A = amylase, B = lactase, C = maltase, D = invertases

15. Which one of the following is the correct matching of the site of action on the given substrate, the enzyme acting upon it and the end product?

    (a) *Stomach* : Fats $\xrightarrow{\text{Lipase}}$ micelles

    (b) Duodenum : Triglycerides $\xrightarrow{\text{Trypsin}}$ monoglycerides

    (d) Small intenstine : Starch $\xrightarrow{\propto \text{Amylase}}$ Disaccharide (Maltose)

    (d) *Small intestine* : Proteins $\xrightarrow{\text{pepsin}}$ Amino acid

16. What will happen if the secretion of parietal cells of gastric glands is blocked with an inhinbitor?

    (a) Enterokinase will not be released from the duodenal mucosa and so trypsinogen is not converted to trypsin

    (b) Gastric juice will be deficient in chymosin

    (c) Gastric juice will be deficient in pepsinogen

    (d) In the absence of HCl secretion, inactive pepsinogen is not converted into the active enzyme pepsin.

17. When breast feeding is replaced by less nutritive food low in proteins and calories; the infants below the age of one year are likely to suffer from :

    (a) Pellagra   (b) Marasmus

    (c) Rickets   (d) Kwashiorkor

18. Aggregates of lymphoid tissue present in the distal portion of the small intestine are known as

    (a) Villi

    (b) Peyer's patches

    (c) Rugae

    (d) Choroid plexus

19. Fructose is absorbed into the blood through mucosa cells of intestine by the process called:

    (a) Active transport

    (b) Facilitated transport

    (c) Simple diffusion

    (d) Co-transport mechanism

20. In **Coprophagus** mammals the cellulose is digested in

    (a) Rumen and Reticulum

    (b) Abomasum

    (c) Large intestine

    (d) Small intestine

21. An adult person consumes boiled potato. Mark the correct statement regarding the digestion of food compoments

    (a) Cellulose will be digested by cellulase

    (b) Starch will not be digested

    (c) Lactase will digest carbohydrates

    (d) DNA will be digested by pancreatic enzymes

22. If the bile-pancreatic duct is blocked, the following will not be affected

    (a) Digestion of proteins

    (b) Emulsification of fats

    (c) Level of blood glucose

    (d) Digestion of starch

ANSWER KEY																			
1	(d)	2	(d)	3	(a)	4	(a)	5	(a)	6	(d)	7	(c)	8	(b)	9	(b)	10	(a)
11	(d)	12	(b)	13	(d)	14	(d)	15	(c)	16	(d)	17	(b)	18	(b)	19	(b)	20	(c)
21	(d)	22	(c)																

Breathing and Exchange of Gases

1. Every 100 ml of oxygenated blood delivers following amount of O_2 to the tissues under normal physiological condition
   (a) 5 ml
   (b) 25 ml
   (c) 50 ml
   (d) More the 50 ml

2. Presence of large number of alveoli around alveolar ducts opening into bronchioles in mammalian lungs is
   (a) Inefficient system of ventilation with little of residual air
   (b) Inefficient system of ventilation with high percentage of residual air
   (c) An efficient system of ventilation with no residual air
   (d) An efficient system of ventilation with little residual air

3. The stage when the lungs are collapsed, specially the alveoli due to deficiency of surfactant, it is called
   (a) Atelactasis
   (b) Poliomyelitis
   (c) Asthma
   (d) Epistaxis

4. During CO_2 transport, HCO_3^- diffuses from erythrocyges to plasma and in turn upsets the ionic equilibrium momentary. In order to keep the ionic balance, and equal number of Cl^- ions pass into the erythrocytes from plasma. This process is known as
   (a) Bicarbonate shift
   (b) Carbonation
   (c) Hamburger phenomenon
   (d) Carbo-chlorosis

5. The correct match for kind of respiration is

	Animal		Respiration
A.	Earthworm	1.	Pulmonary
B.	Human	2.	Branchial
C.	Prawn	3.	Tracheal
D.	Insects	4.	Cutaneous

   (a) 1-A, 2-B, 3-C, 4-D
   (b) 4-A, 2-B, 1-C, 3-D
   (c) 4-A, 1-B, 2-C, 3-D
   (d) 3-A, 2-B, 4-C, 1-D

6. Hamburger phenomenon is also known as
   (a) Calcium shift
   (b) Bohr effect
   (c) Chloride shift
   (d) Na^+-K^+ pump

7. Vital capacity of lungs in terms of IRV (Inspiratory Reserve Volume), ERV (Expiratory Reserve Volume), TV (Tidal Volume) and RV (Residual Volume) can be represented as

   (a) IRV + ERV + TV + RV

   (b) IRV + ERV + TV

   (c) IRV + ERV

   (d) IRV + ERV + TV - RV

8. During oxygen transport the oxyhaemoglobin at the tissue level liberates oxygen to the cells because in tissue

   (a) O_2 concentration is high and CO_2 is low

   (b) O_2 concentration is low and CO_2 is high

   (c) O_2 tension is high and CO_2 tension is low

   (d) O_2 tension is low and CO_2 tension is high

9. Blood analysis of a patient reveals an unusually high quantity of carboxyhaemoglobin content. Which of the following conclusions is most likely to be correct? The patient has been inhaling polluted air containing usually high content of

   (a) Chloroform

   (b) Carbon dioxide

   (c) Carbon monoxide

   (d) carbon disulphide

10. Formation of non-functional methaemoglobin causes blue-baby syndrome. This is due to

    (a) excess of arsenic concentration in drinking water

    (b) excess of nitrates in drinking water

    (c) deficiency of iron in food

    (d) increased methane content in the atmosphere.

11. Match the disorders given in column I with symptoms under column II. Choose the answer which gives the correct combination of alphabets with numbers.

	Column I		Column II
A.	Asthma	1.	Inflammation of nasal tract
B.	Bronchitis	2.	Spasm of bronchial muscles
C.	Rhinitis	3.	Fully blown out alveoli
D.	Amphysema	4.	Inflammation of bronchi
		5.	Cough with blood strained sputum

   (a) A = 4, B = 2, C = 5, D = 1

   (b) A = 5, B = 3, C = 2, D = 1

   (c) A = 3, B = 1, C = 5, D = 4

   (d) A = 2, B = 4, C = 1, D = 3

12. Ascent to high mountains may cause altitude sickness in men. The prime cause of this is

    (a) excess of CO_2 in blood

    (b) decreased efficiency of haemoglobin

    (c) decreased partial pressure of oxygen

    (d) decreased proportion of oxygen in air

13. In lungs, there is definite exchange of ions between RBC and plasma. Removal of CO_2 from blood involves

    (a) influx of Cl^- ions into RBC

    (b) influx of HCO_3^- ions into RBC

    (c) efflux of Cl^- ions from RBC

    (d) efflux of HCO_3^- ions from RBC

14. Listed below are four respiratory capacities (a-d) and four jumbled respiratory volume of a normal human adult:

	Respiratory capacities	Respiratory volumes
(a)	Residual volume	2500 mL
(b)	Vital capacity	3500 mL
(c)	Inspiratory reserve volume	1200 mL
(d)	Inspiratory capacity	4500 mL

15. A large proportion of oxygen is left unused the human blood even after its uptake by the body tissues. This O_2
    (a) Helps in releasing more O_2 to the epithelium tissues
    (b) Acts as a reserve during muscular exercise
    (c) Raises the pCO_2 of blood to 75 mm of Hg
    (d) Is enough to keep oxyhaemoglobin saturation at 96%

16. Hiccups can be best described as:
    (a) Forceful sudden expiration
    (b) Jerky incomplete inspiration
    (c) Vibration of the soft palate during breathing
    (d) Sign of indigestion

17. When you hold your breath, which of the following gas changes in blood would first lead to the urge to breathe?
    (a) Falling O_2 concentration
    (b) Rising CO_2 concentration
    (c) Falling CO_2 concentration
    (d) Rising CO_2 and falling O_2 concentration

18. Partial pressures of oxygen and carbon dioxide in healthy human lung alveoli are, respectively, nearest to:
    (a) 140 and 40 mm of Hg
    (b) 90 and 20 mm of Hg
    (c) 40 and 45 mm of Hg
    (d) 159 and 0.3 mm of Hg

19. The pneumotaxic centre and respiratory rhythm centres are respectively present in:
    (a) Pons and Medulla oblongata
    (b) Corpus callosum and Pons
    (c) Medulla oblongata and Hypothalamus
    (d) Diencephalon and Pons

20. If the volume of CO_2 liberated during respiration is more than the volume of O_2 used, the respiratory substrate will be :
    (a) Fat   (b) Organic acid
    (c) Protein   (d) Carbohydrate

21. Following is the correct order of diffusion rate of oxygen, carbon–dioxide and nitrogen from lungs to blood through the respiratory membrane
    (a) $CO_2 > O_2 > N_2$
    (b) $CO_2 > N_2 > O_2$
    (c) $O_2 > CO_2 > N_2$
    (d) $O_2 > N_2 > CO_2$

ANSWER KEY																			
1	(a)	2	(d)	3	(a)	4	(c)	5	(c)	6	(c)	7	(b)	8	(d)	9	(c)	10	(b)
11	(d)	12	(c)	13	(d)	14	(d)	15	(b)	16	(b)	17	(b)	18	(a)	19	(a)	20	(b)
21	(a)																		

Body Fluids and Circulation

1. Mark incorrect statement regarding normal ECG

   (a) Patient is connected to three electrical leads (one to each wrist and to the left ankle)

   (b) 'T' wave represents atrial repolarization

   (c) Q marks the beginning of ventricular systole

   (d) R represents ventricular depolarization

2. Given below are four statements (a-d) regarding human blood circulatory system

   A. Arteries are thick-walled and have narrow lumen as compared to veins

   B. Angina is acute chest pain when the blood circulation to the brain is reduced

   C. Persons with blood group AB can donate blood to any person with any blood group under ABO system

   D. Calcium ions play a very important role in blood clotting

   Which two of the above statements are correct?

   (a) A & D

   (b) A & B

   (c) C & C

   (d) C & D

3. Fastest distribution of some injectible material/ medicine and with no risk of any kind can be achieved by injecting it into the

   (a) Muscles

   (b) Arteries

   (c) Veins

   (d) Lymph vessels

4. The heartbeat of a person increases at the time of an interview due to secretion of

   (a) Renin

   (b) Adrenaline

   (c) ADH

   (d) ACTH

5. Which of the following cations is required for the conversion of prothrombin into active thrombin by thromboplastin?

   (a) Cu^{2+}

   (b) Fe^{3+}

   (c) Fe^{2+}

   (d) Ca^{2+}

6. Which of the following carries blood rich in food materials, such as glucose and amino acids, from intestine to liver?

(a) Dorsal aorta

(b) Mesenteric artery

(c) Renal portal vein

(d) Hepatic portal vein

7. Which one of the following is a matching pair?

(a) **Lubb**-Sharp closure of AV valves at the beginning of ventricular systole

(b) **Dup**-Sudden opening of semilunar valves at the beginning of ventricular diastole

(c) Pulsation of the radial artery-Valves in the blood vessels

(d) Initiation of the heart beat-**Purkinje fibres**

8. Which is the correct route through which pulse making impulse travels in the heart?

(a) SA node → AV node → Bundle of His → Purkinje fibres

(b) AV node → Bundle of His → SA node → Purkinje fibres → heart muscles

(c) AV node → SA node → Purkinje fibres → Bundle of His → heart muscles

(d) SA node → Purkinje fibres → Bundle of His → AV node → heart muscles

9. Different factors play important roles in coagulation of blood, some of the factors are listed in list -I and their nomenclatures are given in list-II. Find out the accurate matching

	List -I		List - II
A.	factor II	1.	Thromboplastin
B.	factor III	2.	Prothrombin
C.	factor VIII	3.	Hageman factor
D.	factor XII	4.	Antiheaemophilic globulin

(a) A : 2, B : 1, C : 4, D : 3

(b) A : 1, B : 2, C : 3, D : 4

(c) A : 3, B : 4, C : 2, D : 1

(d) A : 4, B : 4, C : 2, D : 1

10. A drop of each of the following, is placed separately on four slides. Which of them will not coagulate?

(a) Whole blood from pulmonary vein

(b) Blood plasma

(c) Blood serum

(d) Sample from the thoracic duct of lymphatic system

11. Consider the following statements about biomedical technologies:

A. During open heart surgery blood is circulated in the heart-lung machine

B. Blockage in coronary arteries is removed by angiography

C. Computerised Axial Tomography (CAT) shows detailed internal structure as seen in a section of body

D. X-ray provides clear and detailed images of organs like prostate glands and lungs

Which two of the above statements are *correct*?

(a) A and B

(b) B and D

(c) C and D

(d) A and C

12. In humans, blood passes from the post caval to the diastolic right atrium of heart due to:

(a) pressure difference between the post caval and atrium

(b) pushing open of the venous valves

(c) suction pull

(d) stimulation of the sino auricular node

13. In a standard ECG which one of the following alphabets is the *correct* representation of the respective activity of the human heart?

    (a) P-depolarisation of the atria

    (b) R-repolarisation of ventricles

    (c) S-start of systole

    (d) T-end of diastole

14. If a person is loosing blood continuously due to injury then the effect on his pulse and BP will be initially

    (a) Pulse and BP both will fall

    (b) Pulse will fall and BP will rise

    (c) Both pulse and BP will rise

    (d) Pulse will rise and BP will fall.

ANSWER KEY																			
1	(b)	**2**	(a)	**3**	(c)	**4**	(b)	**5**	(d)	**6**	(d)	**7**	(a)	**8**	(a)	**9**	(a)	**10**	(c)
11	(d)	**12**	(a)	**13**	(a)	**14**	(d)												

Excretory Products and their Elimination

1. Match the animals with their corresponding excretory structures

	Animal		Excretory structure
(1)	Amphioxus	A.	Pronephros kidney
(2)	Cockroach	B.	Protonephridia
(3)	Prawn	C.	Metanephridia
(4)	Earthworm	D.	Green glands
		E.	Malpighian tubules
		F.	Antennal glands

(a) 1 – B, 2 – E, 3 – D, 4 – C
(b) 1 – A, 2 – C, 3 – D, 4 – B
(c) 1 – B, 2 – E, 3 – F, 4 – C
(d) None of these

2. In which one of the following organisms its *excretory organs* are **correctly** stated?
   (a) Humans – Kidneys, sebaceous glands and tear glands
   (b) Earthworm – P h a r y n g e a l , integumentary and septal nephridia
   (c) Cockroach – Malpighian tubules and enteric caeca
   (d) Frog – Kidneys, skin and buccal epithelium

3. In the renal tubules the permeability of the distal convoluted tubule and collecting duct to water is controlled by
   (a) aldosterone (b) vasopressin
   (c) growth hormone (d) renin

4. The phenomenon which helps in maintaining a constant internal environment in living organism is
   (a) homeostasis (b) entropy
   (c) apoptosis (d) haemolysis

5. Hippuric acid, creatinines and ketones are added to urine through
   (a) Reabsorption (b) Glomerular filtration
   (c) Tubular secretion (d) Both (b) and (c)

6. The part of the nephron that helps in active reabsorption of sodium is
   (a) Bowman's capsule
   (b) Distal convoluted tubules
   (c) Ascending limb of Henle's loop
   (d) Proximal convoluted tubules

7. Expulsion of urine become voluntary when it is present in
   (a) urethra (b) ureters
   (c) urinary bladder (d) pelvis of kidneys

8. Match the excretory functions of section I with the parts of the excretory system in section II. Choose the correct combination from among the answers given.

	Section I (function)		Section II (parts of excretory systems)
1.	ultra filtration	A.	Henle's loop
2.	concentration of urine	B.	ureter
3.	transport of urine	C.	urinary bladder
4.	storage of urine	D.	malpighian corpuscle
		E.	proximal convoluted tubule

(a) 1 - D, 2 - A, 3 - B, 4 - C
(b) 1-D, 2 - C, 3 - B, 4 - A
(c) 1 - E, 2 - D, 3 - A, 4 - C
(d) 1-E, 2 - D, 3 - A, 4 - B

9. Refer the following diagram and identify the parts of a kidney indicated

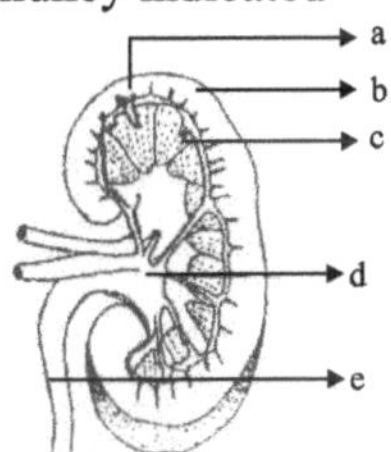

(a) a = cortex, b = nephron, c = pelvis, d = medulla, e = ureter
(b) a = cortex, b = medulla, c = nephron, d = pelvis, e = ureter
(c) a = nephron, b = cortex, c = medulla, d = ureter, e= pelvis
(d) a = nephron, b = cortex, c = medulla, d = pelvis, e = ureter

10. Match the entries in column I with those in column II and choose the correct answer from the followings

	Column I		Column II
A.	uremia	1.	excess of protein in urine
B.	hematuria	2.	presence of high ketone bodies in urine
C.	ketonuria	3.	presence of blood cells in urine
D.	glycosuria	4.	presence of glucose in urine
E.	proteinuria	5.	excess of urea in blood

(a) A - 5, B -3, C - 2, D - 4, E - 1
(b) A - 4, B - 5, C - 3, D - 2, E - 1
(c) A - 5, B -3, C - 4, D - 2, E - 1
(d) A - 3, B -5, C - 2, D - 1, E - 4

11. Match the column I with the column II

	Column I		Column II
A.	Earthworm	I.	Malpighian tubules
B.	Cockroach	II.	Green glands
C.	Amphioxus	III.	Solenocytes
D.	Prawn	IV.	Holonephridia
		V.	Coxal glands

(a) A-IV, B-I, C-III, D-II
(b) A-I, B-V, C-IV, D-II
(c) A-IV, B-I, C-V, D-II
(d) A-III, B-I, C-II, D-V

12. If two solutions, differing in osmolarity, are separated by a semipermeable membrane, then
(a) Flow of water will take place from hypotonic to hypertonic solution
(b) Solute will pass from hypertonic to hypotonic solution
(c) Both (a) and (b) correct
(d) No change in osmolarity will take place

13. Atrial natriuretic factor (**ANF**) is released in response to the increase in blood volume and blood pressure. Which of the followings is not the function of ANF?
(a) Stimulates aldosterone secretion
(b) Inhibits the release of renin from JGA
(c) Stimulates salt loss in urine
(d) Inhibits sodium reabsorption from collecting duct

ANSWER KEY																			
1	(c)	**2**	(b)	**3**	(b)	**4**	(a)	**5**	(d)	**6**	(c)	**7**	(c)	**8**	(a)	**9**	(d)	**10**	(a)
11	(a)	**12**	(a)	**13**	(a)														

Locomotion and Movement

1. Mark the incorrect statement in the followings
   (a) All movements lead to locomotion
   (b) Ciliary movement help in passage of ova through female reproductive tract
   (c) Microfilaments are involved in amoeboid movement
   (d) In *Paramecium* the cilia help in movement of food through cytopharynx and in locomotion as well

2. Match the bones of column A with their corresponding number in column B

	Column A		Column B
A.	True ribs	1.	14
B.	Cervical vertebrae	2.	12
C.	Cranium bones	3.	8
D	Vertebrochondral ribs	4.	6

   (a) Ab, Be, Ca, Dd
   (b) Aa, Be, Cc, Dd
   (c) Ab, Bc, Cd, Dc
   (d) Aa, Bc, Cb, Dd

3. Read the following A to D statements and select the one option that contains both correct statements

   A. Z-line is present in the centre of the light band.
   B. Thin filaments are firmly attached to the M-line
   C. The central part of thick filaments, not overlapped by thin filaments is called Z-band
   D. Light band contains only thin filaments
   (a) A and D
   (b) B and C
   (c) A and C
   (d) B and D

4. Look at the following sets of bones and the type of joints, and select the correct combination of the two sets

   A. Atlas and Axis   1.   Cartilaginous joint
   B. Two Parietals   2.   Fibrous joint
   C. Two pubis bones   3.   Saddle joint
   D. First carpal and   4.   Pivot joint
       first metacarpal
   (a) Ab Ba   (b) Bb Cc
   (c) Cb Dc   (d) Dc Ad

5. Which one of the following pairs of structures is correctly matched with their correct description ?

	Structures	Description
(a)	Tibia and fibula	– Both form parts of knee joint
(b)	Cartilage and cornea	– No blood supply but do require oxygen for respiratory need
(c)	Shoulder joint and elbow joint	– Ball and socket type of joint
(d)	Premolars and molars	– 20 in all and 3-rooted

6. Which of the following pairs, is **correctly** matched?

(a)	Hinge joint	-	between vertebrae
(b)	Gliding joint	-	between zygapophyses of the successive vertebrae
(c)	Cartilaginous joint	-	skull bones
(d)	Fibrous joint	-	between phalanges

7. Contractile tissues have the following features

(i) Mesodermal in orign

(ii) They contain stretch receptors.

(iii) Rhythmic contractions are seen in them

(iv) They do not fatigue during the life of the animal

Which of the above are characteristics of sphincters?

(a) All the four

(b) Only (i), (ii) and (iii)

(c) Only (i), (ii) and (iv)

(d) Only (i), (iii) and (iv)

8. In the given diagram of skull, what does "a" represent?

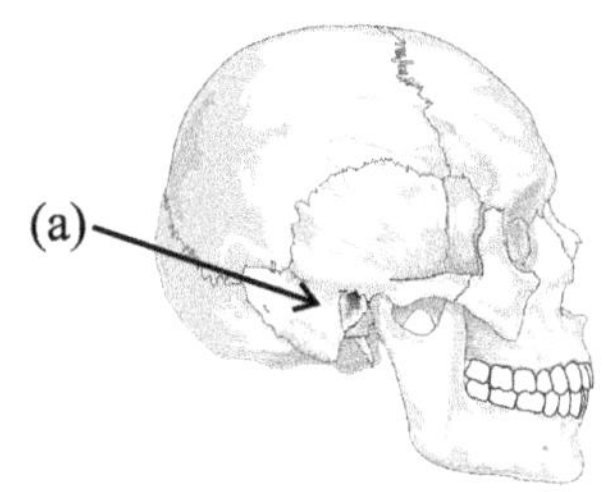

(a) frontal bone   (b) temporal bone

(c) occipital bone   (d) parietal bone

9. The phosphogen that helps the regeneration of ATP from ADP during muscle contraction in vertebrates is

(a) creatinine phosphate (b) arginine phosphate

(c) ADP   (d) inositol phosphate

10. Look at the diagram given below.

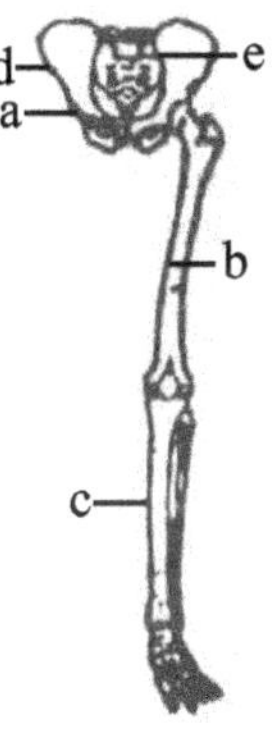

Parts labelled as 'a', 'b', 'c', 'd' and 'e' respectively indicate

(a) ilium, femur, tibia, pubis and sacrum

(b) pubis, tibia, femur, ilium and sacrum

(c) ilium, femur, tibia, pubis, and sacrum

(d) pubis, femur, tibia, ilium and sacrum

11. Hensan's disc are found is

(a) myofibril of striated muscle

(b) myofibril of unstriated muscle

(c) myofibril of heart muscle

(d) none of the above

12. The peg like process in the axis that allows the rotatory movement of the skull is

(a) atlas   (b) odontoid process

(c) condyles   (d) synovial capsule

13. Which one of the following is the *correct* matching of three items and their grouping category ?

	Items		Group
(a)	cytosine, uracil, thiamine	–	pyrimidines
(b)	malleus, incus, cochlea	–	ear ossicles
(c)	ilium, ischium,	–	coxal bones of pelvic girdle
(d)	actin, myosin, rhodopsin	–	muscle proteins

14. Which one of the following pairs of structures is correctly matched with their correct description?

	Structures	Description
(a)	Tibia and fibula –	Both form parts of knee joint
(b)	Cartilage and cornea –	No blood supply but do require oxygen for respiratory need
(c)	Shoulder joint and elbow joint –	Ball and socket type of joint
(d)	Premolars and molars –	20 in all and 3–rooted

15. Select the **correct** statement regarding the specific disorder of muscular or skeletal system :

(a) *Myasthenia gravis* - Auto immune disosrder which inhibits sliding of myosin filaments

(b) *Gout* - inflammation of joints due to extra deposition of calcium

(c) *Muscular dystrophy* - age related shortening of muscles

(d) *Osteoporosis* - decrease in bone mass and higher chances of fractures with advancing age

16. The characteristics and an example of a synovial joint in humans is

	Characteristics	Examples
(a)	Fibrous cartilage between two bones, limited movements	Knee joint
(b)	Fluid filled between two joints, provides cushion	Skull bones
(c)	Fluid filled synovial cavity between two bones	Joint between atlas and axis
(d)	Lymph filled between two bones, limited movement	Gliding joint between carpals

17. Select the correct matching of the type of the joint with the example in human skeletal system:

	Type of joint	Example
(a)	Cartilaginous joint	Between frontal and parietal
(b)	Pivot joint	Between third and fourth cervical vertebrae
(c)	Hinge joint	Between humerus and pectoral girdle
(d)	Gliding joint	Between carpals

18. Match the locomotory structure of column I with the name of phylum in column II

	Column I		Column II
A.	Parapodia	I.	Mollusca
B.	Muscular foot	II.	Echinodermata
C.	Pseudopodia	III.	Protozoa
D.	Tube feet	IV.	Annelida
		V.	Arthropoda

(a) A-V, B-IV, C-III, D-II

(b) A-IV, B-I, C-III, D-II

(c) A-V, B-I, C-III, D-II

(d) A-IV, B-II, C-III, D-V

19. In the following disorder the synovial membrane starts secreting abnormal granules called **Pannus** which cause erosion of cartilage

(a) Osteoarthritis

(b) Gouty arthritis

(c) Rheumatoidal arthritis

(d) Osteoporosis

20. **Foramen transversarium**, also known as vertebro- arterial canal, is present in all

(a) Cervical vertebrae (b) Sacral vertebrae

(c) Lumber vertebrae (d) Caudal vertebrae

21. The striated muscle fibres are united in parallel bundles, the fasciculi. Each fasciculus is in turn surrounded by a connective tissue sheath known as

(a) Perimysium (b) Epimysium

(c) Endomysium (d) Exomysium

22. The joint between two pubis bones of hip girdle is

(a) Fixed type (b) Synovial joint

(c) Imperfect joint (d) Fibrous joint

23. The cross arm that forms the cross bridges during muscle contraction, is formed by

(a) HMM

(b) LLM

(c) Troponin

(d) Both 1 and 2

24. Read the following A to D statements and select the one option that contains both correct statements

A. Z-line is present in the centre of the light band.

B. Thin filaments are firmly attached to the M-line

C. The central part of thick filaments, not overlapped by thin filaments is called Z-band

D. Light band contains only thin filaments

(a) A and D (b) B and C

(c) A and C (d) B and D

25. Three of the following pairs of the human skeletal parts are correctly matched with their respective inclusive skeletal category and one pair is not matched. Identify the non-matching pair.

	Pairs of skeletal parts	Category
(a)	Humerus and ulna	Appendicular skeleton
(b)	Malleus and stapes	Ear ossicles
(c)	Sternum and Ribs	Axial skeleton
(d)	Clavicle and Glenoid cavity	Pelvic girdle

26. Which one of the following is the correct description of a certain part of a normal human skeleton?

(a) Parietal bone and the temporal bone of the skull are joined by fibrous joint

(b) First vertebra is axis which articulates with the occipital condyles

(c) The 9th and 10th pairs of ribs are called the floating ribs

(d) Glenoid cavity is a depression to which the thigh bone articulates

27. The **Krause membrane** is associated with:

(a) Simple epithelium (b) Nervous tissue

(c) Muscular tissue (d) Connective tissue

ANSWER KEY																			
1	(a)	**2**	(b)	**3**	(a)	**4**	(d)	**5**	(b)	**6**	(b)	**7**	(b)	**8**	(b)	**9**	(a)	**10**	(d)
11	(a)	**12**	(b)	**13**	(c)	**14**	(b)	**15**	(d)	**16**	(c)	**17**	(d)	**18**	(b)	**19**	(c)	**20**	(a)
21	(a)	**22**	(c)	**23**	(a)	**24**	(a)	**25**	(d)	**26**	(a)	**27**	(c)						

Neural Control and Coordination

1. Sodium – Postassium pump across membrance, actively transports
   (a) 2-Na ions outwards and 3 K ions into the cell
   (b) 3-Na ions outwards and 2 K ions into the cell
   (c) 2-K ions out wards and 3 Na ions into the cell
   (d) 3 K ions outwards and 2 Na ions into the cell

2. Mark the correct statement
   (a) The space between cornea and lens is filled with transparent gel
   (b) When all cones are stimulated equally a sensation of no light (dark) is produced
   (c) Rhodopsin is purplish red protein, hence called visual purple
   (d) The anterior transparent portion of choroid is called cornea

3. Mark the appropriate word for the box in the follwoing statement. The ripples in basilar membrane press the hair cells against the [　　　　] to generate nerve impulse for auditory cortex
   (a) Macula
   (b) Otolith
   (c) Round window
   (d) None of these

4. A person feels no sensation when he puts his hand over flame the part of the brain which has damaged is
   (a) Cerebellum
   (b) Medulla oblongata
   (c) Diencephalon
   (d) Hypothalamus

5. If ophthalmic branch of trigeminal cuts, what will be the effect?
   (a) Frog dies
   (b) Blindness appears
   (c) Frog loses its capacity of sensing
   (d) None of these

6. The potential difference between outside and inside of a nerve before excitation is known as
   (a) Spike potential
   (b) Reaction potential
   (c) Action potential
   (d) Resting potential

7. Absolute refractory period during nerve impulse conduction is the period of :
   (a) repolarization
   (b) depolarization
   (c) both repolarization and depolarization
   (d) neither repolarization nor depolarization

8. Anaesthetics reduce pain by blocking nerve conduction due to
   (a) Blocking neurotransmitter receptors
   (b) Blocking Na^+ channels
   (c) Blocking K^+ channels
   (d) All the above

9. Which of the following ions are required for nerve conduction ?
   (a) Ca^{++}, Na^+ and K^+ (b) Ca^{++} and Mg^{++}
   (c) Mg^{++} and K^+ (d) Na^+ and K^+

10. Release of cathecholamines from adrenal medulla (human) is controlled by the action of:
    (a) post-ganglionic sympathetic nerves
    (b) pre-ganglionic sympathetic nerves
    (c) pre-ganglionic parasympathetic nerves
    (d) post-ganglionic parasympathetic nerves

11. In frog, the nerve that innervates the retractor bulbi muscles of eye
    (a) pathetic (b) optic
    (c) oculomotor (d) abducens

12. The photosensitive pigments viz., erytrolabe, chlorolabe and cyanolabe are sensitive to the colours respectively:
    (a) red, green and blue
    (b) blue, green and red
    (c) green, red and blue
    (d) blue, red and green

13. In rabbit, optic lobes are small because the eye sight is controlled by
    (a) frontal lobe (b) occipital lobe
    (c) temporal lobe (d) parietal lobe

14. A frog has its brain crushed. But when pinched on the leg, it draws away. It is an example of
    (a) simple reflex
    (b) conditioned reflex
    (c) automated motor response
    (d) neurotransmitter induced response

15. Which part of the brain is involved in loss of control when a person drinks alcohol?
    (a) Thalamus (b) Cerebrum
    (c) Pons varolii (d) Cerebellum

16. Which of the following communicates to the central canal of the spinal cord?
    (a) Fifth ventricle (b) Third ventricle
    (c) Fourth ventricle (d) Lateral ventricle

17. In mammalian cochlea, the thin-walled sloping roof of the scala media is referred to as:
    (a) organ of Corti
    (b) scala tympani
    (c) basilar membrance
    (d) Ressner's membrance

18. Thermoregulatory centre in the body of homeothermal animals and man is found in
    (a) Skin (b) Diencephalon
    (c) Hypothalamus (d) Pituitary

19. A person is wearing spectacles with concave lenses for correcting vision. While not using the glasses, the image of a distant object in his case will be formed:
    (a) on the blind spot (b) behind the retina
    (c) on the yellow spot (d) in front of the retina

20. Parkinson's disease (characterized by tremors and progressive rigidity of limbs) is caused by degeneration of brain neurons that are involved in movement control and make use of neurotransmitter
    (a) acetylcholine (b) norepinephrine
    (c) dopamine (d) GABA

21. In the resting state of the neural membrane, diffusion due to concentration gradients, if allowed would drive :
    (a) K^+ into the cell
    (b) Na^+ into the cell
    (c) Na^+ out of the cell
    (d) K^+ and Na^+ out of the cell

22. Column I lists the parts of the human brain and colum II lists the functions. Match the two columns and identify the correct choice from those given.

	Column I		Column II
A.	Cerebrum	p.	controls the pituitary
B.	Cerebellum	q.	controls vision and hearing
C.	Hypothalamus	r.	controls the rate of heart beat

D.	Midbrain	s.	seat of intelligence
		t.	maintains body posture

(a) A = t; B = s; C = q; D = p

(b) A = s; B = t; C = r; D = p

(c) A = t; B = s; C = r; D = q

(d) A = t; B = t; C = p; D = q

23. Find out the correct answer from the following statements. The main functions of the cerebrum of human brain are

(A) to control the contraction of voluntary muscles through the frontal lobe

(B) to control the sensitivity, movement, memory, vocabulary etc. through the frontal lobe

(C) to control the temperature, taste, touch, pain etc. through the parietal lobe

(D) to control the vision and adaptation through the occipital and frontal lobes

  (a) A, B, D   (b) C, D, A

  (c) A, B, C   (d) B, C, D

24. If after cutting through the dorsal root of a spinal nerve of a mammal, an associated receptor in the skin were stimulated, the animal would

(a) still be able to feel the stimulation

(b) show no response

(c) show a normal but slow response

(d) respond but only at a different level of spinal cord

25. Match the following human spinal nerves in column I with the number of pairs in column II and choose the correct options

	Column I		Column II
A.	cervical nerves	1.	5 pairs
B.	thoracic nerves	2.	1 pair
C.	lumbar nerves	3.	12 pairs
D.	coccygeal nerves	4.	8 pairs

(a) A - 2, B - 4, C - 1, D - 3

(b) A - 4, B - 3, C - 1, D - 2

(c) A - 3, B - 1, C - 2, D - 4

(d) A - 4, B - 1, C - 2, D - 3

26. In the given diagram which stage of conduction of nerve impulse through nerve fibre is observed?

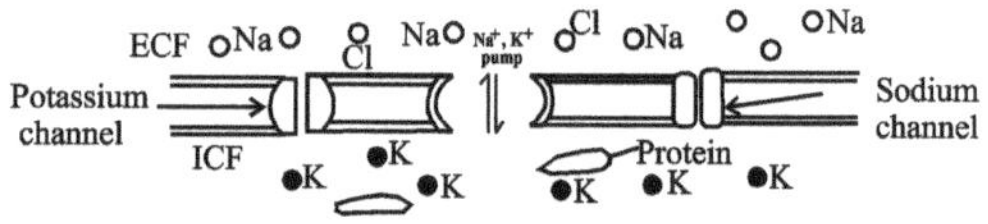

  (a) polarization   (b) resting potential

  (c) repolarization   (d) depolarization

27. Match the entries in column I with those in column II and choose the correct combination from the options given.

	Column I		Column II
A.	diencephalon	1.	cerebellum
B.	telencephalon	2.	medulla
C.	myelencephalon	3.	amygdala
D.	metencephalon	4.	thalamus

(a) A–4, B–3, C–1, D–2

(b) A–3, B–4, C–1, D–2

(c) A–4, B–3, C–2, D–1

(d) A–1, B–2, C–3, D–4

28. During the transmission of nerve impulse through a nerve fibre, the potential on the inner side of the plasma membrane has which type of electric charge?

(a) First positive, then negative and again back to positive

(b) First negative, then positive and again back to negative

(c) First positive, then negative and continue to be negative

(d) First negative, then positive and continue to be positive

29. Which one of the following is the correct difference between rod cells and cone cells of our retina.

		Rod Cells	**Cone Cells**
(a)	Distribution	More concentrated in centre of retina	Evenly distributed all over retina
(b)	Visual acuity	High	Low
(c)	Visual pigment contained	Iodopsin	Rhodopsin
(d)	Over all function	Vision in poor light	Colour vision and detailed vision in bright light

30. Select the answer with correct matching of the structure, its location and function

	Structure	**Location**	**Function**
(a)	Eustachian tube	Anterior part of internal ear	Equalizes air pressure on either sides of tympanic membrane
(b)	Cerebellum	Mid brain	Controls respiration and gastric secretions
(c)	Hypothalamus	Fore brain	Controls body temperature, urge for eating and drinking
(d)	Blind spot	Near the place where optic nerve leaves the eye	Rods and cones are present but inactive here

31. The primary neurotransmitter at the neruromuscular junction is:
(a) Dopamine (b) Adrenaline
(c) Acetylcholine (d) Acetaldehyde

32. If eyeball is shorter and lens is thin, then probable defect would be:
(a) Astigmatism (b) Presbyopia
(c) Short-sightedness (d) Long-sightedness

33. In man the speed of recognition of a particular taste with a protruded tongue compared to the tongue *in situ* is:
(a) faster
(b) slower
(c) unchanged
(d) initially faster then slower

34. Select the answer with *correct matching* of the structure, its location and function

	Structure	**Location**	**Function**
(a)	Eustachian tube	Anterior part of internal ear	Equalizes air pressure on either sides of tympanic membrane
(b)	Cerebellum	Mid brain	Controls respiration and gastric secretions
(c)	Hypothalamus	Fore brain	Controls body temperature, urge for eating and drinking
(d)	Blind spot	Near the place where optic nerve leaves the eye	Rods and cones are present but inactive here

ANSWER KEY																		
1	(d)	**2**	(c)	**3**	(d)	**4**	(d)	**5**	(c)	**6**	(d)	**7**	(a)	**8**	(d)	**9**	(a)	**10**	(a)
11	(d)	**12**	(a)	**13**	(b)	**14**	(a)	**15**	(d)	**16**	(c)	**17**	(d)	**18**	(c)	**19**	(d)	**20**	(c)
21.	(b)	**22**	(d)	**23**	(a)	**24**	(b)	**25**	(b)	**26**	(b)	**27**	(c)	**28**	(b)	**29**	(d)	**30**	(c)
31	(c)	**32**	(d)	**33**	(b)	**34**	(c)												

Chemical Coordination and Integration

1. Alloxan treatment destroys
   - (a) α-Cells of islets of Langerhans
   - (b) Sertoli cells
   - (c) Leydig's cells
   - (d) β-cells of islets of Langerhans

2. Alertness, pupillary dilation and piloerection are due to the effect of
   - (a) Melatonin
   - (b) Corticoids
   - (c) Catecholamines
   - (d) Thyroxine

3. In hormone a ction, if receptor molecules are removed from target organ, the target organ will
   - (a) Continue to respond to hormone
   - (b) Not respond to hormone
   - (c) Continue to respond but requires higher concentration
   - (d) Continue to respond but in the opposite way

4. The hormone that supports pregnancy and stimulates mammary glands for the formation of alveoli for storing milk, is secreted from
   - (a) Ant. Pituitary
   - (b) Post. Pituitary
   - (c) Graafian follicle
   - (d) Corpus luteum

5. Which hormone interacts with membrane bound receptor and does not normally enter the target cell
   - (a) FSH
   - (b) Estrogen
   - (c) Thyroxin
   - (d) Cortisol

6. If thyroxine is added in a beaker which has some small tadpoles then:
   - (a) all tadpoles die
   - (b) they metamorphose very fast
   - (c) they develop small body
   - (d) they develop a giant body

7. The "biological clock" in higher vertebrates is regulated by:
   - (a) thymus
   - (b) cerebral cortex
   - (c) the pituitary gland
   - (d) supra-chiasmatic nucleus in hypothalamus

8. The lorain-levi syndrome is due to

(a) hyper functioning of pituitary

(b) hypothyroidism

(c) hyperthyroidism

(d) deficiency of growth hormone

9. In a normal pregnant woman, the amount of total gonadotropin activity was assessed. The result expected was

(a) High levels of FSH and LH in uterus to stimulate endometrial thickening

(b) High level of circulating HCG to stimulate estrogen and progesterone synthesis

(c) High level of circulating FSH and LH in the uterus to stimulate implantation of the embryo

(d) High level of circulating HCG to stimulate endometrial thickening

10. In heart cells, which one serves as a second messenger, speeding up muscle cell contraction in response to adrenaline?

(a) cAMP

(b) cGMP

(c) GTP

(d) ATP

11. Secretion of which of the following structure is preparing inner wall of uterus of implantation

(a) ovary

(b) pituitary gland

(c) corpus luteum

(d) ovarian follicle

12. The hormones that initiate ejection of milk, stimulates milk production and growth of ovarian follicles, are respectively known as

(a) PRL, OT and LH

(b) OT, PRL and FSH

(c) LH, PRL and FSH

(d) PRH, OT and LH

13. The Chemical messengers which are released out side the body to alter the functioning of other members of the same species are called

(a) Parahormones

(b) Pheromones

(c) Hormones

(d) All of these

14. Both adrenaline and cortisol are secreted in response to stress. Which of the following statement is also true for both of these hormones?

(a) They are secreted by adrenal cortex

(b) They act to increase blood sugar

(c) Their secretion is stimulated by adrenocorticotropins

(d) All of these

15. The receptor for insulin hormone is a tetramer protein having 4-subunits, 2-α units and 2-β units. Which of the following statement regarding this receptor is correct?

(a) 2-α subunits protrude out from the surface of the cell and 2-β subunits protrude into the cytoplasm

(b) 2-β subunits protrude out from the surface of the cell and 2-α subunits protrude into the cytoplasm

(c) One α and one β subunits protrude out from surface of the cell and One α and one β subunits protrude into the cytoplasm

(d) All 4-subunits protrude out from the surface of the cells to bind insulin

16. Female intersexes develop when foetus is exposed to copious (plentiful) supply of

(a) Estrogen from adrenal

(b) Estrogen from ovary

(c) Androgen from Testes

(d) Androgen from Adrenal

17. Mark the correct matching of the hormone and the endocrine cells

I.	C-Cell	A	Inhibin
II.	β-cell	B	Calcitonin
III.	Leydig cell	C	Insulin
IV.	Sertoli cells	D	Testosterone

(a) I-A, II-C, III-D, IV-B

(b) I-C, II-B, III-D, IV-A

(c) I-A, II-C, III-B, IV-D

(d) I-B, II-C, III-D, IV-A

18. Which of the following hormones stimulates epithelium lining of the crop of both male and female birds for the secretion of '**pigeon milk**'?

(a) Estrogen

(b) Prolactin

(c) Thymosin

(d) Growth hormone

19. Match the hormone in column I with their function in column II.

	Column I		Column II
A.	FSH	1.	prepare endometrium for implantation
B.	LH	2.	develops female secondary sexual characters
C.	progesterone	3.	contraction of uterine wall
D.	estrogen	4.	development of corpus luteum
		5.	maturation of graafian follicle

(a) A–5, B–4, C–1, D–2

(b) A–4, B–5, C–2, D–1

(c) A–4, B–3, C–2, D–5

(d) A–5, B–1, C–2, D–4

20. Match the source gland with its respective hormone as well as the function

	Source gland	Hormone	Function
(a)	Thyroid	Thyroxine	Regulates blood calcium level
(b)	Anterior pituitary	Oxytocin	Contraction of uterus muscles during child birth
(c)	Posterior pituitary	Vasopressin	Stimulates resorption of water in the distal tubules in the nephron
(d)	Corpus luteum	Estrogen	Supports pregnancy

21. Column I lists the endocrine structure and column II lists the corresponding hormones. Match the two columns. Identify the correct option from those given

	Column I		Column II
A.	hypothalamus	p.	relaxin
B.	anterior pituitary	q.	estrogen
C.	testis	r.	FSH and LH
D.	ovary	s.	testosterone
		t.	gonadotropin releasing hormone

(a) A = t, B = r, C = s, D = q

(b) A = t, B = r, C = q, D = s

(c) A = p, B = q, C = s, d = r

(d) A = r, B = t, C = s, D = q

22. A tadpole with surgically removed thyroid gland can be made to metamorphose if

(a) Given an injection of TSH

(b) Given an injection of oxytocin

(c) Given an injection of thyroxine

(d) Feed on dried thyroid gland.

23. Which of the following is related to obesity, low plasma Na^+, high K^+ and increased blood pressure?

(a) Growth hormone (b) Cortisol

(c) Thyroxine (d) Adrenaline

24. A person has protruding eyes, tachycardia and higher body temperature. He is suffering from

(a) Cretinism

(b) Hyperthyroidism

(c) Myxoedema

(d) Acromegaly

25. Substances formed at one place and expressing effect at a distant place are called

(a) Pheromones

(b) Enzymes

(c) WBC

(d) Hormones.

26. If both the ovaries of rat are removed which of the following hormones will be deficient ?

(a) Prolactin

(b) Oestrogen

(c) Oxytocin

(d) Gonadotrophic hormone

27. Select the *correct* matching of a hormone, its source and function.

	Hormone	Source	Function
(a)	Vasopressin	Posterior pituitary	Increases loss of water through urine
(b)	Norepine-phrine	Adrenal medulla	Increases heart beat, rate of respiration and alertness
(c)	Glucagon	Beta-cells of Islets of langerhans	Stimulates glycogenolysis
(d)	Prolactin	Posterior Pituitary	Regulates growth of mammary glands and milk formation in females

28. Match the list -I with list II

	List - I		List -II
A.	adenohypophysis	1.	epinephrine
B.	adrenal medulla	2.	somatotropin
C.	parathyroid gland	3.	thymosin
D.	thymus gland	4.	calcitonin

(a) A : 3, B : 1, C : 4, D : 2

(b) A : 1, B : 2, C : 3, D : 4

(c) A : 2, B : 1, C : 4, D : 3

(d) A : 4, B : 3, C : 2, D : 1

ANSWER KEY																			
1	(d)	2	(c)	3	(b)	4	(d)	5	(a)	6	(b)	7	(d)	8	(d)	9	(b)	10	(a)
11	(c)	12	(b)	13	(b)	14	(b)	15	(a)	16	(d)	17	(d)	18	(b)	19	(a)	20	(c)
21	(a)	22	(c)	23	(b)	24	(b)	25	(d)	26	(b)	27	(b)	28	(c)						

Reproduction in Organisms

23

1. Which one of the following is not vegetative propagule?
   - (a) Rhizome and sucker
   - (b) Tuber and offset
   - (c) Bulbil (*e.g., in Agave*), leaf buds, bulb
   - (d) Antherozoid

2. Examine the figures given below and select the right options out of (1 - 4); in which all the 4 items A, B, C and D are identified correctly

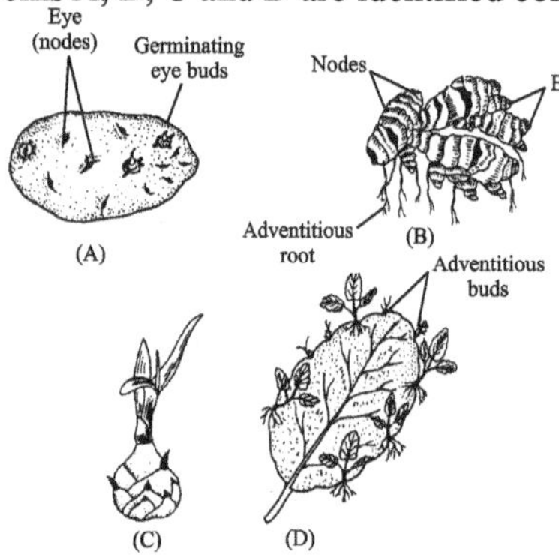

	(A)	**(B)**	**(C)**	**(D)**
(a)	Tuber	Rhizome	Bulb	Leaf buds
(b)	Offset	Sucker	Stolon	Leaf buds
(c)	Offset	Sucker	Stolon	Leaf buds
(d)	Tuber	Rhizome	Bulbil	Leaf buds

3. A number of short stalked sporangia attached to placenta and covered by indusium is called
   - (a) ramenta (b) sorus
   - (c) sporophyll (d) cone

4. During the process of fertilization it is usually found that of the two male gametes, one fuses with the egg and the second with the secondary nucleus. This is known as
   - (a) simple fertilization
   - (b) double fertilization
   - (c) fusion
   - (d) None of the above

5. Which one of the plants using 'Foliar adventitious buds' as method for vegetative propagation?
   - (a) Banana (b) Ginger
   - (c) *Bryophyllum* (d) *Colocasia*

6. The plant material which is widely used in the preparation of culture medium is
   - (a) *Cycas revoluta* (b) *Cocus nucifera*
   - (c) *Pinus longifolia* (d) *Borassus flabellifer*

7. Match the following and mark the correct set

	Column I		**Column II**
A.	Arum	I.	Vegetative reproduction
B.	Micro-propagation	II.	Fly-trap mechanism
C.	Heterothallic	III.	Entomophilly
D.	Coloured petal and nectar	IV.	Sexual reproduction

   - (a) A–I; B–II; C–III; D–IV
   - (b) A–II; B–I; C–IV; D–III
   - (c) A–III; B–II; C–IV; D–I
   - (d) A–I; B–III; C–IV; D–II

8. What is common is *Bryophyllum, Sansevieria* and *Lilium*?
   (a) All are members of family liliaceae.
   (b) All reproduce only sexually.
   (c) All reproduce through leaves vegetatively.
   (d) All lack heterospory.

9. In which of the following does the whole leafblade regenerate into a new individual?
   (a) Rose   (b) Money plant
   (c) Mango   (d) *Kalanchoe*

10. Why inarching is an improved methods of vegetative multiplication?
    (a) Seeds are not formed.
    (b) Stock and scion remain intact.
    (c) Improved seed formation.
    (d) All of these.

11. The gemmule formation is the form of sexual reproduction in class of porifera.
    (a) Calcarea
    (b) Demospongia
    (d) Hexactinellida
    (c) All of the above

12. In *Ipomoea batatas*, the modified roots are
    (a) clustered   (b) fasciculated
    (c) paired   (d) single

13. Match the columns

Column I		Column II
A. Phanerophytes	I.	Buds are situated close to the ground
B. Chamaephytes	II.	Buds completely hidden in the soil
C. Crytophytes	III.	Buds naked or covered with scale
D. Therophytes	IV.	Seasonal plants completing their life cycle in a single favourable season

   (a) A – I; B–II; C–III; D–IV
   (b) A–III; B–I; C–II; D–IV
   (c) A–III; B–II; C–I; D–IV
   (d) A–I; B–III; C–II; D–IV

14. In *Amorphophallus* and *Colocasia*, vegetative reproduction is carried out through
    (a) rhizome
    (b) bulbils
    (c) corms
    (d) offsets

15. Identify the option which correctly indicates the type of gametes.

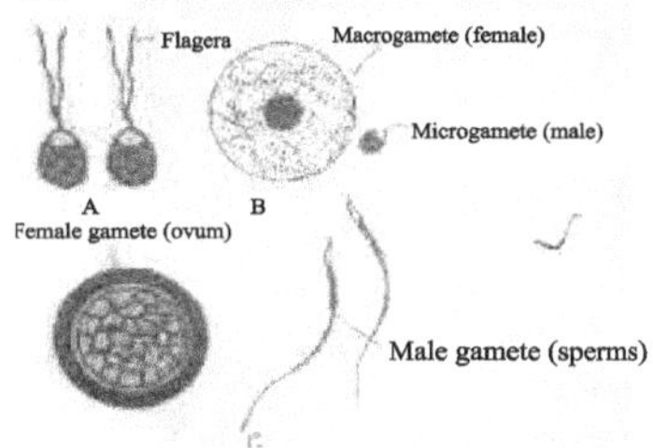

    (a) A-Heterogametes, B-Isogametes, C-Homogametes
    (b) A-Homogametes, B-Isogametes, C-Heterogametes
    (c) A-Isogametes, B-Heterogametes, C-Homogametes
    (d) A-Heterogametes, B-Homogametes, C-Isogametes

16. Identify the events (A, B, D and E) in life of general reproduction-

    (a) A-Gamete transfer, B-Gametogeneis, D-Zygote formation, E-Embryogenesis
    (b) A-Gametogeneis, B-Gamete transfer, D-Zygote formation, E-Embryogenesis
    (c) A-Gametogeneis, B-Zygote formation, D-Gamete transfer, E-Embryogenesis
    (d) A-Gametogeneis, B-Gamete transfer, D-Embryogenesis, E-Zygote formation.

17. Match the following and choose the correct combination from the options given.

Column I (Name of the organism)		Column II (Chromosome number in meiocyte ($2n$))
A. Housefly	I.	20
B. Fruit fly	II.	34
C. Apple	III.	8
D. Maize	IV.	12

    (a) A – I; B – II; C – III; D – IV
    (b) A – II; B – III; C – IV; D – I
    (c) A – III; B – IV; C – II; D – I
    (d) A – IV; B – III; C – II; D – I

18. Which one of the following pairs is wrongly matched while the remaining three are correct?
(a) *Penicillium* - Conidia
(b) Water hyacinth - Runner
(c) *Bryophyllum* - Leaf buds
(d) *Agave* - Bulbils

19. Which one of the following is correctly matched
(a) Onion - Bulb
(b) Ginger - Sucker
(c) *Chlamydomonas* - Conidia
(d) Yeast - Zoospores

20. Match list I with list II and select the correct option.

	List I		List II
A.	Gemmules	I.	*Agave*
B.	Leaf-buds	II.	*Penicillium*
C.	Bulbil	III.	Water hyacinth
D.	Offset	IV.	Sponges
E.	Conidia	V.	*Bryophyllum*

(a) A – IV; B – V; C – I; D – III; E – II
(b) A – IV; B – III; C – II; D – I; E – V
(c) A – III; B – V; C – IV; D – II; E – I
(d) A – IV; B – I; C – V; D – III; E – II

21. Match column I with column II and select the correct option.

	Column I (Name of the organism)		Column II (Haploid chromosome number in gamete)
A.	*Ophioglossum*	I.	23
B.	Rice	II.	24
C.	Potato	III.	12
D.	Man	IV.	630

(a) A – I; B – II; C – III; D – IV
(b) A – II; B – III; C – IV; D – I
(c) A – III; B – IV; C – II; D – I
(d) A – IV; B – III; C – II; D – I

22. Match the items in column I with those in column II and choose the correct option.

	Column I		Column II
A.	Binary fission	I.	Algae
B.	Zoospore	II.	*Amoeba*
C.	Conidium	III.	*Hydra*
D.	Budding	IV.	*Penicillium*
E.	Gemmules	V.	Sponge

(a) A – I; B – IV; C – V; D – III; E – II
(b) A – II; B – I; C – IV; D – III; E – V
(c) A – II; B – IV; C – III; D – V; E – I
(d) A – I; B – IV; C – III; D – II; E – V

23. Based on cellular mechanisms there are two major types of regeneration found in the animals. Which one of the following is the correct example of the type mentioned?
(a) Morphallaxis - Regeneration of two transversely cut equal pieces of a Hydra into two small Hydras.
(b) Epimorphosis - Replacement of old and dead erythrocytes by the new ones.
(c) Morphallaxis - Healing up of a wound in the skin.
(d) Epimorphosis - Regeneration of crushed and filtered out pieces of a Planaria into as many new Planarians.

24. Pick the correct set

	Column I		Column II
A.	Bamboos	I.	Bronchial allergy
B.	Microspore	II.	Die after flowering
C.	Cleistozamous	III.	Orchids
D.	Micropropagation	IV.	flowers which never open

(a) A–I; B–II; C–III; D–IV
(b) A–II; B–I; C–IV; D–III
(c) A–IV; B–II; C–III; D–I
(d) A–I; B–IV; C–II; D–III

ANSWER KEY																			
1	(d)	**2**	(d)	**3**	(b)	**4**	(b)	**5**	(c)	**6**	(b)	**7**	(b)	**8**	(c)	**9**	(d)	**10**	(b)
11	(b)	**12**	(d)	**13**	(b)	**14**	(a)	**15**	(c)	**16**	(b)	**17**	(d)	**18**	(b)	**19**	(a)	**20**	(a)
21	(a)	**22**	(b)	**23**	(a)	**24**	(b)												

Sexual Reproduction in Flowering Plants

24

1. Identified A, B, C and D.

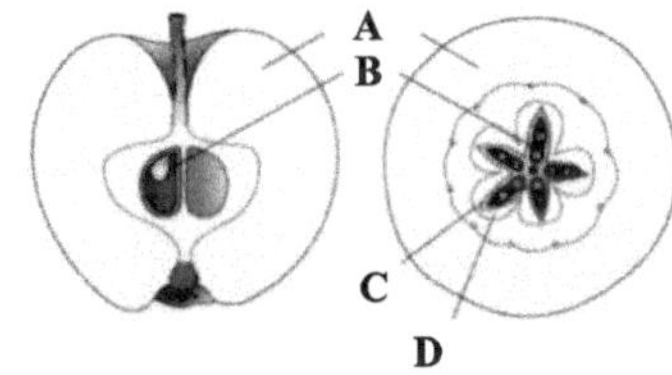

   (a) A – Mesocarp; B – Endocarp; C – Seed;
       D – Thalamus
   (b) A – Seed; B – Thalamus; C – Mesocarp;
       D – Endocarp
   (c) A – Thalamus; B – Seed; C – Endocarp;
       D – Mesocarp
   (d) Mesocarp; B – Endocarp; C – Seed;
       D – Thalamus

2. Identified A, B, C and D of a flower.

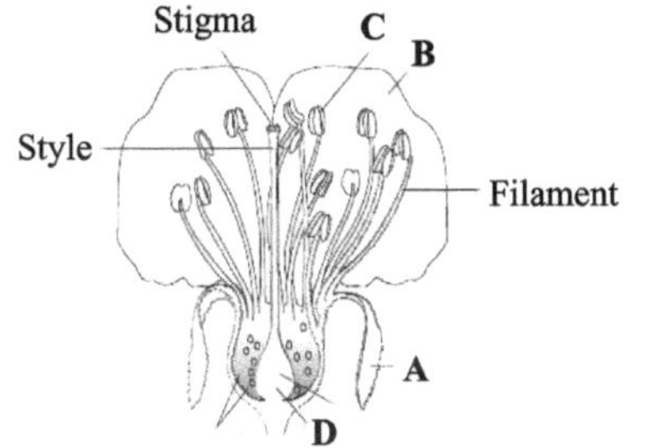

   (a) A – Sepal; B – Petal; C – Anther; D – Ovary
   (b) A – Petal; B – Sepal; C – Anther; D – Ovary
   (c) A – Sepal; B – Petal; C – Ovary; D – Anther
   (d) A – Sepal; B – Ovary; C – Petal; D – Anther

3. Match the following and choose the correct option

	Column I		Column II
A.	Ovary	I.	Groundnut, mustard
B.	Ovule	II.	Guava, orange, mango
C.	Wall of ovary	III.	Pericarp
D.	Fleshy fruits	IV.	Seed
E.	Dry fruits	V.	Fruit

   (a) A-V ; B-IV ; C-III ; D-II ; E-I
   (b) A-I ; B-II ; C-III ; D-IV ; E-V
   (c) A-I ; B-III ; C-II ; D-IV ; E-V
   (d) A-V ; B-IV ; C-I ; D-II ; E-III

4. The cause of dormancy for sometime in fertilized ovule is
   (a) presence of hormone, Auxin.
   (b) zygote divides only after certain amount of endosperm is formed.
   (c) presence of growth inhibitor ABA.
   (d) presence of least amount of water.

5. Choose correct option for A, B, C and D of a dicot embryo.

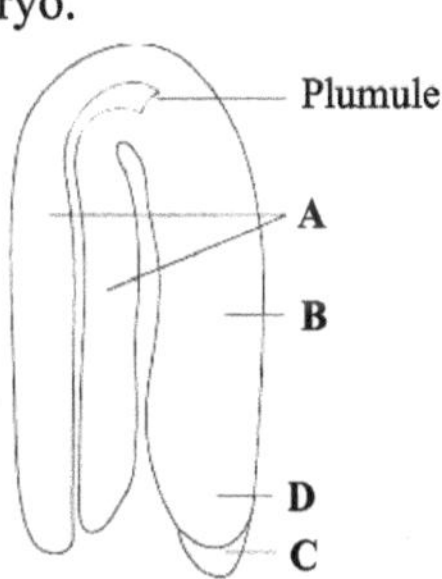

(a) A–Hypocotyl; B–Cotyledons; C–Rootcap; D – Radicle

(b) A–Cotyledons; B–Hypocotyl; C–Rootcap; D – Radicle

(c) A–Cotyledons; B–Hypocotyl; C–Radicle; D – Root cap

(d) A–Cotyledons; B–Radicle; C–Hypocotyl; D – Root cap.

6. Match the following and choose the correct option.

	Column I		Column II
A.	Funicle	I.	Mass of cells with in ovule with more food
B.	Hilum	II.	Basal part of ovule
C.	Integument	III.	One or two protective layers of ovule
D.	Chalazal end	IV.	Region where body of ovules fuses with funicle
E.	Nucellus	V.	Stalk of ovule

(a) A-I ; B-II ; C-III ; D-IV ; E-V

(b) A-V ; B-IV ; C-III ; D-II ; E-I

(c) A-IV ; B-II ; C-I ; D-III ; E-V

(d) A-I ; B-III ; C-V ; D-II ; E-IV

7. Choose correct option for A, B, C and D of a monocot embryo.

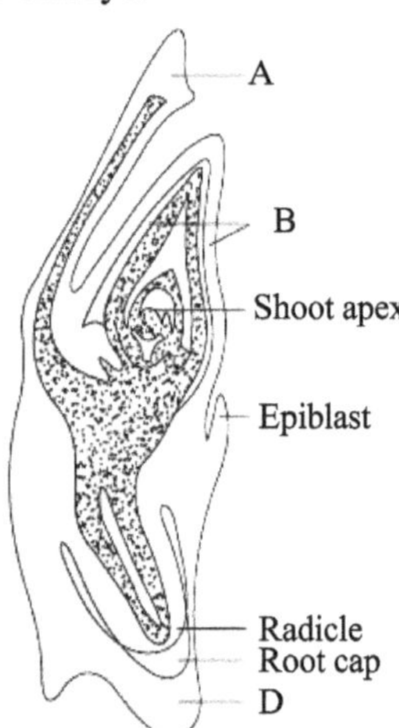

(a) A – Coleoptile; B – Scutellum; C – Epiblast; D – Coleorhiza

(b) A – Scutellum; B – Coleoptile; C – Coleorhiza; D – Epiblast

(c) A – Scutellum; B – Epiblast; C – Coleoptile; D – Coleorhiza

(d) A – Scutellum; B – Coleoptile; C – Epiblast; D – Coleorhiza

8. Match the following and choose the correct option.

	Column I		Column II
A.	Megasporo-genesis	I.	Monosporic development
B.	Megagameto-genesis	II.	Fatty substance
C.	Sporopollenin	III.	Embryo sac formation
D.	Typical embryo & ac	IV.	Megaspore formation

(a) A-I; B-II; C-III; D-IV

(b) A-IV; B-III; C-II; D-I

(c) A-IV; B-I; C-II; D-III

(d) A-III; B-II; C-I; D-IV

9. Pollens are considered as 'well preserved fossils' due to the presence of

(a) exine   (b) intine

(c) mexine   (d) protein

10. Match the following columns.

	Column I		Column II
A.	Calyx	I.	Female gamete
B.	Corolla	II.	Protection
C.	Stamen	III.	Attraction
D.	Carpel	IV.	Male gamete

Codes

(a) A-I; B-II; C-III; D-IV

(b) A-II; B-III; C-IV; D-I

(c) A-IV; B-III; C-II; D-I

(d) A-I; B-II; C-IV; D-III

11. The position of the middle layer in the transverse section of a young anther is between

(a) epidermis and endothecium

(b) endothecium and tapetum

(c) tapetum and sporogenous tissue

(d) cells of sporogenous tissue

12. Double fertilisation was discovered by

(a) Nawaschin

(b) Starsburger

(c) Emerson

(d) None of the above

13. In some organisms, karyokinesis is not followed by cytokinesis as a result of which, multinucleate condition arises leading to the formation of syncytium. The perfect example for this is

(a) appearance of a furrow in cell membrane

(b) liquid endosperm in coconut

(c) sexual reproduction

(d) fertilisation

14. The fruit is chambered, developed from inferior ovary and has seeds with succulent testa in
    (a) pomegranate
    (b) orange
    (c) guava
    (d) cucumber

15. What is the main function of filiform apparatus present at the micropylar part of the ovule?
    (a) It prevents the entry of more than one pollen tube into the embryo sac.
    (b) It brings about opening of the pollen tube.
    (c) It helps in the entry of pollen tube into an antipodal cell.
    (d) It guides the entry of pollen tube into a synergid and discharge the male gametes.

16. If root of a flowering plant has 24 chromosomes, then its gamete has how many chromosomes?
    (a) 24
    (b) 12
    (c) 4
    (d) 8

17. Match the following Columns.

Column - I (Pollination technique)		Column - II (Pollinator)	
A.	Chiropterophily	I.	Ant
B.	Anemophily	II.	Bat
C.	Myrmecophily	III.	Snail
D.	Malacophily	IV.	Wind

    (a) A – III; B – II; C – I; D – IV
    (b) A – II; B – IV; C – I; D – III
    (c) A – IV; B – III; C – II; D – I
    (d) A – I; B – III; C – II; D – IV

18. Match the following and choose the correct option.

	Column-I		Column-II
A.	Zoophily	I.	Pollination by birds
B.	Ornithophily	II.	Pollination by insects
C.	Entomophily	III.	Pollination by bats
D.	Chiropterophily	IV.	Pollination by animals

    (a) (A) – (III); (B) – (II); (C) – (I); (D) – (IV)
    (b) (A) – (I); (B) – (II); (C) – (III); (D) – (IV)
    (c) (A) – (IV); (B) – (I); (C) – (II); (D) – (III)
    (d) (A) – (IV); (B) – (II); (C) – (III); (D) – (I)

19. Identify A to G respectively in the figure given below:

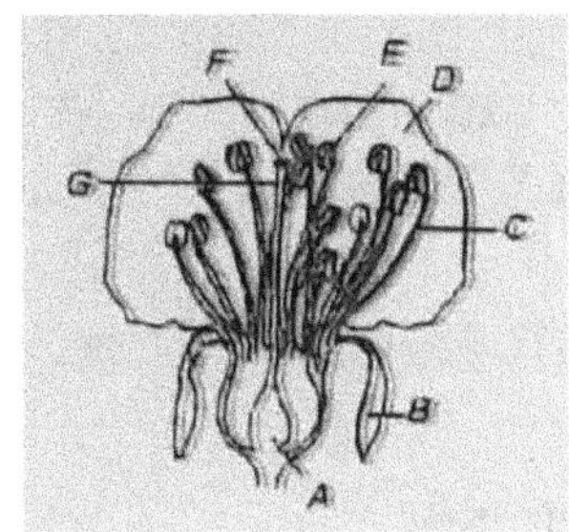

    (a) A-Sepal, B-Ovary, C-Petal, D-Filament, E-Anther, F-Stigma, G-Style.
    (b) A-Ovary, B-Filament, C-Sepal, D-Petal, E-Style, F-Stigma, G-Anther
    (c) A-Ovary, B-Sepal, C-Filament, D-Petal, E-Anther, F-Stigma, G-Style
    (d) A-Petal, B-Sepal, C-Stigma, D-Style, E-Anther, F-Ovary, G-Filament

20. Raphe is
    (a) ridge formed by union of funicle with body of ovule.
    (b) distance between chalaza and micropyle.
    (c) distance between hilum and microphyle.
    (d) area between hilum and chalaza.

21. On culturing the young anther of a plant a botanist got a few diploid plants alongwith haploid plants. Which of the following might have give rise to diploid plants?
    (a) Exine of pollen grain
    (b) Vegetative cell of pollen
    (c) Cells of anther wall
    (d) Generative cell of pollen

22. Sequence of development during the formation of embryo sac is
    (a) Archesporium ⟶ Megaspore ⟶ Megaspore mother cell ⟶ Embryo sac.
    (b) Megasporocyte ⟶ Archesporium ⟶ Megaspore ⟶ Embryo sac.
    (c) Megaspore ⟶ Megaspore mother cell ⟶ Archesporium ⟶ Embryo sac.
    (d) Archesporium ⟶ Megaspore mother cell ⟶ Megaspore ⟶ Embryo sac.

23. Tissue culture technique can produce indefinite number of new plants from a small parental tissue. The economic importance of the technique is in raising
   (a) variants through picking up somaclonal variations.
   (b) genetically uniform population of an elite species.
   (c) homozygous diploid plants.
   (d) development of new species.

24. Match the following columns and choose the correct option.

	Column I		Column II
A.	Coleorhiza	I.	Grapes
B.	Food storing tissue	II.	Mango
C.	Parthenocarpic fruit	III.	Maize
D.	Single seeded fruit developing from monocarpellary superior ovary	IV.	Radicle
E.	Membranous seed coat	V.	Endosperm

   (a) A-III; B-I; C-IV; D-II; E-V
   (b) A-IV; B-II; C-V; D-I; E-III
   (c) A-V; B-I C-III; D-IV; E-II
   (d) A-IV; B-V; C-I; D-II; E-III

25. Match the following columns.

Column I		Column II
A. Monocarpellary	I.	Locule
B. Multicarpellary	II.	Free pistil
C. Syncarpous	III.	Fused pistil
D. Apocarpous	IV.	Many pistil
E. Ovarian cavity	V.	Single pistil

   Codes
   (a) A-I; B-II; C-III; D-IV; E-V
   (b) A-V; B-IV; C-III; D-II; E-I
   (c) A-V; B-III; C-IV; D-II; E-I
   (d) A-V; B-III; C-IV; D-II; E-I

26. Collar-like outgrowth developing from bases of ovule and forming a sort of third integument is
   (a) caruncle   (b) aril
   (c) coma   (d) operculum

27. Polygonum type of embryo sac/typical female gametophyte of angiosperms is
   (a) 7-celled, 7-nucleate
   (b) 7-celled, 8-nucleate
   (c) 8-celled, 7-nucleate
   (d) 8-celled, 8-nucleate

28. Ovule is inverted with body fused to funicle, micropyle lying close to hilum and facing the placenta. It is
   (a) hemitropous   (b) orthotropous
   (c) anatropous   (d) campylotropous

29. Match the following column

Column I		Column II	
A.	Outer integuments	I.	Testa
B.	Inner integuments	II.	Tegman
C.	Ovules	III.	Fruit
E.	Nucellus	IV.	Seed
F.	Ovary wall	V.	Perisperm
		VI.	Pericarp

   Codes
   (a) A-I; B-III; C-II; D-IV; E-VI; F-V
   (b) A-VI; B-V; C-VI; D-III; E-II; F-I
   (c) A-I; B-II; C-III; D-IV; E-V; F-VI
   (d) A-VI; B-III; C-II; D-I; E-V; F-VI

30. Identify the correct modes of entry of pollen tube represented by the three diagrams given below.

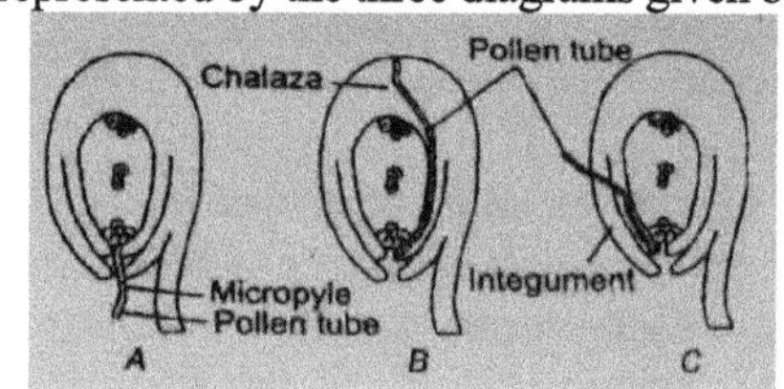

   (a) A-Mesogamy, B-Chalazogamy, C-Porogamy
   (b) A-Chalazogamy, B-Porogamy, C-Mesogamy
   (c) A-Porogamy, B-Chalazogamy, C-Monogamy
   (d) A-Porogamy, B-Chalazogamy, C-Mesogamy

31. While planning for an artificial hybridization programme involving dioecious plants, which of the following steps would not be relevant?
   (a) Bagging of female flower.
   (b) Dusting of pollen on stigma.
   (c) Emasculation.
   (d) Collection of pollen.

32. In a flower, if the megaspore mother cell forms megaspores without undergoing meiosis and if one of the megaspores develops into an embryo sac, its nuclei would be
   (a) haploid
   (b) diploid
   (c) a few haploid and a few diploid
   (d) with varying ploidy

33. Match the following columns.

Column I (Agents of Pollination)	Column II (Technical Term)
A. Wind	I. Anemophily
B. Water	II. Hydrophily
C. Insects	III. Entomophily
D. Birds	IV. Ornithophily
E. Bats	V. Chiropterophily
F. Snails	VI. Malacophily
G. Larger animals	VII. Zoophily including man

Codes
(a) A-I; B-II; C-III; D-IV; E-V; F-VI: G-VII
(b) A-I; B-III; C-II; D-IV; E-V; F-VII; G-VI
(c) A-VII; B-VI; C-IV; D-IV; E-III; F-II; G-I
(c) A-V; B-VI; C-VII; D-I; E-II; F-III; G-IV

34. The condition of maturation of stigma before anthers of the same flower is
(a) protandry   (b) herkogamy
(c) protogyny   (d) prepotency

35. To avoid self-pollination and provide contrivance for cross pollination, the pollen grains of some flowers have no fertilizing effect on the stigma of the same flower but causes death. What is this condition known as?
(a) Homogamy
(b) Dicliny
(c) Self sterility
(d) Dichogamy

36. In which of the following is wall curvature more pronounced and embryo sac become horse shoe shaped?
(a) amphitropous
(b) anatropous
(c) campylotropous
(d) orthotropous

37. After penetrating stigmatic and stylar tissue the pollen tube usually grows down towards the egg cell because
(a) the egg cell attracts pollen tube
(b) it grows under the influence of ovum
(c) it has no other passage to follow
(d) the filiform apparatus of synergids attract the pollen tubes

38. Match Column-I with Column-II and choose the correct answers

Column I	Column II
A. Coleorhiza	I. Grapes
B. Food storing tissue	II. Mango
C. Parthenocarpic fruit	III. Maize
D. Single seeded fruit developing from monocarpellary superior ovary	IV. Radicle
E. Membraneous seed coat	V. Endosperm

(a) A-III, B-I, C-IV, D-II, E-V
(b) A-IV, B-II, C-V, D-I, E-III
(c) A-V, B-I, C-III, D-IV, E-II
(d) A-I, B-III, C-II, D-V, E-IV

39. What is the product of double fertilization and triple fusion in *Capsella*?
(a) $3 \times$ Oospore and $2 \times$ endosperm
(b) $2 \times$ Oospore and $2 \times$ endosperm
(c) $2 \times$ Oospore and $3 \times$ endosperm
(d) $3 \times$ Oospore and $3 \times$ endosperm

ANSWER KEY																			
1	(c)	**2**	(a)	**3**	(a)	**4**	(b)	**5**	(b)	**6**	(b)	**7**	(d)	**8**	(b)	**9**	(a)	**10**	(b)
11	(b)	**12**	(a)	**13**	(b)	**14**	(a)	**15**	(d)	**16**	(b)	**17**	(b)	**18**	(c)	**19**	(c)	**20**	(a)
21	(c)	**22**	(d)	**23**	(b)	**24**	(d)	**25**	(b)	**26**	(b)	**27**	(b)	**28**	(c)	**29**	(c)	**30**	(c)
31	(c)	**32**	(b)	**33**	(a)	**34**	(c)	**35**	(c)	**36**	(a)	**37**	(d)	**38**	(d)	**39**	(c)		

Human Reproduction

25

1. Arrange the following events in order of their occurrence: Gestation (G), Implantation (I), Fertilization (F) and parturition (P)
   (a) FIGP
   (b) IFPG
   (c) FGIP
   (d) IPFG

2. The release of semen into vagina is called
   (a) Ejaculation
   (b) Impotency
   (c) Implantation
   (d) Insemination

3. Milk secreted from the cells of alveoli of mammary lobes reaches nipple through lactiferous duct(L), Mammary duct(M), Mammary tubule(T) and Mammary ampulla(A) in the following order
   (a) TMAL
   (b) MTLA
   (c) MTAL
   (d) ATML

4. Which of the following statement regarding human development is correct?
   (a) Amnion acts as a urinary bladder
   (b) Chorion develops from inner cell mass
   (c) Inner cell mass contains stem cells
   (d) Primitive streak is formed after differentation of three germ layers

5. The first movements of foetus and appearance of hair on head are observed during
   (a) 3rd month
   (b) 4th month
   (c) 5th month
   (d) 6th month

6. Which does not form the component of external genitalia or Vulva in female?
   (a) Clitoris
   (b) Labia majora
   (c) Mons pubis
   (d) Ampulla

7. Which Accessory duct of male reproductive system is completely inside abdominal cavity?
   (a) Vas deferens
   (b) Epididymis
   (c) Ejaculatory duct
   (d) Urethera

8. Development in all multicellular animals happens in this sequence
   (a) Gastrula – blastula – cleavage – germ layers formation
   (b) Cleavage – gastrula – blastula – germ layers formation
   (c) Cleavage – blastula – gastrula – formation of primary germ layers
   (d) Formation of primary germ layers – cleavage – blastula - gastrula

9. Match the following with correct combination.

   A. Hyaluronidase — p. acrosomal reaction
   B. Corpus luteum — q. morphogenetic movements
   C. Gastrulation — r. progesterone
   D. Capacitiation — s. mammary gland
   E. Colostrum — t. sperm activation

   (a) A - t, B - q, C - s, D - p, E - r
   (b) A - p, B - r, C - q, D - t, E - s
   (c) A - r, B - q, C - t, D - s, E - p
   (d) A - p, B - q, C - r, D - s, E - t

10. Mark the correct sequence of the parts labelled A, B, C and D

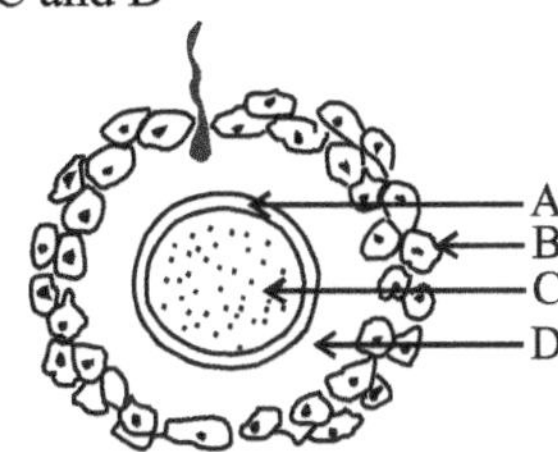

(a) A - Zona pellucida, B - corona radiata, C - ovum, D - perivitelline space

(b) A - Perivitelline space, B - corona radiata, C - Primary oocyte, D - perivitelline space

(c) A - Corona radiata, B - zona pellucida C - secondary oocyte, D - perivitelline space

(d) A -Perivitelline space, B - corona radiata, C - ovum, D - zona pellucida

11. Signals from fully developed foetus and placenta ultimately lead to parturition which requires the release of

(a) estrogen from placenta

(b) oxytocin from maternal pituitary

(c) oxytocin from foetal pituitary

(d) relaxin from placenta

12. If a germ cell in a female gonad and a germ cell in a male gonad are undergoing meiosis simultaneously, what will be the ratio of ova and sperms produced?

(a) 1 : 1   (b) 1 : 2

(c) 1 : 4   (d) 2 : 1

13. Abnormal condition when mammary glands of man become female like

(a) gynaecomastism   (b) feminization

(c) gynochorism   (d) gynosism

14. Choose the correct combination of labelling of seminiferous tubule of testis

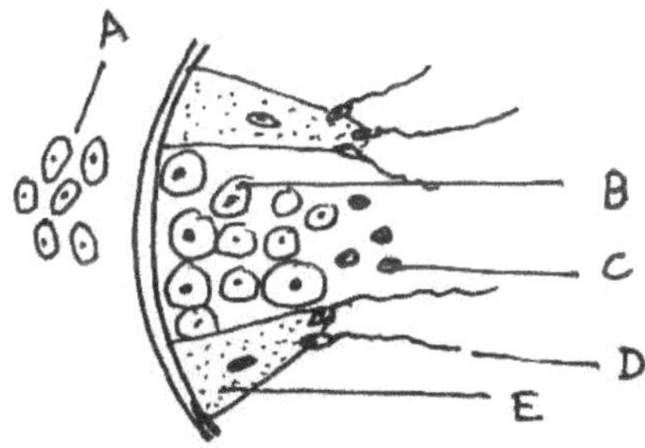

(a) A - sertoli cell, B - spermatogonium, C - spermatid, D - intestitial cell, E - spermatozoa

(b) A - interstitial cell, B - spermatid, C - spermatogonium, D - spermatozoa, E - sertoli cell

(c) A - interstitial cell, B - spermatid, c - spermatozoa, D - spermatogonium, E - sertoli cell

(d) A - interstitial cell, B - spermatogonium, C - spermatid, D - spermatozoa, E - sertoli cell

15. Due to the presence of higher amount of yolk, the zygote is divided into two incomplete halves. This type of cleavage is not found in

(a) Peacock, duck billed Platypus and crocodile

(b) *Hemidactylus, coyotes and varanus*

(c) Jungle fowl, dove and duck

(d) Amphioxus, salamander and rana

16. During embryonic development the establishment of polarity along anterior/ posterior, dorsal/ventral or medial/lateral axis is called

(a) anamorphosis

(b) organizer phenomena

(c) pattern formation

(d) axis formation

17. Which one of the following is the *correct* matching of the events occurring during menstrual cycle?

(a) Menstruation : breakdown of myometrium and ovum not fertilised

(b) Ovulation : LH and FSH attain peak level and sharp fall in the secretion of progesterone.

(c) Proliferative : Rapid regeneration of phase myometrium and maturation of Graafian follicle.

(d) Development of : Secretory phase and corpus luteum increased secretion of progesterone.

18. Which one of the following is the most likely root cause why menstruation is not taking place in regularly cycling human female?
    (a) Retention of well-developed corpus luteum
    (b) Fertilisation of the ovum
    (c) Maintenance of the hypertrophical endometrial lining
    (d) Maintenance of high concentration of sex hormones in the blood stream

19. Amphimixis is
    (a) reaction of antifertilizin & fertilizin
    (b) fusion of male and female pronuclei
    (c) formation of reception cone by ovum
    (d) penetration of sperm into ovum

20. Withdrawal of which of the following hormones is the immediate cause of menstruation?
    (a) FSH   (b) FSH-RH
    (c) Progesterone   (d) Estrogen

21. Which of the following represents a condition where the mobility of the sperms is highly reduced?
    (a) Oligospermia   (b) athenospermia
    (c) Azoospermia   (d) polyspermy

22. What happens during fertilisation in humans after many sperms reach close to the ovum?
    (a) Cells of corona radiata trap all the sperms except one
    (b) Only two sperms nearest the ovum penetrate zona pellucida
    (c) Secretions of acrosome helps one sperm enter cytoplasm of ovum through zona pellucida

    (d) All sperms except the one nearest to the ovum lose their tails

23. The shared terminal duct of the reproductive and urinary system in the human male is
    (a) Urethra   (b) Ureter
    (c) Vas deferens   (d) Vasa efferentia

24. Match column I with column II and select the correct option using the code given below

Column I		Column II
A. Mons pubis	I.	Embryo formation
B. Antrum	II.	Sperm
C. Trophectoderm	III.	Female external genitalia
D. Nebenkern	IV.	Graafian follicle

    (a) A–I; B–IV; C–III; D–II
    (b) A–III; B–IV; C–II; D–I
    (c) A–III; B–IV; C–I; D–II
    (d) A–III; B–I; C–IV; D–II

25. Which of the following depicts the correct pathway of transport of sperms?
    (a) Efferent ductules- Rete testis- Vas deferens- Epididymis
    (b) Rete testis- Efferent ductules- Epididymis- Vas deferens
    (c) Rete testis- Epididymis- Efferent ductules- Vas deferens
    (d) Rete testis- Vas deferens- Efferent ductules- Epididymis

26. Lens of eyes is derived from
    (a) ectoderm   (b) mesoderm
    (c) endoderm   (d) Both (b) and (c)

ANSWER KEY																			
1	(a)	**2**	(d)	**3**	(a)	**4**	(c)	**5**	(c)	**6**	(d)	**7**	(c)	**8**	(c)	**9**	(b)	**10**	(d)
11	(b)	**12**	(c)	**13**	(a)	**14**	(d)	**15**	(d)	**16**	(d)	**17**	(d)	**18**	(b)	**19**	(b)	**20**	(c)
21	(b)	**22**	(c)	**23**	(a)	**24**	(c)	**25**	(b)	**26**	(a)								

Reproductive Health

1. Which of the following is the method of traditional contraception?

(a) Implantation

(b) Lactational amenorrhoea

(c) Condoms

(d) Sterilization

2. Which statement regarding 'Saheli', a new contraceptive, is correct?

(a) It has estrogen and progesterone combination

(b) It is an implant with longer contraceptive effect

(c) It was developed at CDRI, Lucknow

(d) It is a steroidal contraceptive and is used once a week

3. For avoiding conception, one should abstain from coitus for about a week, starting from

(a) 4th day to 10th day of menstrual cycle

(b) 11th day to 17th day of menstrual cycle

(c) 18th day to 25th day of menstrual cycle

(d) The end of luteal phase

4. Female condom, also called as 'Femidom', is different from Cervical cap, as the former

(a) Is a barrier contraceptive

(b) Disposable

(c) Does not allow the entry of sperms into uterus

(d) Is prepared from silicon

5. PID stands for

(a) Penile inflammatory disorder

(b) Pesticide influenced disorder

(c) Pelvic inflammatory disease

(d) Psychological infertility disorder

6. Impotency and low sperm count can be corrected by

(a) Artificial insemination

(b) GIFT

(c) ICSI

(d) ZIFT

7. MTP is performed when pregnancy is due to

(a) Casual unprotected intercourse

(b) Rape

(c) Failure of contraceptive

(d) Any of the above cause

8. Given below are four methods (A-D) and their modes of action (I - IV) in achieving contraception.

   Select their correct matching from the four options that follow :

Method		Mode of Action
A.	The pill	I.	Prevents sperms reaching cervix
B.	Condom	II.	prevents implantation
C.	Vasectomy	III.	prevents ovulation
D.	Copper T	IV.	Semen contains no sperms

   (a) A – II; B – III; C – I; D – IV

   (b) A – III; B – I; C – IV; D – II

   (c) A – IV; B – I; C – II; D – III

   (d) A – III; B – IV; C – I; D – II

9. Consider the statements given below regarding contraception and answer as directed thereafter

   A. Medical Termination of Pregnancy (MTP) during first trimester is generally safe

   B. Generally chances of conception are nil until mother breast-feeds the infant upto two years

   C. Intrauterine devices like copper-T are effective contraceptives

   D. Contraception pills may be taken upto one week after coitus to prevent conception

   Which two of the above statements are *correct*?

   (a) A, B   (b) B, C

   (c) C, D   (d) A, C

10. One of the legal methods of birth control is

    (a) Abortion by taking an appropriate medicine

    (b) By abstaining from coitus from day 10 to 17 of menstrual cycle

    (c) By having coitus at the time of day break

    (d) By a premature ejaculation during coitus

11. Which of the following approaches does not give the defined action of contraceptive?

    (a) Vasectomy- prevents spermatogenesis

    (b) Barrier methods- prevent fertilization

    (c) Intra- uterine devices- increase phagocytosis, suppress motility and fertilizing capacity of sperms

    (d) Hormonal contraceptives- prevent/ retard entry of sperms, prevent ovulation and fertilization

12. A childless couple can be assisted to have a child through a technique called GIFT. The full form of this technique is:

    (a) Gamete intra fallopian transfer

    (b) Gamete internal fertilization and transfer

    (c) Germ cell internal fallopian transfer

    (d) Gamete inseminated fallopian transfer

13. Foetal sex can be determined by examining cells from the amniotic fluid by looking for

    (a) Barr bodies   (b) Autosomes

    (c) Chiasmata   (d) Kinetochore

14. Depo-provera refers to

    (a) injectible contraceptive

    (b) intra uterine device

    (c) implant

    (d) oral contraceptive

15. What is true for an ideal contraceptive?

    A. It should be user-friendly.

    B. It should be easily available.

    C. It should be ineffective and reversible with least side effects.

    D. It should be effective and reversible with least side effects.

    E. It should interfere with the sexual act of the user.

    (a) All   (b) A, B, C

    (c) A, B, D   (d) A, B, D, E

16. Match the following and choose the correct option

Column I		**Column II**
A.	Non-medicated IUDs	I. Lippes loop
B.	Hormone releasing IUDs	II. Multiload 375
C.	Copper releasing IUDs	III. CuT
		IV. Cu7
		V. LNG - 20
		VI. Progestasert

(a) A – I; B– II,VI; C – III, IV, V

(b) A– I; B – V, VI; C – II, III, IV

(c) A – I; B – V, VI; C – I, III, IV

(d) A – II; B – I, VI; C – III, IV, V

17. Match the following and choose the correct option

Column-I		**Column-II**
A.	Hepatitis B	I. Vitamin E
B.	Saheli	II. 7'April, 1948
C.	Normal functioning of reproductive organs	III. CDRI, Lucknow
D.	World Health organisation	IV. Detection of antibody/antigen
E.	ELISA technique	V. Hepatitis B virus

(a) A – V; B – III; C – I; D – II; E – IV

(b) A – V; B – II; C – I; D – III; E – IV

(c) A – V; B – III; C – IV; D – II; E – I

(d) A – V; B – II; C – IV; D – III; E – I

18. Using which contraceptive also provides protection from contracting STDs and AIDS ?

(a) Diaphragms

(b) Spermicidal foams

(c) Condoms

(d) Lactational amenorrhoea

19. Choose the correct option–

A. RTI - Reproductive Tract Infections

B. VD - Venereal Diseases

C. STD - Sexually Transmitted Diseases

D. IVF - Intra Vaginal Fertilization

(a) All   (b) A, B, C

(c) B, C   (d) A, B

20. The first case of IVF-ET technique success, was reported by :

(a) Bayliss and Starling Taylor

(b) Robert Steptoe and Gilbert Brown

(c) Louis Joy Brown and Banting Best

(d) Patrick Steptoe and Robert Edwards

21. What role do contraceptive pills carry out?

A. They inhibit ovulation and implantation.

B. They alter the quality of cervical mucus to prevent or retard the entry of sperms.

C. They prevent the ejaculated semen from entering the female vagina.

D. They inhibit spermatogenesis.

(a) A, B and D   (b) A, B and C

(c) A and B   (d) A, B, C and D

22. Reproductive health in society can be improved by –

A. Introduction of sex education in schools.

B. Increased medical assistance.

C. Awareness about contraception and STDs.

D. Equal opportunities to male and female child.

E. Ban on aminocentesis.

F. Encouraging myths and misconceptions.

(a) All   (b) A, B, D, F

(c) A, B, C, D, E   (d) B,

ANSWER KEY

1	(b)	2	(c)	3	(b)	4	(b)	5	(c)	6	(a)	7	(d)	8	(b)	9	(d)	10	(b)
11	(a)	12	(a)	13	(a)	14	(a)	15	(c)	16	(b)	17	(a)	18	(c)	19	(b)	20	(d)
21	(c)	22	(c)																

Principles of Inheritance and Variation

27

1. Harmful mutations does not get eliminated from gene pool because
   (a) they are recessive and carried by homozygous individuals.
   (b) they are recessive and carried by heterozygous individuals.
   (c) they are formed repeatedly.
   (d) they show genetic drift.

2. Bateson used the terms coupling and repulsion for linkage and crossing over. Name the correct parental or coupling type along with its cross over or repulsion:
   (a) Coupling aaBB, aabb; Repulsion AABB, aabb
   (b) Coupling AABB, aabb; Repulsion AABB, AAbb
   (c) Coupling AAbb, aaBB; Repulsion AaBb, aabb
   (d) Coupling AABB, aabb; Repulsion AAbb, aaBB

3. Which of the following is suitable for experiments on linkage?
   (a) AABB × aabb   (b) AaBb × AaBb
   (c) aaBB × aaBB   (d) AAbb × AaBB

4. '□ □' in pedigree represents
   (a) Dizygotic twins
   (b) Monozygotic twins
   (c) Either of two
   (d) Sibling brothers

5. In case of *Bonellia*, a marine worm, the sex determination mechanism is
   (a) Epigamic   (b) Syngamic
   (c) Haploidy – diploidy (d) None of these

6. The fruit fly *Drosophila melanogaster* was found to be very suitable for experimental verification of chromosomal theory of inheritance by Morgan and his colleagus because:
   (a) It reproduces parthenogenetically
   (b) A single mating produces two young flies
   (c) Smaller female is easily recognisable from larger male
   (d) It completes life cycle in about two weeks

7. The genetic make-up of the following determines the sex in the child:
   (a) Sperm
   (b) Sperm and egg both
   (c) Eggs
   (d) Autosomes

8. Study the pedigree chart of a certain family given below and select the correct conclusion which can be drawn for the character

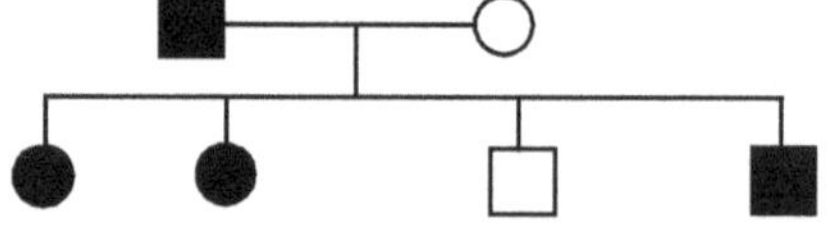

   (a) The female parent is heterozygous
   (b) The parents could not have had a normal daughter for this character
   (c) The trait under study could not be colourblindness
   (d) The male parent is homozygous dominant

9. How many of the following statements regarding Thalassemia are correct?
   A. α-Thalassemia is controlled by genes present on 16th chromosome
   B. β-Thalassemia is controlled by genes present on 11th chromosome
   C. It is a qualitative disorder of globin
   D. It is an autosomal recessive disorder
   (a) One   (b) Two
   (c) Three   (d) All four

10. G-6-P dehydrogenase deficiency is associated with haemolysis of:
    (a) Leucocytes   (b) Lymphocytes
    (c) Platelets   (d) RBCs

11. A haemophilic man marries a normal homozygous woman. What is the probability that their son will be haemophilic?
    (a) 100%   (b) 75%
    (c) 50%   (d) 0%

12. The "cri-du-chat" syndrome is caused by change in chromosome structure involving
    (a) deletion   (b) duplication
    (c) inversion   (d) translocation

13. The correct pathway for the synthesis of skin pigment is
    (a) tyrosine - melanin - dopaquinone - dopa
    (b) tyrosine - dopa - dopaquinone - melanin
    (c) tyrosine - dopa - melanin - dopaquinone
    (d) tyrosine - dopaquinone - dopa -melanin

14. Which one of the following techniques is employed in human genetic counselling?
    (a) serological technique
    (b) pedigree analysis
    (c) genetic engineering
    (d) amniocentesis.

15. In *Drosophila,* gene for white eye mutation is also responsible for depigmentation of body parts. Thus a gene that controls several phenotypes is called
    (a) oncogene   (b) epistatic gene
    (c) hypostatic gene (d) pleiotropic gene

16. Haemophilic female marries normal male, the theoretical ratio of their offsprings regarding haemophilia will be
    (a) all offsprings are haemophilic
    (b) all girls are haemophilic
    (c) all sons are haemophilic
    (d) half daughters and half sons are haemophilic

17. Blackening of urine when exposed to air is a metabolic disorder in human beings. This is due to
    (a) phenylalanine
    (b) valine replacing glutamine
    (c) glutamine replacing valine
    (d) homogentisic acid.

18. Which one of the following is an example of polygenic inheritance ?
    (a) Production of male honey bee
    (b) Pod shape in garden pea
    (c) Skin colour in humans
    (d) Flower colour in *Mirabilis jalapa*

19. Given below is a highly simplified representation of the human sex chromosomes from a karyotype. The gene a and b could be of

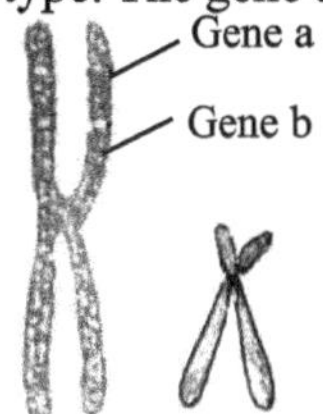

    (a) colour blindness and body height
    (b) attached ear lobe and Rhesus blood group
    (c) haemophilia and red-green colour blindness
    (d) phenylketonuria and haemophilia

20. Kappa particles indicate:
    (a) nuclear inheritance
    (b) cytoplasmic inheritance
    (c) mutation
    (d) nucleo-cytoplasmic inheritance

21. Gynandromorphs are animals having
    (a) same sex in all cells of the body
    (b) different sexes in all cells of the body
    (c) same sex in different cells of the body
    (d) different sexes in different cells of the body

22. In Shepherd's Purse, the fruit shape is controlled by
    (a) supplementary genes
    (b) complementary genes
    (c) duplicate genes
    (d) polymeric genes

23. In multiple allele system a gamete possesses
    (a) two alleles   (b) three alleles
    (c) one allele   (d) several alleles

24. Which of the following is an X- linked recessive trait with locus in Xq 28 and related with factor VIII?
    (a) Haemophilia A   (b) Haemophilia B
    (c) Christmas disease (d) Both (a) and (b)

25. Which one of the followings is correctly matched with their chromosomal condition?
    (a) Sickle cell anaemia – Heterozygous condition of Hbs gene
    (b) Down's syndrome – Trisomy of chromosome 22
    (c) Turner's syndrome – XO condition
    (d) Klinefelter's syndrome – failure of cytokinesis after telophase

26. In blood group typing in human, if an allele contributed by one parent is IA and an allele contributed by the other parent is i, the resulting blood group of the offspring will be
(a) A   (b) B
(c) AB   (d) O

27. A person with unknown blood group under ABO system, has suffered much blood loss in an accident and needs immediate blood transfusion. His one friend who has a valid certificate of his own blood type, offers for blood donation without delay. What would have been the type of blood group of the donor friend?
(a) Type A   (b) Type B
(c) Type AB   (d) Type O

28. A man and a woman, who do not show any apparent signs of a certian inherited disease, have seven children (2 daughters and 5 cons). Three of the sons suffer from the given disease but none of the daughters are affected. Which of the following mode of inhertiance do you suggest for this disease?
(a) Autosomal dominant
(b) Sex-linked dominant
(c) Sex-linked recessive
(d) Sex-linked recessive

29. Human skin colour is controlled by several gene pairs. Let us assume here that there are just three gene pairs on different chromosomes and that for each pair there are two alleles- an incompletely dominant one that codes for melanin deposition and an incompletely recessive one that codes for no melanin deposition. If a very dark skinned person marries a very light skinned woman, what will be the chance that their offspring will have very dark skin?
(a) 0   (b) 1/4
(c) 5/8   (d) 9/64

30. If two persons with 'AB' blood group marry and have sufficiently large number of children, these children could be classified as 'A' blood group, 'AB' blood group, 'B' blood group in 1: 2: 1 ratio. Modern technique of protein electrophoresis reveals the presence of both 'A' and 'B' type proteins in 'AB' blood group individuals. This is an example of:
(a) Codominance
(b) Incomplete dominance
(c) Partial dominance
(d) Complete dominance

31. In order to lessen the suffering of Phenylketonurics their diet should have
(a) No phenylalanine and no tyrosine
(b) Low phenylalanine and normal requirement of tyrosine
(c) Normal recommended amount of phenylalanine
(d) Normal recommended amount of phenylalanine and tyrosine

32. The nuclear structure observed by Henking in 50% of the insect sperms after spermatogenesis was:
(a) X-body   (b) Autosome
(c) Y-chromosome   (d) Nucleolus

33. Which of the following statement (s) is/are correct for epistatic gene?
(a) epistatic gene is nonallelic.
(b) epistatic gene never expresses itself independently.
(c) epistatic and hypostatic genes are present at different loci.
(d) all the above.

34. What will be the first three children. If the parents are hetrozygous albino, the first three childrent will be
(a) some normal, heterozygous and albino
(b) normal
(c) heterozygous albino
(d) abnormal

35. Which blood group Can safely be transfused in emergency when there is no time to analyse the blood group of recipient?
(a) O and Rh$^-$ (b) O and Rh$^+$
(c) B and Rh$^-$ (d) AB and Rh$^+$

36. If the blood group of the mother and the child is O and B respectively. Then the person of the following blood group cannot be the father of this child
(a) O and A   (b) A, B or O
(c) AB only   (d) O only

37. Given pedigree shows that the trait is inherited as autosomal dominant. Trace the genotype of Mother and Father

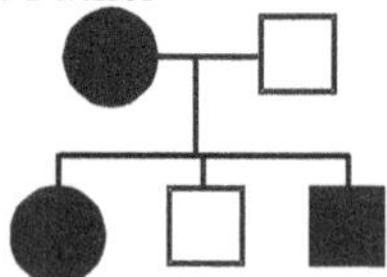

(a) Father AA, Mother aa
(b) Father AA, mother Aa
(c) Father aa, Mother AA
(d) Father aa, Mother Aa

38. A man whose genotype for blood group is I^AI^B marries a lady of genotype I^BI^O. They have two daughters. If one daughter has blood group B, what is the probability that the other daughter will also have the same blood group.
 (a) 50% (b) 25%
 (c) 12.5% (d) None of these

39. Mongoloid idiocy is due to
 (a) Monosomy of a sex chromosome
 (b) Trisomy of an autosome
 (c) Monosomy of 21st chromosome
 (d) None of these

40. Match the terms in Column- I with their description in Column- II and choose the correct option

Column- I		Column- II
A.	Dominance	I. Many genes govern a single character
B.	Co-dominance	II. In heterozygous only one allele expresses itself
C.	Pleiotropy	III. In heterozygous organism both alleles express themselves
D.	Polygenic Inh.	IV. Single gene influences many characters

 (a) A–IV; B–III; C–I; D–II
 (b) A–II; B–I; C–IV; D–III
 (c) A–II; B–III; C–IV; D–I
 (d) A–IV; B–I; C–II; D–III

41. Given below is a pedigree chart showing the inheritance of a certain sex-linked trait in humans

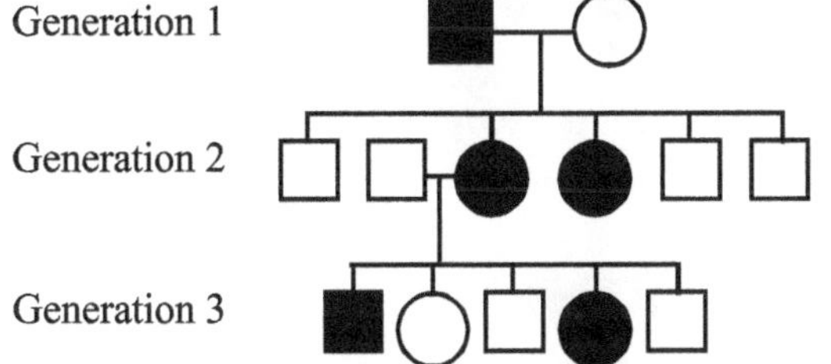

Key :

 Unaffected male  Affected male

◯ Unaffected female ● Affected female

The trait traced in the above pedigree chart is
 (a) dominant X - linked
 (b) recessive X-linked
 (c) dominant Y - linked
 (d) recessive Y-linked

42. Match the following and choose the correct option –

	Column – A		Column – B
A.	ABO blood	I.	Dihybrid cross groups
B.	Law of segregation	II.	Monohybrid cross
C.	Law of Independent	III.	Base pairs substitution assortment
D.	Gene mutation	IV.	Multiple allelism

 (a) A – II; B – I; C – IV; D – III
 (b) A – IV; B – I; C – II; D – III
 (c) A – IV; B – II; C – I; D – III
 (d) A – II; B – III; C – IV; D – I

43. Match the following and choose the correct option–

	Column – I		Column – II
A.	Linkage	I.	Recombination of genes
B.	Mutation	II.	More than two sets of chromosome
C.	Crossing over	III.	Morgan
D.	Polyploidy	IV.	Hugo de Vries

 (a) A – II; B – III; C –I; D – IV
 (b) A– III; B – IV; C–I; D – II
 (c) A – II; B – IV; C – III; D –I
 (d) A – II; B – IV; C –I; D – III

ANSWER KEY																			
1	(b)	2	(d)	3	(b)	4	(a)	5	(a)	6	(d)	7	(a)	8	(a)	9	(c)	10	(d)
11	(d)	12	(a)	13	(b)	14	(b)	15	(d)	16	(c)	17	(d)	18	(c)	19	(c)	20	(b)
21	(d)	22	(c)	23	(c)	24	(a)	25	(c)	26	(a)	27	(d)	28	(d)	29	(a)	30	(a)
31	(b)	32	(a)	33	(d)	34	(a)	35	(a)	36	(a)	37	(d)	38	(a)	39	(b)	40	(c)
41	(a)	42	(c)	43	(b)														

Molecular Basis of Inheritance

28

1. The given figure shows *lac* operon and its functioning. Select the option which correctly labels A, B, X,Y and Z.

	A	B	X	Y	Z
(a)	Repressor	Inducer	Permease	Beta-galactosidase	Transacetylase
(b)	Inducer	Repressor	Beta-galactosidase	Permease	Transacetylase
(c)	Inducer	Repressor	Beta-galactosidase	Transacetylase	Permease
(d)	Repressor	Inducer	Beta-galactosidase	Permease	Transacetylase

2. Given diagram represent the components the components of a transcription unit. Select the correct answer regarding it.

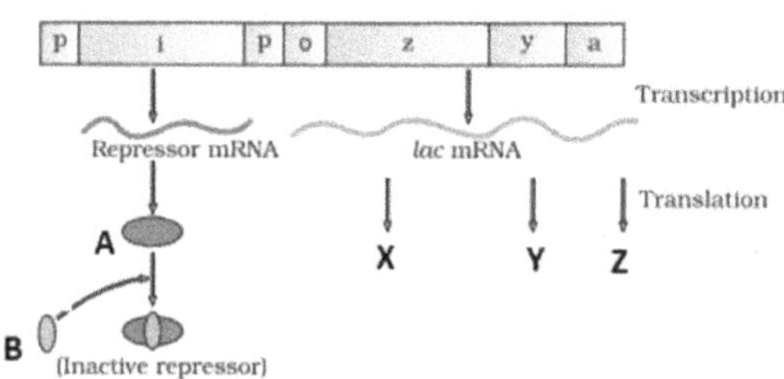

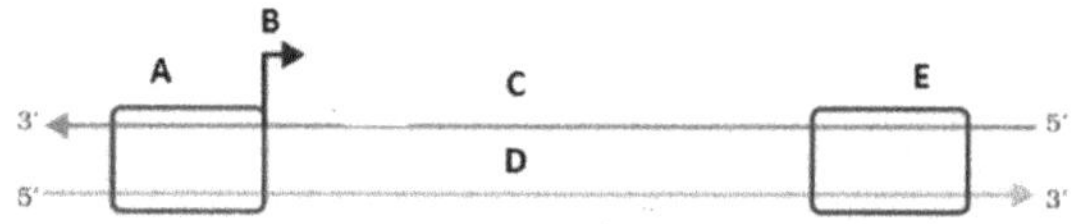

	A	B	C	D	E
(a)	Terminator	Promoter	Template strand	Coding strand	Transcription start site
(b)	Promoter	Terminator	Coding Strand	Template strand	Transcription start site
(c)	Transcription start site	Coding Strand	Template strand	Promoter	Terminator
(d)	Terminator	Transcription start site	Template strand	Coding strand	Promoter

3. Which of the following is/are correct matching(s)?

	Codon	Amino acid
(i)	$^5{}'AUG^{3'}$	Serine
(ii)	$^5{}'AUG^{3'}$	Tyrosine
(iii)	$^5{}'AUG^{3'}$	Methionine
(iv)	$^5{}'GUG^{3'}$	Valine

(a) (i) and (iii)
(b) All of these
(c) (ii), (iii) and (iv)
(d) (i), (ii) and (iii)

4. Match column-I with column-II and select the correct answer using the codes given below.

Column-I		Column-II
A. Operator site	I.	Binding site for RNA polymerase
B. Promoter site	II.	Binding site for repressor molecule
C. Structure gene	III.	Codes for enzyme protein
D. Regulator gene	IV.	Codes for repressor molecules

(a) A-II; B-I; C-III; D-IV
(b) A-II; B-I; C-IV; D-III
(c) A-IV; B-III; C-I; D-II
(d) A-II; B-III; C-I; D-IV

5. Identify the labels A, B, C and D in the given structure of t RNA and select the correct option.

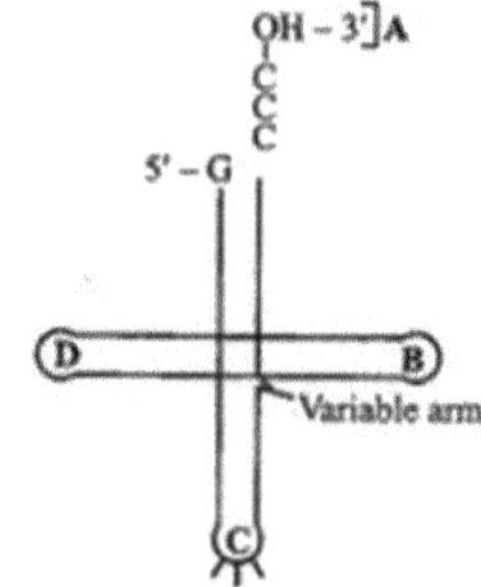

	A	B	C	D
(a)	Anticodon loop	TυC loop	AA binding site	DHU loop
(b)	AA binding site	TC loop	Anticodon loop	DHU loop
(c)	AA binding site	DHU loop	Anticodon loop	TC loop
(d)	AA binding site	DHU loop	TC loop	Anticodon loop

6. During infection of *E. coli* cells by bacteriophage T_2,
   (a) proteins are the only phage components that actually enter the infected cell.
   (b) both proteins and nucleic acids enter the cell.
   (c) only proteins from the infecting phage can also be detected in progeny phage.
   (d) only nucleic acids enter the cell.

7. The correct order of events for synthesis of the lagging strand is
   (a) Primase adds RNA primer, DNA polymerase III creates a stretch, DNA polymerase I removes the primer, and ligase seals the gaps.
   (b) Primase adds primer, DNA polymerase I removes the primer, DNA polymerase extends the segment, and ligase seals the gap.

(c) Ligase adds bases to the primase, the primase generates the polymerase 1, polymerase III adds to the stretch, helicase winds the DNA.

(d) Helicase unwinds the DNA, primase creates a primer, DNA polymerase I elongates the stretch, DNA polymerase III removes the primer, and ligase seals the gaps in the DNA.

8. Human Genome Project (HGP) is closely associated with the rapid development of a new area in biology called as

(a) biotechnology   (b) bioinformatics

(c) biogeography   (d) bioscience

9. Before the discovery of DNA, why was the hereditary material thought to be made of proteins and not nucleic acids?

(a) Nucleic acids are made up of 20 different bases, while proteins are made up of only 5 amino acids.

(b) Protein subunits can combine to form larger proteins.

(c) Proteins seemed to be much more diverse chemically.

(d) Proteins can be enzymes.

10. What are the three major properties of genes that are explained by the structure of DNA?

(a) They contain information, direct the synthesis of proteins, and are contained in the cell nucleus.

(b) They contain nitrogenous bases, direct the synthesis of RNA, and are contained in the cell nucleus

(c) They encode the organisms phenotype, are passed on from one generation to the next, and contain nitrogenous bases.

(d) They contain information, replicate exactly, and change to produce a mutation.

11. The error rate of changing an incorrect base with another incorrect base during proofreading is

(a) 1 in 10 bases   (b) 1 in 100 bases

(c) 1 in 1,000 bases   (d) 1 in 10,000 bases

12. SNP which is pronounced as "snips" stands for

(a) small nuclear protein

(b) single nucleotide particle

(c) single nucleotide polymorphism

(d) small nicking points

13. The wild type *E. coli* cells are growing in normal medium with glucose. They are transferred to a medium containing only lactose as sugar. Which of the following changes takes place?

(a) The lac operon is repressed

(b) All operons are induced

(c) The lac operon is induced

(d) *E.coli* cells stop dividing

14. Operon model of gene regulation and organisation of prokaryotes was proposed by

(a) Messelson and Stahl (b) Wilkins and Franklin

(c) Beadle and Tatum (d) Jacob and Monod

15. If a nucleotide lacking a hydroxyl group at the 3' end is added to a PCR, result would be

(a) no additional nucleotides would be added to a growing strand containing that nucleotide.

(b) strand elongation would proceed as normal.

(c) nucleotides would only be added at the 5' end.

(d) *Thermus aquaticus* DNA polymerase would be denatured.

16. A mutation at one base of first codon of a gene forms a nonfunctional protein is

(a) nonsense mutation

(b) reverse mutation

(c) frame shift mutation

(d) mis-sense mutation

17. Information flow or central dogma of modern biology is

(a) RNA $\longrightarrow$ Proteins $\longrightarrow$ DNA

(b) DNA $\longrightarrow$ RNA $\longrightarrow$ Proteins

(c) RNA $\longrightarrow$ DNA $\longrightarrow$ Proteins

(d) DNA $\longrightarrow$ RNA $\longrightarrow$ Proteins.

18. DNA with labelled thymidine is added to a medium where Escherichia coli is growing. After 5 minutes of growth

(a) all the DNA strands of parents and daughters will show DNA with labelled thymidine

(b) only parental strands will show thymidine labelled DNA

(c) all the strands of daughters will be thymidine labelled

(d) half the daughter strands will have labelled and half strands without labelled thymidine

19. In Meselson and Stahl's experiment, DNA extracted from the culture of one generation after the transfer from ^{15}N to ^{14}N medium had a hybrid (or intermediate density).
Choose the correct reasoning.
   (a) Since the generation time of E. coli (culture) was about 20 minutes.
   (b) Since it would take 20 minutes for DNA translation.
   (c) Since it would take 20 minutes for replication of DNA to RNA (transcription)
   (d) Since it would take 20 minutes for translation RNA to protein.

20. *E.coli* cells with a mutated z gene of the lac operon cannot grow in medium containing only lactose as the source of energy because:
   (a) the lac operon is constitutively active in these cells
   (b) they cannot synthesize functional beta-galactosidase
   (c) in the presence of glucose, *E.coli* cells do not utilize lactose
   (d) they cannot transport lactose from the medium into the cell

21. Antibiotic inhibiting interaction between tRNA and mRNA during protein synthesis in bacteria is
   (a) tetracycline   (b) neomycin
   (c) erythromycin   (d) streptomycin

22. Which antibiotic inhibits interaction between RNA and mRNA during bacterial protein synthesis?
   (a) Neomycin   (b) Streptomycin
   (c) Tetracycline   (d) Erythromycin

23. C-value paradox is
   (a) diploid DNA content
   (b) haploid DNA content
   (c) variation in C-value
   (d) constancy of C-value

24. The okazaki fragments in DNA chain growth
   (a) polymerize in the 3' - to - 5' direction and forms replication fork
   (b) prove semi-conservative nature of DNA replication
   (c) polymerize in the 5' - to - 3' direction and explain 3' - to - 5' DNA replication
   (d) result in transcription.

25. Molecular basis of organ differentiation depends on the modulation in transcription by
   (a) ribosome   (b) transcription factor
   (c) anticodon   (d) RNA polymerase.

26. What would be the correct base sequence in mRNA for the given DNA strand?
   5' – AATGCCTTAAGC – 3'

   (a) 5 – GCUUAAGGCAUU – 3'
   (b) 5 – UUACGGAATTCG – 3'
   (c) 3 – UUACGGAAUUCG – 5'
   (d) 3 – AAUGCCUUAUCG – 5'

27. 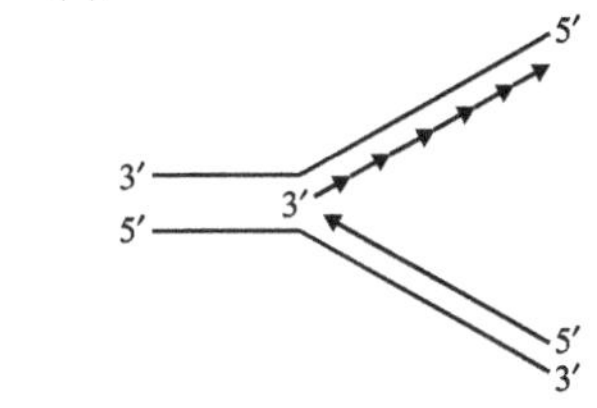

What is the error in above diagram?
   (a) Arrows are wrongly depicted.
   (b) Polarity is incorrect.
   (c) Both arrows and polarity are incorrect.
   (d) None of the above.

28. The double helical model of the DNA was, proposed by Watson and Crick based on what data produced by Wilkins and Franklin?
   (a) hybridization
   (b) DNA sequencing
   (c) Southern blotting
   (d) Fourier's transformation

29. Which one of the following correctly represents the manner of replication of DNA ?
   (a)

   (b)

   (c)

   (d)
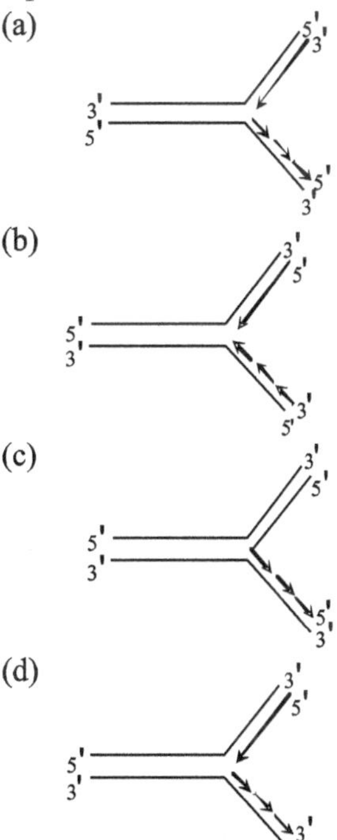

30. ABO blood groups are determined by three different alleles. How many genotypes and phenotypes are possible?

	Genotype	Phenotype
(a)	3	1
(b)	6	4
(c)	4	6
(d)	9	7

31. The diagram shows an important concept in the genetic implication of DNA. Fill in the blanks A to C.

DNA $\xrightarrow{A}$ mRNA $\xrightarrow{B}$ protein $\xrightarrow[C]{\text{Proposed by}}$

(a) A-translation B - transciption C-Erwin Chargaff
(b) A-transcription B - translation C-Francis Crick
(c) A-translation B - extension C-Rosalind Franklin
(d) A-transcription B - replication C-James Watson

32. Select the correct option:

	Direction of RNA synthesis	Direction of reading of the template DNA strand
(a)	5′—3′	3′—5′
(b)	3′—5′	5′—3′
(c)	5′—3′	5′—3′
(d)	3′—5′	3′—5′

33. Match the enzyme in column I with its function in column II and choose the correct option.

	Column I		Column II
A.	β-galactosidase	I.	Joining of DNA fragments
B.	Permease	II.	Peptide bond formation
C.	Ligase	III.	Hydrolysis of lactose
D.	Ribozyme	IV.	Increases permeability to β-galactosidase

(a) A – II; B – I; C – IV; D – III
(b) A – III; B – II; C – I; D – IV
(c) A – II; B – IV; C – I; D – III
(d) A – I; B – II; C – IV; D – III

34. Which of the following is the Pribnow box?
(a) 5′- T A T A A T - 3′
(b) 5′ - T A A T A T - 3′
(c) 5′ - A A T A A T - 3′
(d) 5′ - A T A T T A - 3′

35. Consider these sentences regarding to the structure and nature of DNA.
A. DNA has two pyrimidine bases which contain single ring structure.
B. In DNA, composition of bases should be $\dfrac{A+T}{G+C} = 1$.
C. Each base pair of DNA is 3.4Å apart from other base pair.
D. The nucleosome model of DNA packaging was proposed by Kornberg and Thomas.

Choose the correct statements from given options.
(a) A and C
(b) A, B and C
(c) B, C and D
(d) A, C and D

36. What does the given flow diagram indicate?

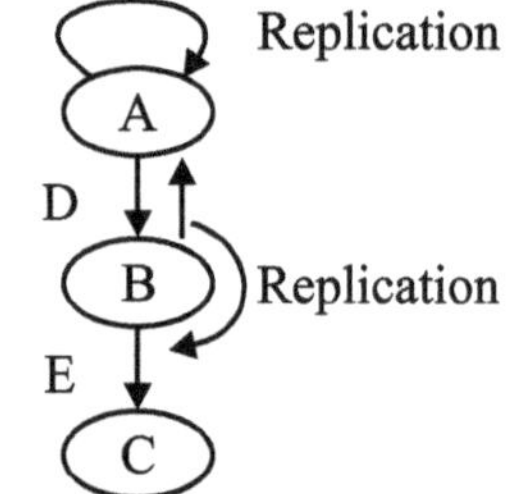

(a) unidirectional flow of information
(b) bidirectional flow of information
(c) both (a) and (b)
(d) sometimes (a) or (b)

ANSWER KEY																			
1	(d)	2	(d)	3	(c)	4	(a)	5	(b)	6	(d)	7	(a)	8	(b)	9	(c)	10	(d)
11	(d)	12	(c)	13	(c)	14	(d)	15	(a)	16	(d)	17	(d)	18	(c)	19	(a)	20	(b)
21	(b)	22	(a)	23	(b)	24	(c)	25	(d)	26	(c)	27	(b)	28	(d)	29	(d)	30	(b)
31	(b)	32	(a)	33	(b)	34	(a)	35	(d)	36	(b)										

Evolution

1. Mark the correct statement/option
   (a) Life appeared about 500 M. yrs after the formation of earth
   (b) Louis Pasteur believed that life appeared only from preexisting life
   (c) Oparin advocated that life came from preexisting non-living organic molecules
   (d) All of these

2. A marsupials evolved from ancestral stock, but all within Australian continent. This represents
   (a) Adaptive radiation like in Darwin's finches
   (b) Adaptive radiation unlike in Darwin's finches
   (c) Convergent evolution like in Darwin's finches
   (d) Convergent evolution unlike in Darwin's finches

3. *Australopithecus* lived in East African grasslands about:
   (a) 3.5 mya   (b) 2 mya
   (c) 1.2 mya   (d) 0.7 mya

4. At a particular locus, frequency of 'A' allele is 0.6 and that of 'a' is 0.4. What would be the frequency of heterozygotes in a random mating population at equilibrium?

   (a) 0.36   (b) 0.16
   (c) 0.24   (d) 0.48

5. Given below are four statements (A-D) each with one or two blanks. Select the option which correctly fills up the blanks in two statements

   Statements :
   (A) Wings of butterfly and birds look alike and are the results of ___(i)___, evolution.
   (B) Miller showed that CH_4, H_2, NH_3 and ___(i)___, when exposed to electric discharge in a flask resulted in formation of ___(ii)___.
   (C) Vermiform appendix is a ___(i)___ organ and an ___(i)___ evidence of evolution.
   (D) According to Darwin evolution took place due to ___(i)___ and ___(ii)___ of the fittest.

   Options :
   (a) (D) – (i) Small variations, (ii) Survival,
        (A) – (i) Convergent
   (b) (A) – (i) Convergent,
        (B) – (i) Oxygen, (ii) nucleosides
   (c) (B) – (i) Water vapour, (ii) Amino acids
        (C) – (i) Rudimentary, (ii) Anatomical
   (d) (C) – (i) Vestigial, (ii) Anatomical
        (D) – (i) Mutations, (ii) Multiplication

6. The contribution of American scientist, S L Miller, regarding origin of life was:

(a) Discovery of complex organic compounds from the analysis of meteorites

(b) Proposition of chemical evolution theory

(c) To show that organic compounds like amino acids could be synthesized non-enzymatically

(d) Laying the foundation of Panspermia

7. The frequent use of antibiotics is making the microbes resistant. This is because:

(a) Microbes are fast- mutating

(b) Most of the antibiotics are synthetic

(c) Of faster selection of resistant forms

(d) Sensitive or virulent forms are fast changing into resistant forms

8. *Archaeopteryx* is known as missing connecting link because it is a fossil and has characters between

(a) Fishes and amphibians

(b) Birds and reptiles

(c) Reptiles and mammals

(d) Chordates and nonchordates

9. The organs of different species that are related to each other through common descent though becomes functionally different are called

(a) analogous

(b) vestigial

(c) homologous

(d) None of these

10. Select the pair that does not match

(a) Linnaeus - species are not immutable

(b) Darwin's finches - Unique to Galapagos

(c) Hugo De Vries - Evolution is discontinuous

(d) Coacervates - aggregates of organic compounds bound by organic membrane

11. The spread of genes from one breeding population to another by migration which may result is change in gene frequency is

(a) genetic drift

(b) gene grequency

(c) gene flow

(d) None of these

12. The gas mixture used by Miller in his experiment comprised

(a) CH_4, CO_2, N_2, H_2O

(b) CH_3, CO_2,H_2O, N_2

(c) CH_2, NH_3,N_2,H_2O

(d) CH_4, NH_3,H_2, H_2O

13. Sickle cell anemia has not been eliminated from the African population because

(a) it is not a fatal disease

(b) it provides immunity against malaria

(c) it is controlled by dominant genes

(d) it is controlled by recessive genes

14. Match the following

	Column-I		**Column-II**
A.	Pliocene	I.	*Sinanthropus pekinensis*
B.	Richard leaky	II.	*Australopithecus*
C.	Mid pleistocene	III.	*Homo neanderthalensis*
D.	Dussel Dorf	IV.	*Homo habilis*
E.	Raymond Dart	V.	*Oreopithecus*

(a) A–V; B – IV; C – I; D – III; E – II

(b) A– V; B – I; C – IV; D – III; E – II

(c) A– V; B – IV; C – I; D – II; E – III

(d) A– V; B – IV; C – III; D – I; E – II

15. When two species of different genealogy come to resemble each other as a result of adaptation, the phenomenon is termed:

(a) Convergent evolution

(b) Divergent evolution

(c) Microevolution

(d) Co-evolution

16. One of the important consequences of geographical isolation is:

(a) Random creation of new species

(b) No change in the isolated fauna

(c) Preventing Speciation

(d) Speciation through reproductive isolation

17. Age of fossils in the past was generally determined by radio-carbon method and other methods involving radioactive elements found in the rocks. More precise methods, which were used recently and led to the revision of the evolutionary period for different groups of organisms, includes:
    (a) Study of carbohydrates and proteins in fossils
    (b) Study of conditions of fossilization
    (c) Electron Spin Resonance and fossil DNA
    (d) Study of proteins and nucleic acids in rocks

18. Which one of the following experiments suggests that simplest living organisms could not have originate0d spontaneously from non-living matter?
    (a) Microbes did not appear in stored meat
    (b) Larvae could appear in decaying organic matter
    (c) Microbes appeared from unsterilized organic matter
    (d) Meat was not spoiled, when heated and kept sealed in a vessel

19. There are two opposing views about origin of modern man. According to one view *Homo erectus* in Asia were the ancestors of modern man. A study of variations of DNA however suggested African origin of modern man. What kind of observation on DNA variation could suggest this?
    (a) Greater variation in Africa than in Asia
    (b) Variation only in Asia and no variation in Africa
    (c) Greater variation in Asia than in Afirca
    (d) Similar variation in Africa and Asia

20. Match the following

Column-I		Column-II
A. Mesozoic	I.	First land vertebrates
B. Devonian	II.	Proliferation of reptiles
C. Palaeocene	III.	Raise of odern mammals
D. Permian	IV.	Radiation of primitive mammals
	V.	160 million years

    (a) A–V; B–IV; C–III; D–II
    (b) A–V; B–I; C–IV; D–II
    (c) A–V; B–I; C–II; D–V
    (d) A–V; B–I; C–IV; D–III

21. Match the following column I with column II

Column I		Column II
A. Darwin	I.	Use and disuse theory
B. Lamarck	II.	Origin of species
C. Hugo De Vries	III.	Origin of life
D. A. I. Oparin	IV.	Mutation theory

    (a) A – I; B – II; C – III; D – IV
    (b) A – II; B -A; C – III; D – IV
    (c) A – IV; B – I; C – II; D – III
    (d) A – II; B – I; C – IV; D – III

22. Which one of the following scientist's name is *correctly* matched with the theory put forth by him ?
    (a) Mendel – Theory of Pangenesis
    (b) Weismann – Theory of continuity of Germplasm
    (c) Pasteur – Inheritance of acquired characters
    (d) de Vries – Natural selection

23. Choose the wrong pair:
    (a) Divergent evolution- Fore limbs of whales, bats, cheetah and human
    (b) Convergent evolution- Flippers of penguins and dolphins
    (c) Homologous structures- Vertebrate hearts
    (d) Analogous structures- Tendrils of Bougainvillea and Cucurbita
    (5) Adaptive radiation- Darwin's finches

24. The potato with high and low sugar contents were selected and grown separately for few generations. The graph depicts the results of these experiments.

This is an example of :

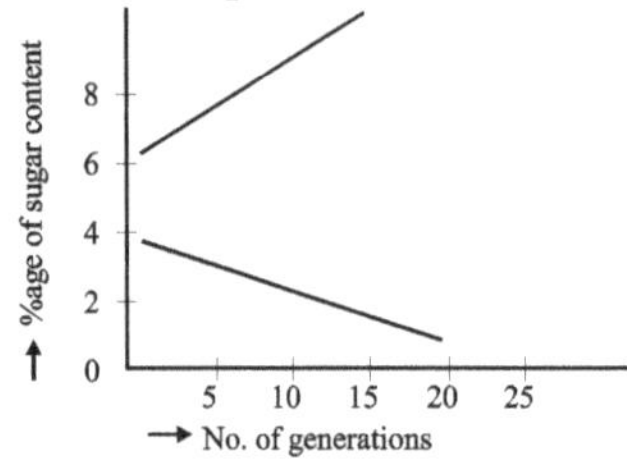

(a) Stabilizing selection
(b) Directional selection
(c) Distruptive selection
(d) Mimicry

25. Which one of the following scientists name is correctly matched with the theory put forth by him?
    (a) Weismann – Theory of continuity of germplasm
    (b) Pasteur – Inheritance of acquired characters
    (c) De Vries – Natural selection
    (d) Mendel – Theory of Pangenesis

26. Lederberg and Lederberg through their replica plating experiment showed that
    (a) Penicillin can induce a change in bacteria for better survival
    (b) Frequency of a particular allele increases with the change of environment
    (c) Penicillin can cause mutations in bacteria
    (d) Species can evolve due to chance factors

27. Correct sequence of stages in evolution of Modern Man/*Homo sapiens sapiens* is
    (a) *Australopithecus*, Neanderthal Man, Cro-Magnon Man, *Homo erectus*, Modern Man
    (b) *Australopithecus*, *Homo erectus*, Neanderthal Man, Cro-Magnon Man, Modern Man
    (c) Neanderthal Man, *Australopithecus*, Cro-Magnon Man, *Homo erectus*, Modern Man
    (d) *Homo erectus*, *Australopithecus*, Neanderthal Man, Cro-Magnon Man, Modern Man.

28. What kind of evidence suggested that man is more closely related with chimpanzee that with other hominoid apes?
    (a) Evidence from DNA extracted from sex chromosomes, autosomes and mitochondria
    (b) Evidence from DNA from sex chromosomes only
    (c) Comparison of chromosomes morphology only
    (d) Evidence from fossil remains and the fosil mitochondrial DNA alone

29. Which of the following sets represents the correct sequence of the evolution of man?
    (a) *Kenyapithecus – Australopithecus – Homo habilis*
    (b) *Kenyapithecus – Australopithecus – Pithecanthropus – Homobabilis – Homo sapiens*
    (c) *Australopithecus – Kenyapithecus – Homo habilis – Pithecanthropus – Homo saiens*
    (d) *Pithecanthropus – Australopithecus – Kenyapithecus – Homo habilis – Homo sapiens*

30. The manuscript '*On the tendencies of varieties to depart indefinitely from the original type*' was written by
    (a) Malthus (b) J.B.S. Haldane
    (c) A.R. Wallace (d) Hugo de Vries

31. Which statement is correct?
    (a) Lamarck's theory - Struggle for existence
    (b) Darwin's theory - Use and disuse of organ
    (c) Biogenetic law -Recapitulation theory
    (d) Lamarck - Theory of continuity of germplasm

ANSWER KEY																			
1	(d)	2	(a)	3	(b)	4	(d)	5	(a)	6	(c)	7	(c)	8	(b)	9	(c)	10	(a)
11	(c)	12	(d)	13	(b)	14	(a)	15	(a)	16	(d)	17	(c)	18	(d)	19	(c)	20	(b)
21	(d)	22	(b)	23	(d)	24	(a)	25	(a)	26	(b)	27	(b)	28	(a)	29	(c)	30	(c)
31	(c)																		

Human Health and Disease 

1. Given below are 4-statements. Read the statements and mark the option that has both correct statements
   A. Heroin, commonly called Smack, is obtained by acetylation of morphine
   B. Cocaine is obtained from the latex of *Papaver somniferum*
   C. Marijuana interferes with the transmission of dopamine
   D. Morphine is an effective sedative and pain killer.
   - (a) A and B
   - (b) A and D
   - (c) B and C
   - (d) C and D

2. A person suffering from a disease caused by *Plasmodium* experiences recurring chill and fever at the time when?
   - (a) The sporozoites released from RBCs are being rapidly killed and broken down inside speen
   - (b) The trophozoites reach maximum growth and give out certain toxins
   - (c) The parasite after its rapid multiplication inside RBCs ruptures them, releasing the stage to enter fresh RBCs.
   - (d) The microgametocytes and megagametocytes are being destroyed by the WBCs

3. Which one of the following can not be used for preparation of vaccines against plague?
   - (a) Formalin-inactivated suspensions of virulent bacteria
   - (b) Avirulent live bacteria
   - (c) Synthetic capsular polysaccharide material
   - (d) Heat-killed suspensions of virulent bacteria

4. The Indian Ayurveda system of medicine believed that person with following humour belonged to hot personality and developed fever:
   - (a) Black bile
   - (b) Yellow bile
   - (c) Phlegm
   - (d) Short breath

5. The adjoining skeletal structure is of:

   - (a) Morphine
   - (b) Phospholipid
   - (c) Marijuana
   - (d) Barbiturate

6. Which one is a correct match ?
- (a) *Culex* - filariasis
- (b) Sand fly - sleeping sickness
- (c) Bed bug - leishmaniasis
- (d) ADH - diabetes mellitus

7. The best HLA (human leukocyte antigen) match for transplants in order of preference is
- (a) sibling > twin > parent > unrelated donor
- (b) twin > unrelated donor > parent > sibling
- (c) twin > sibling > parent > unrelated donor
- (d) sibling > parent > twin > unrelated donor

8. Recognisation and digestion or phagocytosis due to coated surface of antibodies is
- (a) opsonisation
- (b) immunization
- (c) T-cell immunization
- (d) B-cell immunization

9. A person showing unpredictable moods, outbursts of emotion, quarrelsome behaviour and conflicts with other is suffering from
- (a) Borderline personality disorder (BPD)
- (b) Mood disorders
- (c) Addictive disorders
- (d) Schizophrenia

10. Column I lists the components of body defence and column II lists the corresponding descriptions. Match the two columns. Choose the correct option from those given.

	Column I		Column II
A.	active natural immunity	I.	injection of gamma globulins
B.	first line of defence	II.	complement proteins and interferons
C.	Passive natural immunity	III.	direct contact with the pathogens that have entered inside
D.	second line of defence	IV.	surface barriers
		V.	antibodies transferred through the placenta

- (a) A – IV; B – III; C – V; D – II
- (b) A – III; B – IV; C – II; D – V
- (c) A – III; B – IV; C – V; D – II
- (d) A – V; B – III; C – II; D – I

11. Column I lists some disorders associated with brain. Column II lists the causes for these disorders. Match the two columns and identify the correct option from those given.

	Column I		Column II
A.	Epilepsy	I.	degeneration of neurons in the cerebral cortex
B.	Alzheimer's disease	II.	irregular electrical discharge in the neurons
C.	Parkinson's disease	III.	decreased production of acetylcholine
D.	Huntington's chorea	IV.	regeneration of dopamine releasing neurons
		V.	formation of blood clots in brain

- (a) A – V; B – IV; C – III; D – I
- (b) A – II; B – III; C – I; D – IV
- (c) A – II; B – III; C – IV; D – I
- (d) A – II; B – IV; C – III; D – I

12. Column A represent diseases and column B represent their symptoms, which of the following pairs are correct match for them?

	Column A		Column B
A.	asthma	I.	recurring of bronchitis
B.	emphysema	II.	accumulation of WBCs in alveolus
C.	pneumonia	III.	allergy

- (a) A – III; B – I; C – II
- (b) A – II; B – I; C – III
- (c) A – III; B – II; C – I
- (d) A – II; B – III; C – I

13. Match the following

	Set I		Set II
A.	LSD	I.	Euphorian effect
B.	Disulfiram	II.	Parasympathetic
C.	Cocaine	III.	*Cannabis*
D.	Scopolamine	IV.	Ergot alkaloid
E.	Hashish	V.	Antabuse

- (a) A – IV; B – V; C – I; D – II; E – III
- (b) A – IV; B – I; C – V; D – II; E – III
- (c) A – IV; B – V; C – II; D – I; E – III
- (d) A – V; B – IV; C – I; D – II; E – III

14. Which of the following vaccines are injected to babies at the age of 1½, 2½ and 3½ months?
(a) DTP-Hib and Polio
(b) polio and BCG
(c) BCG and DTP-Hib
(d) BCG and hepatitis B

15. A very much publicized treatment method 'DOTS' is being adapted for the cure of:
(a) Dementia   (b) Tuberculosis
(c) AIDS   (d) Tetanus

16. When children play bare footed in pools of dirty water and flood water, they may suffer from diseases like
(a) leptospirosis and bilharizia
(b) malaria, amoebic dysentery and leptospirosis
(c) bilharizia, infective hepatitis and diarrhoea
(d) guinea worm infection, elephantiasis and amoebic dysentery

17. A transplant between individuals of the same species, but with different MHC/HLA alleles is
(a) autograft   (b) isograft
(c) xenograft   (d) allograft

18. If you suspect major deficiency of antibodies in a person, to which of the following would you look for confirmatory evidence?
(a) Haemocytes
(b) Serum albumins
(c) Serum globulins
(d) Fibrinogen in the plasma

19. Patients suffering from cholera are given a saline drip because
(a) Na^+ ions help in stopping nerve impulses and hence, sensation of pain
(b) NaCl is important component of energy supply
(c) NaCl furnishes most of the fuel required for cellular activity
(d) Na^+ ions help in the retention of water in the body tissues

20. Match the disease in Column I with the appropriate items (pathogen/ prevention/ treatment) in column II.

Column I		Column II
A.	Amoebiasis	I. *Treponema pallidum*
B.	Diptheria	II. Use only sterilized food and water
C.	Chloera	III. DPT Vaccine
D.	Syphilis	IV. Use oral rehydration therapy

(a) A–II; B–III;C–IV; D–I
(b) A–I; B–II; C–III; D–IV
(c) A–II; B–IV; C–I; D–III
(d) A–II; B–I; C–III; D–IV

21. Read the following statement having two blanks (A and B) "A drug used for (A) patients is obtained from a species of the organism (B)".
The one correct option for the two blanks is

	Blank-A	Blank-B
(a)	Swine flu	*Monascus*
(b)	AIDS	*Pseudomonas*
(c)	Heart	*Penicillium*
(d)	Organ-transplant	*Trichoderma*

22. In which one of the following options the two examples are correctly matched with their particular type of immunity?

	Examples		Type of immunity
(a)	Saliva in mouth and tears in eyes	–	Physical barriers
(b)	Mucus coating of epithelium lining the	–	Physiological barriers urinogenital tract and the HCl in stomach
(c)	Polymorphonuclear leukocytes and monocytes	–	Cellular barriers
(d)	Anti-tetanus and anti-snake bite injections	–	Active immunity

23. Match the following bacteria with the diseases

Column-I		Column-II
A. *Treponema pallidum*	I.	Plague
B. *Yersinia pestis*	II.	Anthrax
C. *Bacillus anthracis*	III.	Syphilis
D. *Vibrio*	IV.	Cholera

(a) A – III; B – I; C – II; D – IV
(b) A – IV; B – I; C – II; D – III
(c) A – III; B – II; C – I; D – IV
(d) A – I; B – III; C – II; D – IV

24. Morphine, which is used as an analgesic is obtained from
    (a) *Taxus brevifolia*
    (b) *Berberis nilghiriensis*
    (c) *Cinchona officinalis*
    (d) *Papaver somniferum*

25. If you suspect major deficiency of antibodies in a person to which of the following would you look for the confirmatory evidence?
    (a) Serum albumins
    (b) Haemocytes
    (c) Serum globulins
    (d) Fibrinogen in plasma

26. Which of the following is based upon the principle of antigen-antibody interaction?
    (a) PCR   (b) ELISA
    (c) r-DNA technology (d) RNA

27. Read the statements:
    A. IgE antibodies are produced in an allergic reaction,
    B. B-lymphocytes mediate cell mediated immunity,
    C. The yellowish fluid colostrum has abundant IgE antibodies,
    D. Spleen is a secondary lymphoid organ
    Of the above statements:
    (a) Only A is correct
    (b) A and B are correct
    (c) B and C are correct
    (d) A and D are correct

28. Which of the following best explains the difference between an epitope and an antigen?
    (a) An epitope is any foreign substance, an antigen is a foreign protein
    (b) An epitope is the part of an antigen where an antibody or lymphocyte receptor binds
    (c) An antigen is the part of an epitope where an antibody or lymphocyte receptor binds
    (d) Antigens are recognized by B- cells and antibodies, epitopes are recognized by T-cells

29. Gas gangrene is caused by
    (a) *Clostridium botulinum*
    (b) *Xanthomonas campestris*
    (c) *Pseudomonas*
    (d) *Clostridium perfringens*

30. In higher vertebrates, the immune system can distinguish self and non-self-cells. If this property is lost due to genetic abnormality and attacks self-cells, then it leads to
    (a) Active immunity
    (b) Allergic response
    (c) Graft rejection
    (d) Auto immune diseases

31. Match the following sexually transmitted diseases (Column-I) with their causative agents (Column-II) and select the correct option?

	Column- I		Column -II
A.	Gonorrhoea	I.	HIV
B.	Syphilis	II.	Neisseria
C.	Genital warts	III.	Treponema
D.	AIDS	IV.	Human papilloma virus

    (a) A–II; B–III; C–IV; D–I
    (b) A–III; B–IV; C–I; D–II
    (c) A–IV; B–II; C–III; D–I
    (d) A–IV; B–III; C–II; D–I

32. A person is injected with globulin against hepatitis. This is
    (a) naturally acquired active immunity
    (b) naturally acquired passive immnity
    (c) artificially acquired active immunity
    (d) artificially acquired passive immunity

33. Histamines the inflammation producing substance are produced by which cells of the body ?
    (a) mast cells   (b) collagen fibres
    (c) macrophages   (d) sustentacular cells

34. Which one of the following is not correctly matched ?
    (a) *Culex pipiens*   – Filariasis
    (b) *Aedes aegypti*   – Yellow fever
    (c) *Anopheles culifacies*   – Leishmaniasis
    (d) *Glossina palpalis*   – Sleeping sickness

ANSWER KEY																			
1	(b)	**2**	(c)	**3**	(c)	**4**	(a)	**5**	(c)	**6**	(a)	**7**	(c)	**8**	(a)	**9**	(a)	**10**	(c)
11	(c)	**12**	(a)	**13**	(a)	**14**	(a)	**15**	(b)	**16**	(a)	**17**	(d)	**18**	(c)	**19**	(d)	**20**	(a)
21	(d)	**22**	(c)	**23**	(a)	**24**	(d)	**25**	(c)	**26**	(b)	**27**	(d)	**28**	(b)	**29**	(d)	**30**	(d)
31	(a)	**32**	(c)	**33**	(a)	**34**	(c)												

Strategies for Enhancement in Food Production

1. The animal husbandry deals with the care, breeding and management of
   - (a) Domesticated animals
   - (b) Fishes
   - (c) Honey bees and silk worms
   - (d) All of these

2. India and China have more than 70% of world live stock population and produce following percentage of world farm produce
   - (a) 10 %
   - (b) 25 %
   - (c) 40 %
   - (d) 50 %

3. The development and flourishment of fishery industry has lead to
   - (a) Green revolution
   - (b) Blue revolution
   - (c) Silver revolution
   - (d) White revolution

4. Match the column I with the column II and choose the correct option.

	Column I		Column II
A.	Sericulture	I.	Bee keeping
B.	Pisciculture	II.	Rearing of silkworm
C.	Apiculture	III.	Micropropagation
D.	Tissue culture	IV.	Rearing of fishes
E.	Green Revolution	V.	Fish production
F.	White Revolution	VI.	Crop production
G.	Blue Revolution	VII.	Milk production

   - (a) A – IV, B – III, C – II, D – I, E – VI, F – VII, G – V
   - (b) A – IV, B – I, C – II, D – III, E – VII, F – VI, G – V
   - (c) A – I, B – II, C – III, D – IV, E – VI, F – VII, G – V
   - (d) A – II, B – IV, C – I, D – III, E – VI, F – VII, G – V

5. *Hisardale* is a new breed of sheep developed in Punjab by crossing
   - (a) Marino ram and Bikaneri ewe
   - (b) Aseel ram and white leg horn ewe
   - (c) Rhode Island ram and white leg horn ewe
   - (d) Cochin ram and Ghagus ewe

6. Match the column I with column II and choose the correction option.

	Column I		Column II
A.	Many people have deficiencies as they cannot buy fruits & vegetables	I.	Single cell proteins

B.   Crops with higher   II.   Micropropagation
vitamins, proteins
and fats

C.   Growing microbes   III.   Somaclones
as the alternative
source of proteins

D.   Capacity to   IV.   Hidden hunger
generate plant
from a single cell
or explant

E.   Production of   V.   Biofortification
thousand plants
through tissue
culture

F.   Genetically   VI.   Totipotency
identical plants

(a)   A – IV; B – V; C – VI; D – I; E – II;
F – III

(b)   A – IV; B – V; C – VI; D – I; E – III;
F – II

(c)   A – IV; B – V; C – I; D – VI; E – II;
F – III

(d)   A – VI; B – V; C – I; D – IV; E – II;
F – III

7. Correct chronological order of the events occuring during callus culture is

(a)   Callus → Cell division → Explant → Addition of cytokinin → Cells acquire meristematic property

(b)   Explant → Callus → Cell division → Addition of cytokinin → Cells acquire meristematic property

(c)   Explant → Cell division → Callus → Addition of cytokinin → Cells acquire meristematic property

(d)   Callus → Explant → Cell division → Addition of cytokinin → Cells acquire meristematic property

8. Select the correct statements –

(a)   Our present day crop plants are entirely different from their wild ancestors as almost all our present day crops are the result of selections carried out by the prehistoric human beings.

(b)   Almost all our present day crops are the result of selections carried out by the prehistoric human beings.

(c)   Feeding of rarer plants into agriculture and horticulture trade is of great advantage in genetic conservation.

(d)   All of the above

9. Following type of breeding helps in elimination of less desirable genes and exposing the harmful recessive genes:

(a)   Cross breeding   (b)   Inbreeding

(c)   Interbreeding   (d)   Outbreeding

10. Which one of the following types of silk is being produced extensively in South India?

(a)   Eri   (b)   Mulberry

(c)   Tussar   (d)   Muga

11. A plant cell has potential to develop into full plant. This property of the plant cell is called

(a)   tissue culture   (b)   totipotency

(c)   pleuripotency   (d)   gene cloning

12. Consider the following four measures (A-D) that could be taken to successfully grow chickpea in an area where bacterial blight disease is common

(A)   Spray with Bordeaux mixture

(B)   Control of the insect vector of the disease pathogen

(C)   Use of only disease-free seeds

(D)   Use of varieties resistant to the disease

Which two of the above measures can control the disease?

(a)   B and C   (b)   A and B

(c)   C and D   (d)   A and D

13. Bean seeds were planted and put on a sunny windowsill. As the plants grew, their stems bent toward the window. This bending was most likely caused by an
    (a) unequal distribution of auxin in the stem.
    (b) unequal distribution of a neurotransmitter in the stem.
    (c) equal distribution of auxin in the stem.
    (d) equal distribution of a neurotransmitter in the stem.

14. Match the following columns and choose the correct option:

Column-I		Column-II
A.	Mutation breeding	(I)	Laborious and expensive process to obtain gene variation
B.	Selection	(II)	Hybrid vigour can be maintained for several generations
C.	Hybridisation	(III)	Simplest and easiest method of plant improvement
D.	Introduction	(IV)	Oldest breeding method
		(V)	Quick method to obtain gene variation

    (a) A – V; B – IV; C – I; D – II
    (b) A – V; B – IV; C – I; D – III
    (c) A – IV; B – II; C – III; D – I
    (d) A – I; B – II; C – IV; D – V

15. For studying and understanding language of honey bees, the scientist who was awarded Nobel Prize, was:
    (a) Rachael Carson   (b) D. Muller
    (c) Carl Von Frisch   (d) T.A. Loomis

16. Among the following edible fishes, which one is a marine fish having rich source of omega-3 fatty acids?
    (a) Mrigala   (b) Mackerel
    (c) Mystus   (d) Mangur

17. A horse and a donkey can breed to produce mule which is an infertile animal. The infertility is because horse and donkey belong to different.
    (a) class   (b) order
    (c) species   (d) genus

18. Which of the following is incorrectly matched?
    (a) Explant   -   Excised plant part used for callus formation
    (b) Cytokinins   -   Root initiation in callus
    (c) Somatic embryo -   Embryo produced from a vegetative cells
    (d) Anther culture -   Haploid plants

19. Several south indian states raise 2-3 crops of rice annually. The agronomic feature that makes this possible is because of
    (a) shorter rice plant.
    (b) better irrigation facilities.
    (c) early yielding rice variety.
    (d) disease resistant rice variety.

20. Which one of the following combination would a sugarcane farmer look for in the sugarcane crop?
    (a) Thick stem, long internodes, high sugar content and disease resistant.
    (b) Thick stem, high sugar content and profuse flowering.
    (c) Thick stem, short internodes, high sugar content, disease resistant.
    (d) Thick stem, low sugar content disease resistant.

21. On culturing the young anther of a plant a botanist got a few diploid plants alongwith haploid plants. Which of the following might have given the diploid plants ?
    (a) Exine of pollen grain
    (b) Vegetative cell of pollen
    (c) Cells of anther wall
    (d) Generative cell of pollen

22. Choose the correct statements
- A. protoplasts of different cells of the same plant are fused.
- B. protoplasts from cells of different species can be fused.
- C. treatment of cells with cellulase and pectinase is mandatory.
- D. the hybrid protoplast contains characters of only one parental protoplast.

  (a) D and C   (b) A and B
  (c) C and B   (d) B and C

23. Gelatin, a very important raw material for preparation of photographic emulsion, is a biproduct of
  (a) Chicken   (b) Forest
  (c) Fish   (d) Cattle

24. The process of mating of individuals, which are more closely related than the average of the population to which they belong, is called
  (a) inbreeding   (b) hybridization
  (c) heterosis   (d) self breeding

25. Presence of high aspartic acid, low nitrogen and sugar content in maize protects them from
  (a) aphids   (b) fruit borer
  (c) jassids   (d) stem borer

26. Which one of the following is a wrong statement with reference to somatic hybridization?
  (a) Naked protoplasts are used.
  (b) Interspecific hybrids are produced.
  (c) Used protoplasts are identical.
  (d) PEG is used as fusogens.

27. Match the following columns:
- A. *Saccharum barberi*   1. Thicker stems
- B. *Ratna*   2. High yielding *Triticum*
- C. *Saccharum officinarum*   3. Poor stem content
- D. *Sonalika*   4. Semi-dwarf variety *Oryza*

  (a) A-4, B-3, C-2, D-1
  (b) A-3, B-4, C-1, D-2
  (c) A-2, B-1, C-1, D-3
  (d) A-1, B-2, C-3, D-4

28. Match the following columns:
- A. Rapeseed   1. *Pusa sawani*
- B. Flat bean   2. *Pusa sem-2*
- C. *Okra*   3. *Pusa gaurav*

  (a) A-1, B-2, C-3   (b) A-3, B-2, C-1
  (c) A-3, B-1, C-2   (d) A-2, B-1, C-3

29. Match the following columns:

Column I	Column II
A. Atlas 66	(i) Musturd
B. *Pusa gaurav*	(ii) Flat bean
C. *Pusa sawani*	(iii) Wheat
D. *Pusa sem 3*	(iv) Bhindi

  (a) A-(i), B-(ii), C-(iv), D-(iv)
  (b) A-(iii), B-(i), C-(ii), D-(iv)
  (c) A-(iii), B-(i), C-(iv), D-(ii)
  (d) A-(iv), B-(ii), C-(iii), D-(i)

30. Match the following:
- A. Pomato   1. Somaclones
- B. Virus free plants   2. Meristem culture
- C. Genetically identical plants   3. Micro-propagation
- D. Producing thousands of plants   4. Embryo culture
-     5. Somatic hybridisation

  (a) A-4, B-2, C-3, D-1   (b) A-5, B-2, C-1, D-3
  (c) A-1, B-2, C-3, D-5   (d) A-5, B-2, C-2, D-4

ANSWER KEY																			
1	(d)	2	(b)	3	(b)	4	(d)	5	(a)	6	(c)	7	(c)	8	(d)	9	(b)	10	(c)
11	(b)	12	(c)	13	(a)	14	(b)	15	(c)	16	(b)	17	(c)	18	(b)	19	(c)	20	(a)
21	(c)	22	(d)	23	(d)	24	(a)	25	(d)	26	(c)	27	(b)	28	(b)	29	(c)	30	(b)

Microbes in Human Welfare

1. Which bacterium helps in the production of 'Swiss cheese'?
   (a) *Propionibacterium sharmanii*
   (b) *Trichoderma polysporum*
   (c) *Saccharomyces cerevisiae*
   (d) *Aspergillus niger*

2. The technology of biogas production was developed in India mainly due to the efforts of
   (a) Indian Agricultural/ Research. Institute (IARI) and Khadi and Village Industries Commission (KVIC)
   (b) National Botanical Research Institute (NBR1)
   (c) Indian Council of Medical Research (ICMR)
   (d) Indian Council of Agricultural Research (ICAR)

3. The large vessels for growing microbes on an industrial scale are called
   (a) petridish   (b) digestors
   (c) biogas vessel (d) fermentors

4. Conversion of sugar into alcohol during fermentation is due to the direct action of
   (a) temperature
   (b) micro-organisms
   (c) zymase
   (d) concentration of sugar solution

5. In a barren land when the soil has been eroded due to overgrazing and wind. The soil also has been leeched. To restore to fertility of soil we should add
   (a) Legumes to the soil
   (b) inorganic nutrients
   (c) air
   (d) water

6. Drug administered to ....A... patients is obtained from ...B... species. It helps in clearing blood clots inside the blood vessels.
   (a) A-hear, B-*Streptococcus*
   (b) A-organ transplant, B-*Trichoderma*
   (c) A-heart, B-*Pseudomonas*
   (d) A-organ transplant, B-*Monascus*

7. "Upstream process" in preparation of alcohol in biotechnology includes
   (a) all process before fermentation
   (b) all processes during fermentation
   (c) processes after fermentation
   (d) flavouring and ripening of alcohol

8. For biogas production besides dung which one of the following weed is recommended in our country:
   (a) *Eichhornia crassipes*
   (b) *Hydrilla*
   (c) *Mangifera*
   (d) *Solanum nigrum*

9. Match the microbes in column I with their commercial/industrial products in column II and choose the correct answer.

Column I		Column II
A.	*Aspergillus niger*	I. Ethanol
B.	*Clostridium butylicum*	II. Statins
C.	*Saccharomyces cerevisiae*	III. Citric acid
D.	*Trichoderma polysporum*	IV. Butyric acid
E.	*Monascus purpureus*	V. Cyclosporin A

   (a) A – IV; B – V; C – II; D – I; E – III
   (b) A – V; B – IV; C – I; D – II; E – III
   (c) A – III; B – IV; C – I; D – V; E – II
   (d) A – III; B – IV; C – V; D – I; E – II

10. *Trichoderma harzianum* has proved a useful microorganism for
    (a) bioremediation of contaminated soils
    (b) reclamation of wastelands
    (c) gene transfer in higher plants
    (d) biological control of soil-borne plant pathogens

11. Who of the following scientists showed that *Saccharomyces cerevisiae* causes fermentation forming products such as beer and buttermilk ?
    (a) Louis Pasteur
    (b) Alexander Flemming
    (c) Selman Waksman
    (d) Schatz

12. Which one of the following helps in absorption of phosphorus from soil by plants ?
    (a) *Anabaena*
    (b) *Glomus*
    (c) *Rhizobium*
    (d) *Frankia*

13. Read the following statement having two blanks (A and B):
    "A drug used for ———— (A) ———— patients is obtained from a species of the organism ———— (B) ————."
    The one correct option for the two blanks is

	Blank - A	Blank - B
(a)	Heart	*Penicillium*
(b)	Organ-transplant	*Trichoderma*
(c)	Swine flu	*Monascus*
(d)	AIDS	*Pseudomonas*

14. Cyclosporin A, which is used as an immunosuppressive agent, is produced by
    (a) *Aspergillus*   (b) *Clostridium*
    (c) *Saccharomyces*   (d) *Trichoderma*

15. Which among these are produced by distillation of fermented broth?
    A. Whisky   B. Wine
    C. Beer   D. Rum
    E. Brandy
    (a) B and C alone
    (b) A and B alone
    (c) C and E alone
    (d) A, D and E alone

16. A patient brought to a hospital with myocardial infarction is normally immediately given
    (a) Penicillin   (b) Streptokinase
    (c) Cyclosporin-A   (d) Statins

17. Chloramphenicol and erythromycin (broad spectrum antibiotics) are produced by
    (a) Streptomyces   (b) Nitrobacter
    (c) Rhizobium   (d) Penicillium

18. Match the following list of microbes and their importance:

A.	*Sacharomyces cerevisiae*	I.	Production of immunosuppressive agents
B.	*Monascus Purpureus*	II.	Ripening of Swiss cheese
C.	*Trichoderma polysporum*	III.	Commercial production of ethanol
D.	*Propionibacterium sharmanii*	IV.	Production of blood cholesterol lowering agents

  (a) A – IV; B – III; C – II; D – I
  (b) A – IV; B – II; C – I; D – III
  (c) A – III; B – I; C – IV; D – II
  (d) A – III; B – IV; C – I; D – II

19. Which of the following is wrongly matched in the given table ?

	Microbe	Product	Application
(a)	*Trichoderma polysporum*	Cyclosporin A	Immuno-suppressive drug
(b)	*Monascus purpureus*	Statins	lowering of blood cholesterol
(c)	*Streptococcus*	Streptokinase	removal of clot from blood vessel
(d)	*Clostridium butylicum*	Lipase	removal of oil stains

20. Choose the right combination

	Column-I		Column-II
A.	*Escherichia coli*	I.	Nif gene
B.	*Rhizobium melilotae*	II.	Digestive hydrocarbon of crude oil
C.	*Bacillus thuringiensis*	III.	Production of human insulin
D.	*Pseudomonas putida*	IV.	Biological control of fungal disease
		V.	Bio-decomposed insectiside

  (a) A – III; B – I; C – V; D – IV
  (b) A – I; B – II; C – III; D – IV
  (c) A – II; B – I; C – III; D – IV
  (d) A – III; B – I; C – V; D – II

21. Match the columns and choose the correct option–

	Column-I		Column-II
A.	Neomycin	I.	*Streptomyces fradiae*
B.	Terramycin	II.	*Penicillium notatum*
C.	Viridin	III.	*Streptomyces rimosus*
D.	Penicillin	IV.	*Gliocladium virens*

  (a) A-III; B-I; C-IV; D-II
  (b) A-I; B-III; C-IV; D-II
  (c) A-III; B-IV; C-I; D-II
  (d) A-IV; B-I; C-II; D-III

22. Which of the following statements is not true for stirred tank fermentation ?
  (a) Buffer needed to control pH
  (b) Batch and feed possible
  (c) Control dissolved oxygen
  (d) Easy in process sampling

23. Match the items in Column 'I' and Column 'II' and choose correct answer.

	Column-I		Column-II
A.	Lady bird	I.	*Methanobacterium*
B.	Mycorrhiza	II.	*Trichoderma*
C.	Biological control	III.	Aphids
D.	Biogas	IV.	*Glomus*

The correct answer is:
  (a) A-II, B-IV, C-III, D-I
  (b) A-III, B-IV, C-II, D-I
  (c) A-IV, B-I, C-II, D-III
  (d) A-III, B-II, C-I, D-IV

24. Which one of the following statement(s) is/are correct?

    (a) Herbicides kill plants mostly by blocking PS II (Photolysis of water) and occasionally phloem transport.

    (b) Insecticides kill insects mostly through impairment of nerve conduction and sometimes through respiratory arrest.

    (c) Both (a) and (b)

    (d) None of these

25. Which of the following pairs of bacteria is involved in two step conversion of NH_3 into nitrate?

    (a) *Azotobacter* and *Nitrosomonas*

    (b) *Pseudomonas* and *Nitrobacter*

    (c) *Azotobacter* and *Achromobacter*

    (d) *Nitrosomonas* and *Nitrobacter*

26. Match the column I and column II and choose the correct combination of alphabets of the two columns

Column-I		Column-II
Types of Bacteria		**Activity**
A. *Streptomyces*	I.	Food poisoning
B. *Rhizobium*	II.	Source antibiotics
C. *Nitrosomonas*	III.	Nitrogen fixation
D. *Acetobacter*	IV.	Nitrification
	V.	Vinegar synthesis

    (a) A-IV, B-V, C-I, D-III

    (b) A-V, B-I, C-III, D-IV

    (c) A-II, B-III, C-I, D-V

    (d) A-II, B-III, C-IV, D-V

27. Match the following and choose the correct combination.

Column-I		Column-II
A. *Escherichia coli*	I.	'nif' gene
B. *Rhizobium meliloti*	II.	Digests hydrocarbons of crude oil
C. *Bacillus thuringiensis*	III.	Human insulin production
D. *Pseudomonas putida*	IV.	Biocontrol of fungal disease
	V.	Biodegradable insecticide.

    (a) A-III, B-I, C-V, D-II

    (b) A-III, B-I, C-V, D-IV

    (c) A-I, B-II, C-III, D-IV

    (d) A-II, B-I, C-III, D-IV

28. Match the column I and column II and find the correct option.

Column I		Column II
A. Dextran	I.	Clarification of juices
B. Invertase	II.	Used as clot buster
C. Streptokinase	III.	Hydrolysis of sucrose
D. Protease	IV.	Polymerization of simple sugar

    (a) A – IV; B– III; C – II; D – I

    (b) A– III; B– II; C– I; D– IV

    (c) A– I; B– IV; C– III; D– II

    (d) A– II; B– I; C – IV; D – III

ANSWER KEY

1	(a)	2	(a)	3	(d)	4	(c)	5	(a)	6	(a)	7	(a)	8	(a)	9	(c)	10	(d)
11	(a)	12	(b)	13	(b)	14	(d)	15	(d)	16	(b)	17	(a)	18	(d)	19	(d)	20	(d)
21	(b)	22	(c)	23	(b)	24	(d)	25	(d)	26	(d)	27	(a)	28	(a)				

Biotechnology : Principles and Processes

1. Choose the correct option.

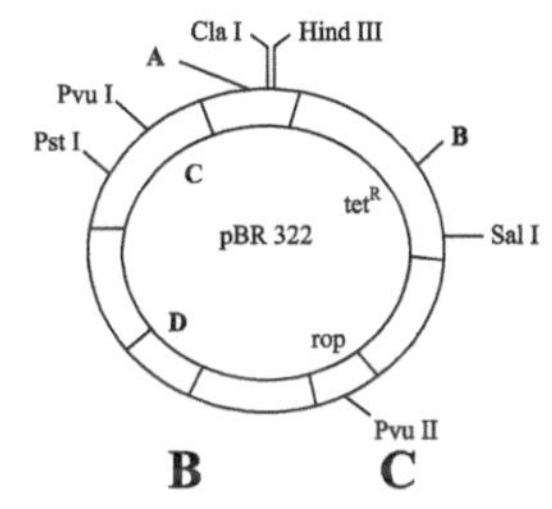

	A	**B**	**C**	**D**
(a)	Hind I	Ecor I	amp^R	ori
(b)	Hind I	Bamh I	kan^R	amp^R
(c)	BamH I	Pst I	ori	amp^R
(d)	EcoR I	BamH I	amp^R	ori

2. *Agrobacterium tumefaciens* is used in genetic engineering for
(a) DNA-mapping
(b) DNA-modification
(c) cloning vector to deliver genes into host
(d) DNA finger printing

3. A genetically engineered bacteria used for clearing oil spills is
(a) *Escherichia coli*
(b) *Bacillus subtilis*
(c) *Agrobacterium tumifaciens*
(d) *Pseudomonas putida*

4. Identify the correct match for the given apparatus.

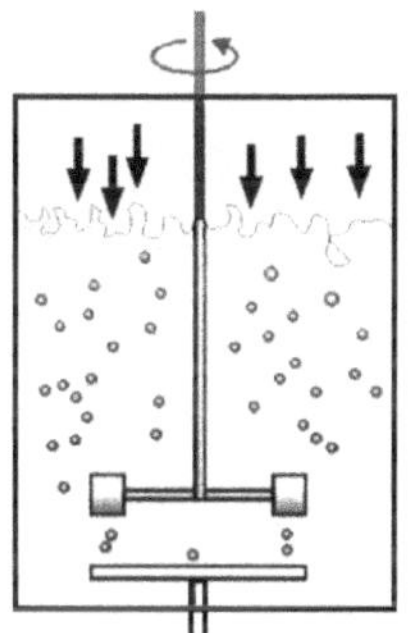

	Apparatus	**Function**
(a)	Gene gun	Vectorless direct gene transfer
(b)	Column chromatography	Separation of chlorophyll pigments
(c)	Sparged tank bioreactor	Carry out fermentation process
(d)	Respirometer	Finding out rate of respiration

5. Choose the correct option.

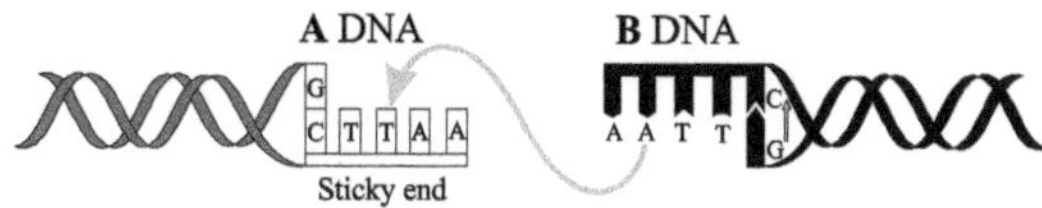

	A DNA	**B DNA**	**Enzyme recognizing palindrome**	**Enzyme the sticky ends joining**
(a)	Vector	Foreign	DNA ligase	EcoRI
(b)	Vector	Foreign	EcoRI	DNA ligase
(c)	Vector	Foreign	Exonuclease	DNA ligase
(d)	Vector	Foreign	DNA ligase	Exo-nuclease

6. Which of these is not correctly matched?

(a) Gene gun—bioplastics

(b) Plasmids—extrachromosomal DNA

(c) DNA ligase—Biological scissors

(d) Bacteriophages—viruses.

7. The prerequisite for biotechnological production of antibiotic is

(a) to isolate antibiotic gene.

(b) to search an antibiotic producing micro-organism.

(c) to join antibiotic gene with *E.coli* plasmid.

(d) All of these.

8. Identify the correct match for the given figure.

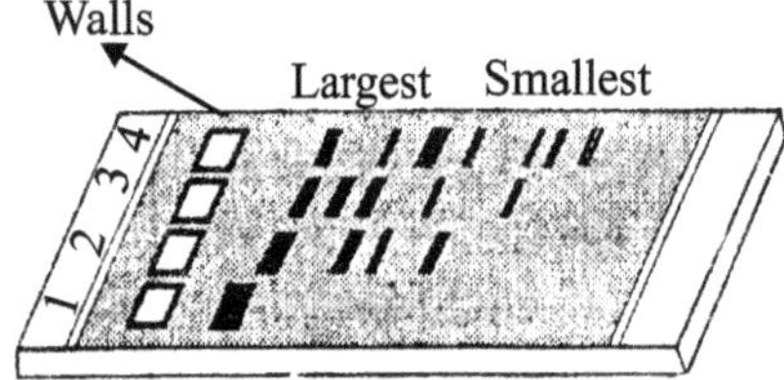

(a) Electrophoresis — Differential migration of DNA fragments.

(b) Column chromatography — Separation of chlorophyll pigments.

(c) Gene cloning — Technique of obtaining identical copies of a particular DNA segment or a gene.

(d) Microinjection — Technique of introducing foreign genes into a host cell.

9. Which of the following features cannot be associated with Ti plasmid of *Agrobacterium tumifaciens* which is modified into a cloning vector?

(a) It is able to deliver genes of our interest into a variety of plants.

(b) It is modified into cloning vector as it can transfer a piece of T-DNA into the plant cells.

(c) It is pathogenic to the plants.

(d) Ti plasmid of *Agrobacterium* is a natural genetic engineer.

10. Two enzymes responsible for restricting the growth of bacteriophages in *Escherichia coli* were isolated. One was methylase and other was restriction endonuclease. What was the significance of methylase?

(a) Able to cut the DNA of bacteriophage at specific sites.

(b) Able to remove the methyl group and hence prevent the action of restriction endonuclease on host DNA.

(c) Protection of host DNA from the action of restriction endonuclease by adding methyl group to one or two bases usually within the sequence recognized by restriction enzyme.

(d) Able to ligate the two cohesive ends of DNA molecule.

11. Identify the figures and choose the correct option.

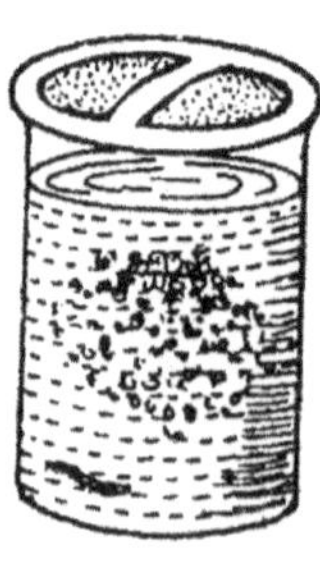

(a) DNA spooling   (b) DNA digestion

(c) DNA recognition   (d) DNA bands

12. Following enzymes / techniques are used in the process of recombinant DNA technology

A. EcoRl to cut the isolated genome

B. DNA ligase

C. Protease and ribonuclease for removal of proteins and RNA from DNA

D. Production of recombinant hosts

E. Lysozyme for isolation of the genetic material (DNA)

F. Gel electrophoresis for separation and isolation of DNA fragments

Mark the correct sequence of their use

(a) C, E, B, F, A, D   (b) E, C, A, B, F, D

(c) E, C, A, F, B, D   (d) A, E, C, B, D, F

13. Identify the correct option.

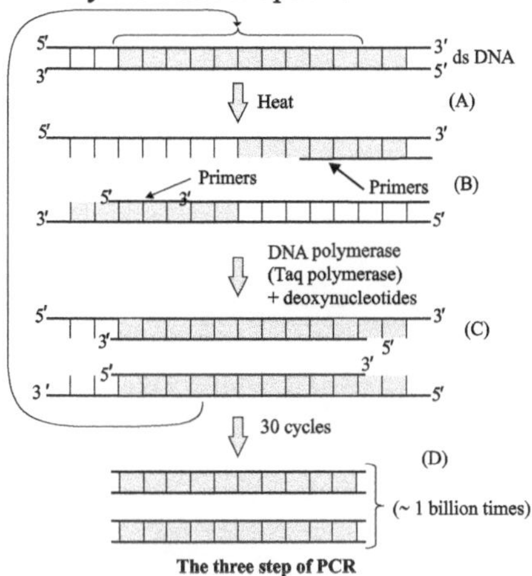

(a) A - Denaturation, B - Annealing, C - Extension, D - Amplified

(b) A - Annealing, B - Denaturation, C - Extension, D - Amplified

(c) A - Denaturation, B - Annealing, C - Amplified, D - Extension

(d) A - Annealing, B - Denaturation, C - Amplified, D - Extension

14. Which one of the following pairs is not correctly matched?

(a) *Spirulina* - Single cell protein

(b) *Rhizobium* - Biofertilizer

(c) *Streptomyces* - Antibiotic

(d) *Serratia* - Drug addiction

15. Match the following columns.

	Column I		Column II
A.	Plasmids	I.	Virus infecting bacteria
B.	Bacteriophages	II.	Natural polymer of D-galactose
C.	Cosmids	III.	Hybrid vector derived from plasmids
D.	Agarose	IV.	Circular extrachromosomal DNA

(a) A–II; B–I; C–III; D–IV

(b) A–IV; B–I; C–III; D–II

(c) A–III; B–II; C–I; D–IV

(d) A–I; B–IV; C–III; D–II

16. Match the following columns.

	Column I		Column II
A.	Arber, Nathan and Hamilton Smith	I.	Isolated first restriction endonuclease from bacteria
B.	Paul Berg	II.	Term biotechnology
C.	Herbert Boyer and Stanley Cohen	III.	Father of genetic engineering
D.	Karl Erkey	IV.	First recombinant DNA

(a) A–I; B–IV; C–III; D–II

(b) A–III; B–II; C–I; D–IV

(c) A–I; B–III; C–IV; D–II

(d) A–IV; B–III; C–I; D–II

17. Bacteria uses restriction endonuclease to protect itself from viral attack. The bacterial DNA does not get degraded by its own enzyme because

(a) DNA of bacteria is able to reintegrate itself

(b) bacterial DNA does not have specific site

(c) bacterial DNA protect itself by changing the configuration of active site

(d) the enzyme cannot identify the sites

18. c-DNA probes are copied from the messenger RNA molecules with the help of
    (a) restriction enzymes
    (b) reverse transcriptase
    (c) DNA polymerase
    (d) adenosine deaminase

19. It is sometimes necessary to genetically modify mammalian cells to produce proteins because they
    (a) can produce larger quantities of protein than bacteria.
    (b) can read eukaryotic genes and bacteria cannot.
    (c) can add sugars to make glycoproteins and bacteria cannot.
    (d) are easier to grow than bacteria.

20. The enzyme which helps to cut one strand of DNA duplex to release tension of coiling of two strands is
    (a) DNA ligase
    (b) DNA polymerase I
    (c) topo-isomerase
    (d) helicase or unwindases

21. Crystals of *Bt* toxin produced by some bacteria do not kill the bacteria themselves because
    (a) bacteria are resistant to the toxin.
    (b) toxin is immature.
    (c) toxin is inactive.
    (d) bacteria enclose the toxin in special sac.

22. *E. coli* with a mutated Z gene of the lac operon cannot grow in medium containing only lactose as the source of energy because
    (a) in the presence of glucose, *e. coli* cells do not utilize lactose
    (b) they cannot transport lactose from the medium into the cell
    (c) the lac operon is constitutively active in these cells
    (d) they cannot synthesize functional β-galactosidase

23. Which of the following is maintained for optimum production of vinegar?
    (a) Anaerobic condition
    (b) Temperature of 65°C
    (c) Aerobic condition
    (d) Microaerophilic condition

24. The figure below is the diagrammatic representation of the *E.Coli* vector pBR 322. Which one of the given options correctly identifies its certain component (s)?

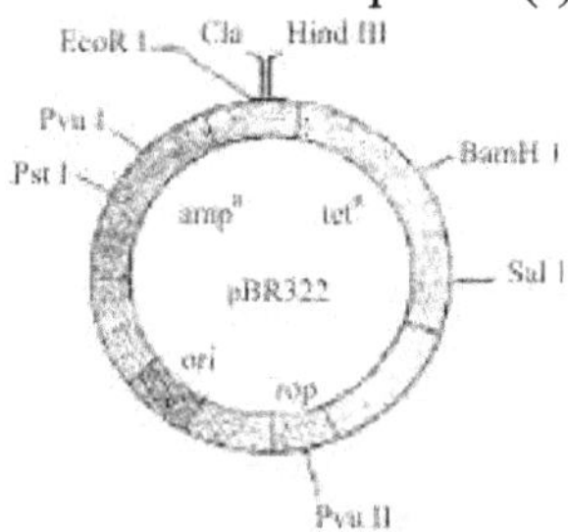

    (a) ori - original restriction enzyme
    (b) rop-reduced osmotic pressure
    (c) Hind III, EcoRI - selectable markers
    (d) amp^R, tet^R - antibiotic resistance genes

25. Which one of the following represents a palindromic sequence in DNA?
    (a) 5' - GAATTC - 3'
        3' - CTTAAG - 5'
    (b) 5' - CCAATG - 3'
        3' - GAATCC - 5'
    (c) 5' - CATTAG - 3'
        3' - GATAAC - 5'
    (d) 5' - GATACC - 3'
        3' - CCTAAG - 5'

26. The colonies of recombinant bacteria appear white in contrast to blue colonies of non-recombinant bateria because of
    (a) Insertional inactivation of alpha-galactosidase in non-recombinant bacteria
    (b) Insertional inactivation of alpha-galactosidase in recombinant bacteria
    (c) Inactivation of glycosidase enzyme in recombinant bacteria
    (d) Non-recombinant bacteria containing beta-galactosidase

27. Human Genome Project (HGP) is closely associated with the rapid development of a new area in biology called as
    (a) biotechnology
    (b) bioinformatics
    (c) biogeography
    (d) bioscience

28. Which of the following enzyme is used in case of fungus to cause release of DNA along with other macromolecules?

   (a) Lysozyme   (b) Cellulase

   (c) Chitinase   (d) Amylase

29. During heat shock to the bacterium, the temperature used for giving thermal shock is

   (a) 82° C   (b) 100°C

   (c) – 196°C   (d) 42°C

30. Which one of the following option is correct?

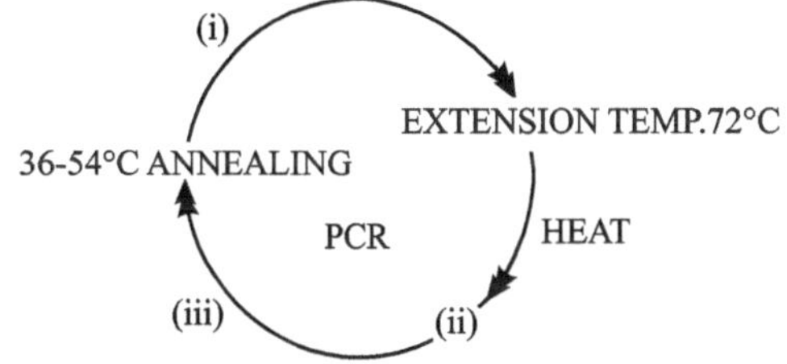

   (a) (i) *Taq* polymerase (ii) Denaturation at 94° C (iii) Primer

   (b) (i)Denaturationat94°C(ii)Taqpoly-merase (iii) Primer

   (c) (i) Primer (ii) Denaturation at 94°C (iii) *Taq* polymerase

   (d) (i) *Taq* polymerase (ii) Extension (iii) Ligation

31. Due to ampicillin resistance gene, one is able to select a transformed cell in the presence of ampicillin. The ampicillin resistance gene in this case is called

   (a) recombinant gene (b) selectable marker

   (c) origin of replication (d) recognition site

32. After the formation of the product in the bioreactors, it undergoes through separation and purification processes before a finished product is ready for marketing. These processes are collectively referred to as

   (a) upstream processing

   (b) downstream processing

   (c) elution

   (d) transformation

33. Which one of the following option is correct for A, B, C and D?

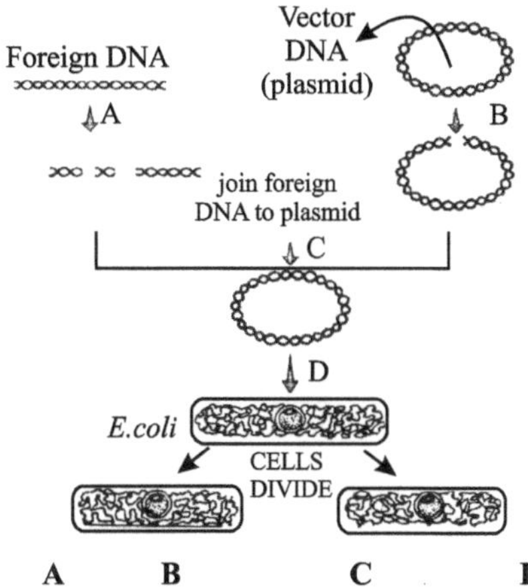

	A	B	C	D
(a)	Exonuclease	Endonuclease	DNA ligase	Transformation
(b)	Exonuclease	Exonuclease	DNA ligase	Transformation
(c)	Exonuclease	Endonuclease	Hydro-lase	Transduction
(d)	Restriction endonuclease	Restriction endonuclease	DNA ligase	Transformation

34. Which of the following pairs are correctly matched?

   (a) Central dogma   —   Codon

   (b) Okazaki fragments   —   Splicing

   (c) RNA polymerase   —   RNA primer

   (d) Restriction enzyme   —   Genetic engineering

35. Which of the following statement is not true?

   (a) Hind II always cut DNA molecules at a particular point by recognising a specific sequence of 4 base pairs.

   (b) Besides Hind II, today we know more than 900 restriction enzymes.

   (c) The name Eco RI comes from *Escherichia coli* - 13.

   (d) Type II restriction endonuclease is most useful in genetic engineering.

36. The transfer of genetic material from one bacterium to another through the mediation of a vector like virus is termed as

   (a) transduction   (b) conjugation

   (c) transformation   (d) translation

                                                                    BIOLOGY

37. Match List I with List II and select the correct option

	List I		List II
A.	*Bacillus thuringiensis*	I.	Production of chitinases
B.	*Rhizobium meliloti*	II.	Scavenging of oil spills
C.	*Escherichia coli*	III.	Incorporation of 'nif' gene
D.	*Pseudomonas putida*	IV.	Production of *Bt* toxin
E.	*Trichoderma*	V.	Production of human insulin

(a) A – II; B – IV; C – I; D – V; E – III
(b) A – II; B – IV; C – V; D – I; E – III
(c) A – IV; B – III; C – V; D – II; E – I
(d) A – III; B – IV; C – V; D – I; E – II

38. Which one of the following pairs is not correctly matched?
(a) Plasmid — Small piece of extrachromosomal DNA in bacteria
(b) Interferon — An enzyme that interferes with DNA replication
(c) Cosmid — A vector for carrying large DNA fragments into host cells
(d) Myeloma — Antibody-producing tumour cells

39. The primary difference between sexual reproduction of plants and animals with bacteria is that
(a) bacterial sexual reproduction involves more than two individuals.
(b) bacterial sexual reproduction does not involve genetic recombination.
(c) bacteria exchange RNA, not DNA.
(d) bacterial sexual reproduction does not produce offspring.

40. Match the following columns.

	Column I		Column II
A.	*Eco RI*	I.	*E. Coli R 245*
B.	*Hind III*	II.	*Bacillus amyloliquefaciens*
C.	*BamHi*	III.	*Haemophilus influenzae*
D.	*EcoRII*	IV.	*Escherichia coli RY13*

(a) A–I; B–II; C–III; D–IV
(b) A–III; B–II; C–I; D–IV
(c) A–IV; B–III; C–II; D–I
(d) A–IV; B–II; C–III; D–I

41. When restriction enzymes cut the strand of DNA a little away from the centre of the palindrome sites between the same two base of opposite strands, it produces
(a) sticky end   (b) blunt end
(c) flush end   (d) noncohesive end

42. Match column I with column II with respect to the nomenclature of enzyme EcoRI and select the correct answer from codes given below.

	Column I		Column II
A.	*E*	I.	1st in order of identification
B.	*co*	II.	Name of genus
C.	R	III.	Name of species
D.	I	IV.	Name of strain

(a) A–III; B–IV; C–I; D–II
(b) A–II; B–III; C–IV; D–I
(c) A–II; B–I; C–IV; D–III
(d) A–II; B–III; C–I; D–IV

ANSWER KEY

1	(d)	2	(c)	3	(d)	4	(c)	5	(b)	6	(c)	7	(a)	8	(a)	9	(c)	10	(c)
11	(a)	12	(c)	13	(a)	14	(d)	15	(b)	16	(c)	17	(c)	18	(b)	19	(c)	20	(c)
21	(c)	22	(d)	23	(a)	24	(d)	25	(a)	26	(d)	27	(b)	28	(c)	29	(d)	30	(a)
31	(b)	32	(b)	33	(d)	34	(d)	35	(a)	36	(a)	37	(c)	38	(b)	39	(d)	40	(c)
41	(a)	42	(b)																

Biotechnology and its Applications

34

1. Select the correct set of the names for A, B, C and D.

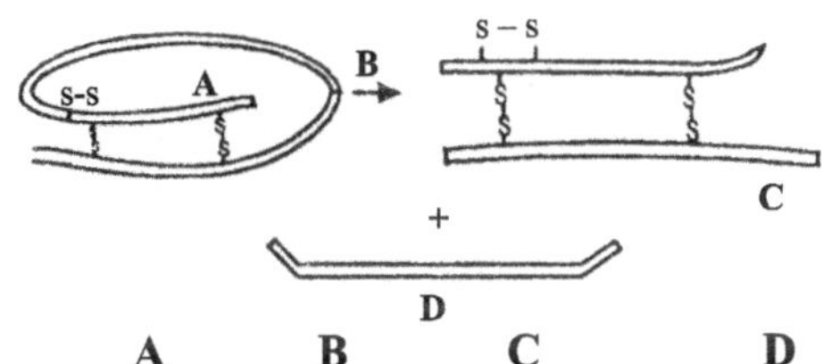

	A	B	C	D
(a)	Proinsulin	Peptide	Free C-Peptide	Insulin
(b)	Proinsulin	Peptidase	Insulin	Free C-Peptide
(c)	Proinsulin	Peptide	Insulin	Free C-Peptide
(d)	Insulin	Peptidase	Proinsulin	Free C-Peptide

2. Which of the following is correct sequence for gene therapy ?
   A. Inject engineered cells into patients bone marrow.
   B. Viral DNA carrying the normal allele inserts into chromosome.
   C. Let retrovirus infect bone marrow cells that have removed from patient and cultured.
   D. Insert RNA version of normal allele into retrovirus

   (a) A, B, C, D   (b) D, C, B, A
   (c) A, B, D, C   (d) D, C, A, B

3. Which one of the following is true about Genetic Engineering Approval committee (GEAC) ?
   (a) It will make decision regarding the validity of GM research.
   (b) It will make the safety of introducing GM - organism for public services.
   (c) It genetic modification of organism can have unpredictable results when such organisms are introduced into the ecosystem. Therefore, the Indian government has set up organisation such as GEAC.
   (d) All of these

4. Match the following and choose the correct option.

	Column I		Column II
A.	Golden Rice	I.	Cry protein
B.	Bt toxin	II.	Rich in vitamin A
C.	RNAi	III.	First trangenic cow
D.	Rosie	IV.	Gene silencing

   (a) A–II; B–I; C–IV; D–III
   (b) A–II; B–I; C–III; D–IV
   (c) A–II; B–III; C–I; D–IV
   (d) A–IV; B–I; C–II; D–III

5. Choose the correct option.

A. gene therapy has been tested on large number of patients with a wider variety of inherited genetic disorders, and in numerous cases it has produced a complete curve.

B. genetic engineering has been used to mass produce insulin for curing the diabetes.

C. DNA hybridization is the base pairing of DNA from two different sources.

D. genetic engineering is a technique of plant breeding.

(a) A, B

(b) B, C

(c) A, B, C

(d) A, B, C, D

6. Match the following and choose the correct option.

	Column I		Column II
A.	Biopiracy	I.	Search for unknown compounds
B.	Bioprospecting	II.	Hybridoma technology
C.	Monoclonal antibodies.	III.	Mobile genetic element
D.	Transposon	IV.	Bioresources

(a) A–II; B–I; C–IV; D–III

(b) A–II; B–I; C–III; D–IV

(c) A–II; B–III; C–I; D–IV

(d) A–IV; B–I; C–II; D–III

7. Match the following and choose the correct option.

	Column I		Column II
A.	Forensic science	I.	AIDS
B.	ELISA	II.	First man made hormone
C.	Humulin	III.	Emphysema
D.	a-1-antitrypsin	IV.	DNA fingerprinting

(a) A–II; B–I; C–IV; D–III

(b) A–II; B–I; C–III; D–IV

(c) A–II; B–III; C–I; D–IV

(d) A–IV; B–I; C–II; D–III

8. Which of the following combinations of risk are associated with genetically modified food ?

A Toxicity

B Allergic reaction

C Antibiotic resistance in micro-organisms present in alimentary canal

(a) A and B   (b) A, B and C

(c) A and C   (d) B and C

9. Golden rice is a promising transgenic crop, when released for cultivation, it will help in

(a) producing petrol like fuel from rice.

(b) alleviation of vitamin A.

(c) pest resistance.

(d) herbicide tolerance.

10. Match the following columns.

	Column I		Column II
A.	Gene therapy	I.	Effort to fix functional gene
B.	Humulin	II.	A single-stranded DNA of RNA tagged with a radioactive molecule
C.	Probe	III.	Diabetes
D.	ELISA	IV.	Diagnostic test

(a) A–I; B–III; C–II; D–IV

(b) A–IV; B–II; C–III; D–I

(c) A–II; B–III; C–I; D–IV

(d) A–III; B–I; C–IV; D–II

11. Which of the following is/are true ?

I. Biowar – Biowar is the use of biological weapons against humans and or their crops and animals.

II. Bioethics – Bioethics is the unauthorised use of bioresources and traditional knowledge related to bioresources for commercial benefits.

III. Biopatent – Exploitation of bioresources of other nations without proper authorization.

(a) II only

(b) I only

(c) I and II only

(d) I and III only

12. Use of transgenic plants as biological factories for the production of special chemicals is called
(a) molecular farming
(b) molecular genetics
(c) molecular mapping
(d) dry farming

13. Lactic acid bacteria (LAB) at suitable temperature converts milk to curd, which improves its nutritional quality by enhancing
(a) vitamin A   (b) vitamin B
(c) vitamin C   (d) vitamin D

14. Somatostatin or human growth hormone (HGH) for the first time was genetically isolated by
(a) Banting and Best (b) Ross
(c) Pasteur   (d) Goeddel

15. Genetic engineering has been successfully used for producing:
(a) transgenic mice for testing safety of polio vaccine before use in humans
(b) transgenic models for studying new treatments for certain cardiac diseases
(c) transgenic cow – rosie which produces high fat milk for making ghee
(d) animals like bulls for farm work as they have super power

16. Consider the following statements (A-D) about organic farming:
A. Utilizes genetically modified crops like *Bt* cotton
B. Uses only naturally produced inputs like compost
C. Does not use pesticides and urea
D. Produces vegetables rich in vitamins and minerals

Which of the above statements are correct?
(a) B, C and D   (b) C and D only
(c) B and C only   (d) A and B only

17. Which one of the following techniques made it possible to genetically engineer living organism?
(a) Recombinant DNA techniques
(b) X-ray diffraction
(c) Heavier isotope labelling
(d) Hybridization

18. Read the following four statements (A-D) about certain mistakes in two of them
A The first transgenic buffalo, Rosie produced milk which was human alpha-lactal albumin enriched.
B Restriction enzymes are used in isolation of DNA from other macro-molecules.
C Downstream processing is one of the steps of R-DNA technology.
D Disarmed pathogen vectors are also used in transfer of R-DNA into the host.

Which are the two statements having mistakes?
(a) Statement B and C (b) Statement C and D
(c) Statement A and C (d) Statement A and B

19. Consumption of which one of the following foods can prevent the kind of blindness associated with vitamin 'A' deficiency?
(a) '*Flavr Savr*' tomato (b) Canolla
(c) Golden rice   (d) Bt-Brinjal

20. Tobacco plants resistant to a nematode have been developed by the introduction of DNA that produced (in the host cells)
(a) both sense and anti-sense RNA
(b) a particular hormone
(c) an antifeedant
(d) a toxic protein

21. RNA interference (RNAi) technique has been devised to protect the plants from nematode is silenced by ______ produced by the host plant.
(a) dsDNA
(b) ssDNA
(c) dsRNA
(d) target proteins

22. Select the correct statement(s)-
    A   IARI has released a mustard variety rich in vitamin C.
    B   Pusa Sawani variety of Okra is resistant to aphids.
    C   Hairiness of leaves provides resistance to insect pests.
    D   Agriculture accounts for approximately 33% of India's GDP and employs nearly 62% of the population.
    (a) (A) and (B)   (b) (B) and (C)
    (c) (A), (C) and (D)   (d) None of these

23. By the use of biotechnology in which of the following bacteria production of B_2 vitamins has been increased to about 20,000 times?
    (a) *Ashbya gossypi*
    (b) *E. coli*
    (c) *Pseudomonas denitrificans*
    (d) *Propionibacterium shermanii*

24. Biotechnology deals with industrial scale production of biopharmaceuticals and biological products using genetically modified
    (a) microbes only
    (b) fungi only
    (c) plants and animals only
    (d) All of these

25. *Bt* toxin genes are isolated from *Bacillus thuringiensis* and incorporated into crop plants making them insecticidal.
    The choice of genes depend upon
    (a) crop plant only
    (b) targeted pest only
    (3) Both (a) and (b)
    (d) neither type of crop nor targeted pest

26. When DNA is transcribed into mRNA, usually the mRNA remains single-stranded, but in some cases an RNA can be made that is complementary to the mRNA. This is called _______ and its main function is to __________.
    (a) antisense RNA, block gene expression
    (b) antisense RNA, amplify mRNA
    (c) antisense RNA, enhance translation
    (d) reverse transcription, enhance translation

27. Which step proved to be the main challenging obstacle in the production of human insulin by genetic engineering?
    (a) Splitting A and B polypeptide chains.
    (b) Addition of C-peptide to pro-insulin.
    (c) Getting insulin assembled into mature form.
    (d) Removal of C-peptide from active insulin.

28. RNA interference (RNAi) technique has been devised to protect the plants from nematode is silenced by _______ produced by the host plant.
    (a) dsDNA   (b) ssDNA
    (c) dsRNA   (d) target proteins

29. A sample of DNA from a person suspected of having sickle-cell anaemia is subjected to DNA hybridization using two probes. One that binds to the normal allele and another that binds to the sickle-cell allele. If both probes bind to the DNA, this individual
    (a) is homozygous dominant for the sickle-cell gene.
    (b) is heterozygous for the sickle-cell gene.
    (c) is heterozygous recessive for the sickle cell gene.
    (d) has sickle cell anaemia.

30. A functional ADA can be introduced into cells of the patients receiving gene therapy by using vector constituted by
    (a) *E. coli*
    (b) *Reovirus*
    (c) *Retrovirus*
    (d) *Agrobacterium*

31. Transgenic animals are produced
    A.   to study-how gene are regulated and how they affect the normal functions of body and its development.
    B.   to study of diseases.
    C.   to obtain useful biological products .
    D.   to test of vaccine safety and chemical safety.
    (a) A, B, C and D
    (b) A and D
    (c) B and D
    (d) Only A

32. Which step of Government of India has taken to cater to the requirement of patent terms and other emergency provisions in this regard?
- (a) Biopiracy act
- (b) Indian patents bill
- (c) RTI act
- (d) negotiable instruments act

33. Today, transgenic models exist for many human diseases which includes
- A. Cancer   B. Cystic fibrosis
- C. Rheumatoid arthritis D. Alzhiemer's disease
- (a) A and C only   (b) B and C only
- (c) A, B and C only   (d) A, B, C and D

34. Which of the following statements is correct?
- (a) The current interest in the manipulation of microbes, plants and animal has raised serious ethical issues.
- (b) One possible risk of genetic engineering is the accidental production of dangerously resistant microorganisms.
- (c) Although risks are possible, genetic engineering appears to offer more of contribution to human welfare than threats.
- (d) All of the above

35. In cloning of cattle, a fertilised egg is taken out of the mother's womb and
- (a) the egg is divided into four pairs of cells, which are implanted into the womb of other cows.
- (b) in the eight cell stage, cells are separated and cultured until small embryos are formed, which are implanted into the womb of other cows.
- (c) in the eight cell stage, the individual cells are separated under electrical field for further development in culture media.
- (d) from this upto eight identical twins can be produced.

36. A person suffering from SCID has a defective gene for the enzyme Adenosine Deaminase (ADA). As a result of which the person lacks .... thus making him prone to infections.
- (a) B-lymphocytes
- (b) phagocytes
- (3) T-lymphocytes
- (d) Both (a) and (b)

37. There are set of healthcare products. Match them with organisms which are genetically engineered for respective product

A.	Insulin	I.	*Escherichia coli / Saccharomyces*
B.	Somatotropin	II.	*Escherichia coli / yeast*
C.	Interferon	III.	GM *Escherichia coli*
D.	Interleukins	IV.	hGR in *Escherichia coli*
		V.	Humulin through *Escherichia coli*

- (a) A–V; B–IV; C–I; D–II
- (b) A–V; B–I; C–II; D–IV
- (c) A–V; B–III; C–IV; D–I
- (d) A–V; B–IV; C–III; D–II

ANSWER KEY

1	(b)	2	(b)	3	(d)	4	(a)	5	(b)	6	(d)	7	(d)	8	(b)	9	(b)	10	(a)
11	(b)	12	(a)	13	(b)	14	(d)	15	(a)	16	(c)	17	(a)	18	(d)	19	(c)	20	(a)
21	(c)	22	(c)	23	(a)	24	(d)	25	(c)	26	(a)	27	(c)	28	(c)	29	(c)	30	(c)
31	(a)	32	(b)	33	(d)	34	(d)	35	(b)	36	(c)	37	(a)						

Organisms and Populations

35

1. Mark the correct identification from the following picture

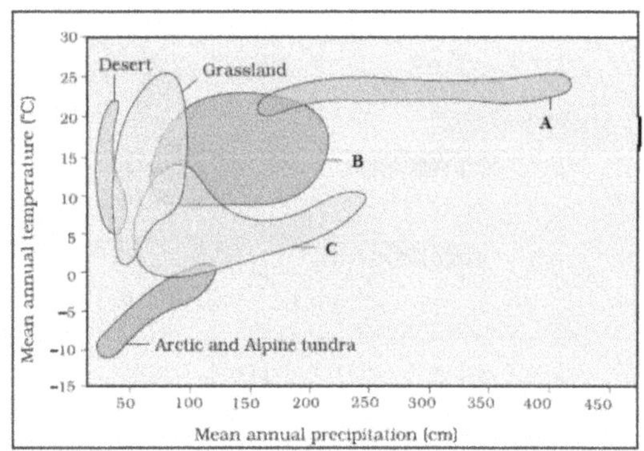

	(A)	(B)	(C)
(a)	Tropical forest	Temperate forest	Coniferous forest
(b)	Temperate forest	Tropical forest	Coniferous forest
(c)	Temperate forest	Coniferous forest	Tropical forest
(d)	Coniferous forest	Tropical forest	Temperate forest

2. A majority of organisms are restricted to a narrow range of temperature, and are called

　　(a) Stenothermal

　　(b) Endothermal

　　(c) Ectothermal

　　(d) Eurythermal

3. Which option gives the correct identification of three types of organisms in response to a biotic factor

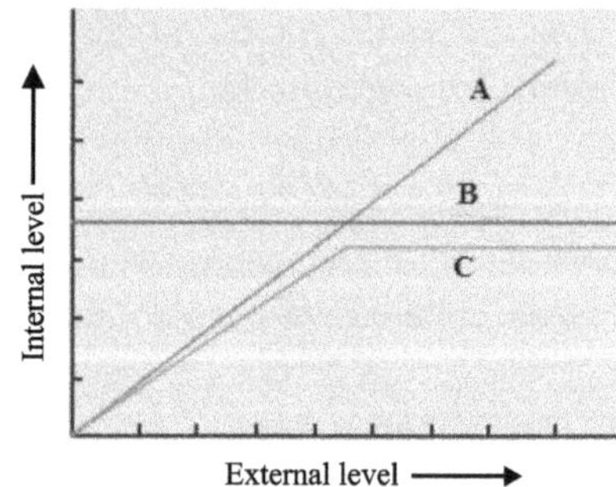

	(A)	(B)	(C)
(a)	Partial regulator	Regulator	Conformers
(b)	Regulator	Conformers	Partial regulator
(c)	Conformer	Regulator	Partial regulator
(d)	Regulator	Partial regulator	Conformers

4. The foraging, reproductive and migratory activities of the organisms are primarily dependent upon

   (a) Light   (b) Temperature

   (b) Water   (c) Soil

5. Mark the correct statement

   (a) The case of bear, going into hibernation during winter, is an example of 'escape in time'

   (b) To prevent desiccation some snails and fishes enter into diapause

   (c) Under unfavourable conditions many zooplankton species go into aestivation

   (d) All of these

6. When one gets settled at higher altitude for quite some time, then

   (a) The binding capacity of haemoglobin is decreased

   (b) No. of RBCs is increased

   (c) Hyperpnea develops

   (d) All of these

7. In exponential growth, the increase or decrease in population size during a unit period is

   (a) $(B + I) - (D + E)$ (b) $(b + d) - N$

   (c) $N \times (b - d)$ (d) $r + N$

8. Verhulst -Pearl logistic growth pattern is

   (a) Sigmoid   (b) J-shaped

   (c) Straight line   (d) Hyperbola

9. Match the association in Column I with the type of interaction given in Column II and mark the correct option:

Column I		Column II	
A.	Barnacles on whale	I.	Predation
B.	Butterfly and birds	II.	Parasitism
C.	Goats and tortoise	III.	Competition
D.	Copepods on marine fish	IV.	Commensalism

   (a) A- (I), B- (IV), C- (III), D- (II)

   (b) A- (IV), B- (I), C- (II), D- (III)

   (c) A- (III), B- (I), C- (IV), D- (II)

   (d) A- (IV), B- (I), C- (III), D- (II)

10. Mark the correct statement:

    (a) Logistic growth pattern is more realistic one and is 'S' shaped

    (b) Exponential growth pattern is more realistic one and is 'J' shaped

    (c) Verhulst- Pearl growth pattern is more realistic one and is 'J' shaped

    (d) Geometric growth pattern is not realistic one and is 'S' shaped

11. What is the sequence of phases in the growth curve?

	(A)	(B)	(C)
(a)	Lag	Log	Inflexion phase
(b)	Lag	Stationary	Log
(c)	Log	Lag	Stationary
(d)	Lag	Log	Stationary

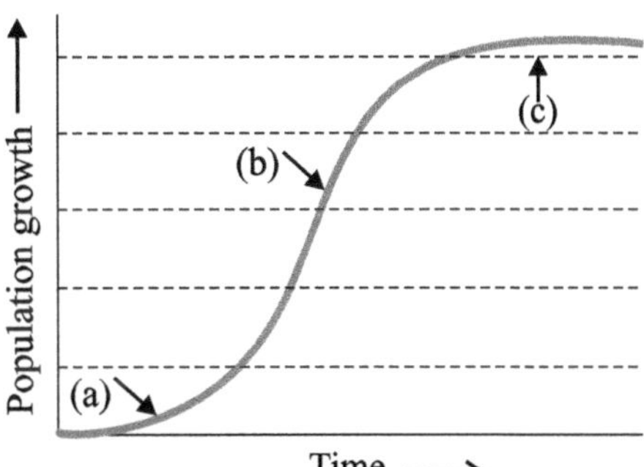

12. A country with a high rate of population growth took measures to reduce it. The figure below shows age-sex pyramids of populations A and B twenty years apart. Select the correct interpretation about them :

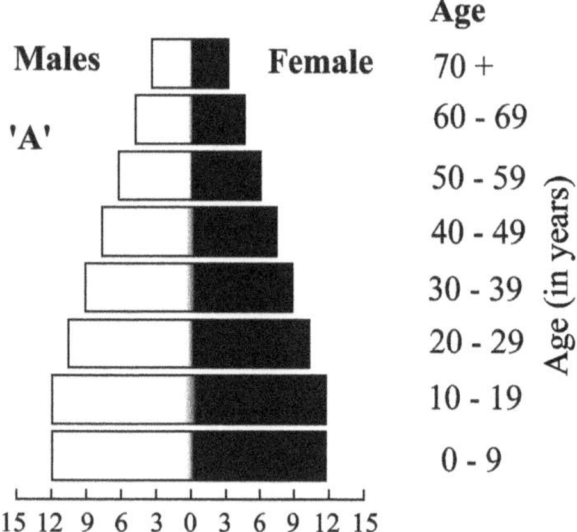

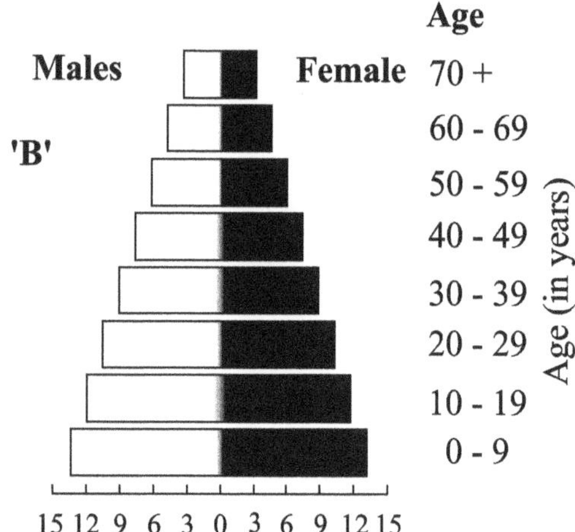

Interpretations

(a) "A" is the earlier pyramid and no change has occurred in the growth rate.

(b) "A" is more recent and shows slight reduction in the growth rate.

(c) "B" is earlier pyramid and shows stabilised growth rate

(d) "B" is more recent showing that population is very young

13. Within biological communities, some species are important in determining the ability of a large number of other species to persist in the community. Such species are called

(a) keystone species   (b) allopatric species

(c) sympatric species (d) threatened species

14. A population growing in a habitat with limited resources shows four phases of growth in the following sequence

(a) Acceleration – deceleration – lag phase – asymptote

(b) Asymptote – acceleration – deceleration – lag phase

(c) Lag phase – acceleration – deceleration – asymptote

(d) Acceleration – lag phase – deceleration – asymptote

15. Consider the following statement (A)-(D) each with one or two blanks.

(A) Bears go into ------I----- during winter to ----- II ----cold weather

(B) A conical age pyramid with a broad base represents----- III------ human population

(C) A wasp pollinating a fig flower is an example of -----IV

(D) An area with high levels of species richness is known as----- V

Which one of the following options, gives the correct fill ups for the respective blank numbers from I to V in the statements?

(a) III - expanding, IV - commensalism, V - biodiversity park

(b) I - hibernation, II - escape, III - expanding, V - hot spot

(c) III - stable, IV - commensalism, V - marsh

(d) I - aestivation, II - escape, III - stable, IV - mutualism

16. Study the given figure and mark the correct answer:

(a) a= logistic plot, b= exponential plot, k= carrying capacity

(b) a= exponential plot, b= logistic plot, k= carrying capacity

(c) a= carrying capacity, b= exponential plot, k= logistic plot

(d) a= carrying capacity, b= logistic plot, k= exponential plot

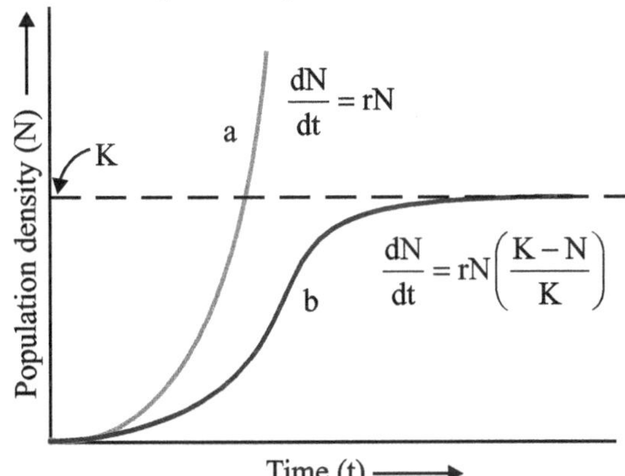

17. Which of the following is correct?

(a) Population change= (Birth + Immigration) – (Death + Emigration)

(b) Population change= (Birth + Immigration) + (Death + Emigration)

(c) Population change= (Birth + Emigration) + (Death + Immigration)

(d) Population change= (Birth + Emigration) – (Death + Immigration)

18. The Verhulst- Pearl logistic growth is described using the equation $\frac{dN}{dT} = rN\left(\frac{K-N}{K}\right)$, in this K stands for:

(a) Temperature in degree Kelvin

(b) Intrinsic rate of natural increase

(c) Carrying capacity

(d) Population density

19. If '+' sign is assigned to beneficial interaction, '-' sign to detrimental and '0' sign to neutral interaction, then the population interaction represented by '+' '-' refers to

(a) Parasitism   (b) Mutualism

(c) Amensalism   (d) Commensalism

20. The density of a population can be calculated by

(a) $D = \dfrac{S\ (Space)}{N\ (Number)}$

(b) $D = \dfrac{N\ (Number)}{S\ (Space)}$

(c) $D = \dfrac{S\ (Size)}{W\ (Weight)}$

(d) None of these

21. Two opposite forces operate in the growth and development of every population. One of them relates to the ability of reproduction at a given rate. The force opposing to it is called

(a) Biotic control

(b) Mortality

(c) Fecundity

(d) Environmental resistances

22. Certain, characteristic demographic features of developing countries are :

(a) high mortality, high density, uneven population growth and a very old age distribution

(b) high fertility, low or rapidly falling mortality rate, rapid population growth and a very young age distribution

(c) high fertility, high density, rapidly rising mortality rate and a very young age distribution

(d) high infant mortality, low fertility, uneven population growth and a very young age distribution

ANSWER KEY																			
1	(a)	**2**	(a)	**3**	(c)	**4**	(a)	**5**	(a)	**6**	(d)	**7**	(c)	**8**	(a)	**9**	(d)	**10**	(a)
11	(d)	**12**	(b)	**13**	(a)	**14**	(c)	**15**	(b)	**16**	(b)	**17**	(a)	**18**	(c)	**19**	(a)	**20**	(b)
21	(d)	**22**	(b)																	

Ecosystem

36

1. Which one of the following statement is correct?
   (a) Decomposition rate is slower if detritus is rich in lignin and chitin, and quicker, if detritus is rich in nitrogen and water - soluble substances like sugars.
   (b) Decomposition rate is slower if detritus is rich in nitrogen and water - soluble substances like sugars, and quicker, if detritus is rich in lignin and chitin.
   (c) Decomposition rate is slower if detritus is rich in cellulose, and quicker, if detritus is rich in phosphorus.
   (d) Decomposition rate is quicker if detritus is rich in lignin, and quicker, if detritus is rich in sulphur.

2. What are the two most important climatic factors that regulate decomposition through their effects on soil microbes?
   (a) Temperature and rainfall
   (b) Temperature and soil moisture
   (c) Temperature and humidity
   (d) Temperature and pressure

3. Which one of the following statement is correct?
   (a) Warm and moist environment favours decomposition whereas low temperature and anaerobiosis inhibit decomposition.
   (b) Warm and moist environment inhibit decomposition whereas low temperature and anaerobiosis favour decomposition.
   (c) Warm and anaerobiosis favour decomposition whereas low temperature favours decomposition.
   (d) Warm and low temperature inhibit decomposition whereas anaerobiosis favours decomposition.

4. Out of the following biogeochemical cycles identify the gaseous type?
   A. Sulphur   B. Phosphorus
   C. Nitrogen   D. Carbon
   (a) Only A   (b) Only B
   (c) Only D   (d) C and D

5. Identified A, B, C and D.

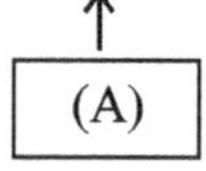

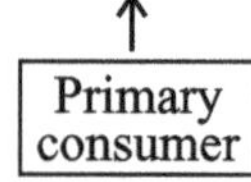

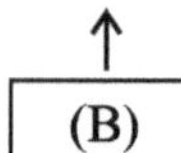

Trophic levels		Examples
Tertiary consumer	Fourth trophic level (Top carnivore)	(D)
(A)	Third trophic level (Carnivore)	Birds, fishes, and wolf
Primary consumer	Second trophic level (Herbivore)	Zooplankton, grasshopper and cow
(B)	First trophic level (C)	Phytoplankton, grass and trees

(a) A – Primary producer; B – Second consumer;C – Man / Lion; D – Plants

(b) A – Secondary consumer; B – Primary producer; C – Man / lion; D – Plants

(c) A – Primary producer; B – Secondary consumer; C – Plants; D – Man / lion

(d) A – Secondary consumer; B – Primary producer; C – Plants; D – Man / lion

6. Identify the activities that result in the release of CO_2 to the atmosphere.

A. Burning of wood.

B. Volcanic activity

C. Combustion of organic matter

D. Fossil fuels

(a) A, B, C and D   (b) C and D

(c) A, C and D   (d) B and C

7. On the basis of vertical changes of temperature, fresh water media is divided into three strata. The correct sequence of the three strata is

(a) epilimnion, thermocline and hypolimnion

(b) hypolimnion, epilimnion and thermocline

(c) thermocline, hypolimnion and epilimnion

(d) epilimnion, hypolimnion and thermocline

8. Identified A, B, C and D of a nutrient cycle.

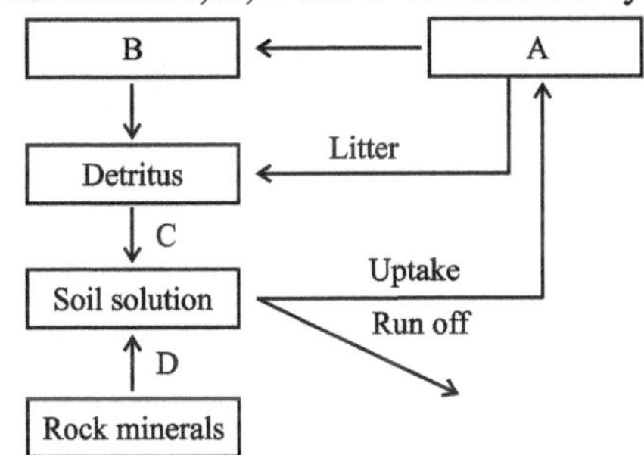

(a) A – Consumers; B – Decomposition; C – Producers; D – Weathering

(b) A – Consumers; B – Weathering; C – Producers; D – Decomposition

(c) A – Producers; B – Consumers; C – Decomposition; D – Weathering

(d) A – Consumers; B – Producers; C – Decomposition D – Weathering

9. Match the following and choose the correct option

	Column I		Column II
A.	Primary succession	I.	Autotrophs
B.	Climax community	II.	Community that has completed succession
C.	Consumer	III.	Colonization of a new environment
D.	Producer	IV.	Animals

(a) A – III; B – II; C – IV; D – I

(b) A – III; B – I; C – IV; D – II

(c) A – I; B – III; C – II; D – IV

(d) A – II; B – III; C – IV; D – I

10. The organisms spending most of the time in transitional area between two communities are called

(a) exotic species   (b) edge species

(c) keystone species   (d) critical link species

11. Match the following columns.

	Column I		Column II
A.	Scavengers	I.	Autotrophs
B.	Parasites	II.	Heterotrophs
C.	Producers	III.	Consumers of dead bodies
D.	Phagotrophs	IV.	Consumers that feed on a small part of a living being

(a) A–III; B–V; C–I; D–II

(b) A–III; B–I; C–II; D–IV

(c) A–I; B–II; C–IV; D–III

(d) A–IV; B–III; C–II; D–I

12. Identify A, B and C from the given flow chart.

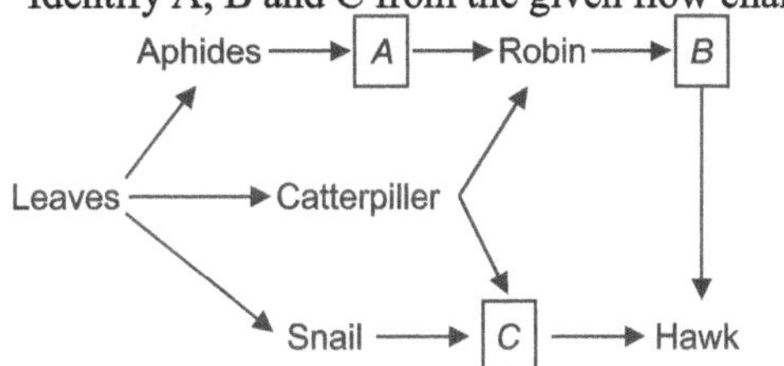

(a) A-Bulbul, B-Snake, C-Monkey

(b) A-Beetle, B-Lizard, C-Praying mantis

(c) A-Ladybird, B-Snake, C-Pigeon

(d) A-Lizard, B-Bird, C-Snake

13. .... shows the relation between producers and consumers in an ecosystem in a graphical manner in the form of a pyramid.

(a) Ecological pyramid

(b) Tropical level

(c) Punnett square

(d) Pyramid of biomass

14. What is represented by this sequence?

Cyanobacteria → Crustose → lichens → Foliose lichens → Mosses → Shrubs → Dicotyledonous plants

(a) Genetic drift

(b) Eltanian pyramid

(c) Ecological succession

(d) Phylogenetic relationships

15. Match the two sets

	Column I		Column II
A.	Pioneers	I.	Vegetation which modifies its own environment and thus causing its own replacement
B.	Autogenic	II.	Replacement of existing community by external conditions.
C.	Allogenic	III.	Establishment succession
D.	Ecesis	IV.	Primary colonisers

(a) A – IV; B – I, C – II; D – III
(b) A – I; B – II, C – III; D – IV
(c) A – II; B – I, C – IV; D – III
(d) A – I; B – IV, C – III; D – II

16. Match the following columns.

	Column I		Column II
A.	Inorganic substances	I.	Light, temperature and humidity
B.	Organic compounds	II.	Soil, pH and minerals.
C.	Climatic factors	III.	Proteins, carbohydrates and lipids, nucleic acid
D.	Edaphic factors	IV.	Carbon, nitrogen, oxygen and water.

(a) A–III; B–I; C–II; D–IV
(b) A–IV; B–III; C–I; D–II
(c) A–I; B–II; C–III; D–IV
(d) A–IV; B–II; C–I; D–III

17. Match the names of organisms given under column I with the ecological names given under column II. Choose the answer which gives the correct combinations of the two columns.

	Column I (Organisms)		Column II (Ecological names)
A.	Grass	I.	Decomposer
B.	Grasshopper	II.	Secondary carnivore
C.	Frog	III.	Producer
D.	Hawk	IV.	Primary consumer
		V.	Primary carnivore

(a) A–III; B–V; C–IV; D–II
(b) A–III; B–IV; C–V; D–II
(c) A–I; B–III; C–IV; D–V
(d) A–III; B–I; C–IV; D–V

18. Match the following and choose the correct option–

	Column I		Column II
A.	Standing state	I.	Perfect
B.	Gaseous cycles	II.	Amount of nutrients
C.	Standing crop	III.	Imperfect
D.	Sedimentary cycles	IV.	Living matter at different trophic levels

(a) A – II, B – I, C – IV, D – III
(b) A – I, B – II, C – III, D – IV
(c) A – III, B – II, C – IV, D – I
(d) A – I, B – IV, C – III, D – II

19. The important step in the process of decomposition in order is
(a) Catabolism → Fragmentation → Leeching → Humification → Mineralization
(b) Catabolism → Fragmentation → Humification → Leeching → Mineralization
(c) Fragmentation → Humification →Catabolism → Leeching → Mineralization
(d) Fragmentation → Leeching → Catabolism → Humification → Mineralization

20. Perturbation of which of the following cycles contributes most to global warming?
(a) The global carbon cycle
(b) The global water cycle
(c) The global nitrogen cycle
(d) All of these cycles contribute equally.

21. In a comparative study of grassland ecosystem and pond ecosystem it may be observed that
(a) the biotic components are almost similar.
(b) the abiotic components are almost similar.
(c) primary and secondary consumers are similar.
(d) both biotic and abiotic components are different.

22. Answer the correct set

	Column I		Column II
A.	Gross primary	I.	Total assimilation productivity
B.	Secondary productivity	II.	Remains mobile and does not remain in-situ
C.	Transducers	III.	Green plants
D.	Food web	IV.	Interlocking pattern

(a) A–I; B–II; C–III; D–IV
(b) A–II; B–III; C–IV; D–I
(c) A–III; B–IV; C–I; D–II
(d) A–I; B–III; C–II; D–IV

23. Study the following columns and choose the correct option.

	Column I		Column II
A.	Population	I.	Parts of the earth consisting of all the ecosystems of the world.
B.	Community	II.	Assemblage of all the individuals belonging to different species occurring in an area
C.	Ecosystem	III.	Group of similar individuals belonging to the same species found in an area.
D.	Ecosphere	IV.	Interaction between the organisms and their physical environment components.
	living	V.	Classification of organisms based on the type of environment.

(a) A–III; B–II; C–I; D–IV
(b) A–V; B–II; C–III; D–IV
(c) A–II; B–III; C–V; D–I
(d) A–III; B–II; C–IV; D–I

24. Choose the correct combination of labelling of the zones in water in a lake

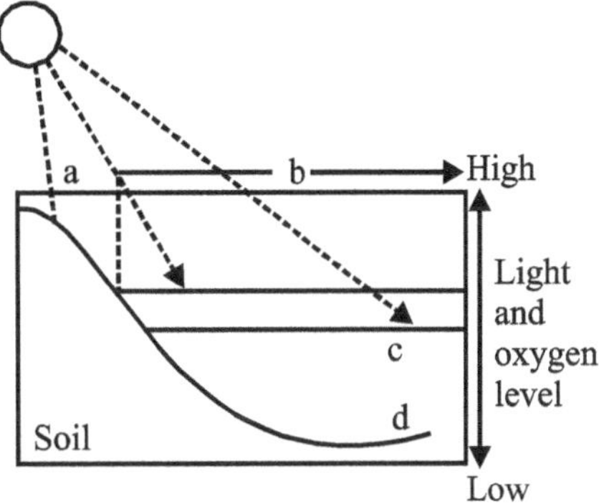

(a) a-Limnetic zone, b-Profundal zone, c-Littoral zone, d-Benthic zone
(b) a-Littoral zone, b-Benthic zone, c-Profundal zone, d-Limnetic zone
(c) a-Littoral zone, b-Limnetic zone, c-Profundal zone, d-Benthic zone
(d) a-Limnetic zone, b-Littoral zone, c-Benthic zone, d-Profundal zone

25. Match the following columns.

	Column I		Column II
A.	Primary consumers	I.	A meat eater that eats primary consumers.
B.	Secondary consumers	II.	A meat eater that eats tertiary consumers.
C.	Tertiary consumers	III.	A organism eater that eats producers.
D.	Quaternary consumers	IV.	A meat eater that eats secondary consumers.

(a) A–I; B–IV; C–II; D–III
(b) A–III; B–I; C–IV; D–II
(c) A–IV; B–II; C–III; D–I
(d) A–II; B–III; C–I; D–IV

26. Consider the following statements about ecological pyramids.

A. Charles Elton developed the concept of ecological pyramid.

B. Ecological pyramids are also called as Eltonian pyramids, named after Charles Elton.

C. It is a numerical representation or pyramid shaped diagram which depicts the number of organisms, biomass and energy at each trophic level.

Which of the statements given above are correct?

(a) A and B
(b) A and C
(c) B and C
(d) A, B and C

27. Match the following columns.

	Column I		Column II
A.	Primary succession	I.	Colonisation of a new environment
B.	Climax community	II.	Ecosystem development
C.	Pioneer community on	III.	Crustose lichens lithosphere
D.	Ecological succession	IV.	Community that has completed succession

(a) A–III; B–II; C–I; D–IV
(b) A–IV; B–III; C–II; D–I
(c) A–I; B–II; C–III; D–IV
(d) A–IV; B–III; C–I; D–II

28. Match the following columns.

	Column I		Column II
A.	First trophic level	I.	Producer
B.	Decomposer	II.	Consumer
C.	Primary productivity	III.	Phytoplankton
D.	Secondary productivity	IV.	Stratification
		V.	Bacteria

(a) A–I; B–V; C–III; D–IV
(b) A–II; B–III; C–IV; D–V
(c) A–III; B–V; C–I; D–II
(d) A–III; B–V; C–II; D–I

29. Match the sets

	Column I		Column II
A.	*Artemisia tridentata*	I.	Grow better in over grazed area
B.	*Capparis spinosa* fires	II.	Dominate in areas destructed by
C.	*Pteridium aquilina* and *Pyronema*	III.	Indicates intense soil erosion
D.	*Amaranthus* and *Chenopodium*	IV.	Saline soils

(a) A–I; B–II; C–III; D–IV
(b) A–II; B–III; C–IV; D–I
(c) A–III; B–I; C–II; D–IV
(d) A–IV; B–III; C–II; D–I

30. Match column A with column B and select the correct option.

	Column I		Column II
A.	Pyramid of energy	I.	Xerosere
B.	First group of	II.	Always plant in bare area inverted
C.	Pyramid of biomass	III.	Hydrosere in aquatic habitat
D.	Succession in	IV.	Pioneers desert area
		V.	Always upright

(a) A – II; B – I; C – V; D – III
(b) A – V; B – IV; C – II; D – I
(c) A– V; B – III; C – II; D – IV
(d) A – II; B – III; C – V; D – I

31. Match the following columns.

	Column I		Column II
A.	Xeroseres	I.	Ecological succession starts on terrestrial habitat.
B.	Hydroseres	II.	Succession begins from open water
C.	Lithoseres	III.	Successions begin on sand
D.	Psammoseres	IV.	Succession start on a bare rock

(a) A – III; B – I, C – II; D – IV
(b) A – IV; B – III, C – I; D – II
(c) A – I; B – II, C – IV; D – III
(d) A – II; B – IV, C – III; D – I

ANSWER KEY																			
1	(a)	**2**	(b)	**3**	(a)	**4**	(d)	**5**	(d)	**6**	(d)	**7**	(d)	**8**	(c)	**9**	(a)	**10**	(b)
11	(a)	**12**	(c)	**13**	(a)	**14**	(c)	**15**	(a)	**16**	(b)	**17**	(b)	**18**	(a)	**19**	(d)	**20**	(a)
21	(a)	**22**	(a)	**23**	(d)	**24**	(c)	**25**	(b)	**26**	(a)	**27**	(c)	**28**	(c)	**29**	(a)	**30**	(b)
31	(c)																		

Biodiversity and its Conservation

1. Following arrangement is correct from the point of view of decreasing biodiversity in angiosperms (N), fungi (F), pteridophytes (P) and algae(A)
   (a) $N > F > P > A$
   (b) $N > F > A > P$
   (c) $F > N > P > A$
   (d) $F > N > A > P$

2. From Origin of life to its diversification on earth, there have occurred following number of episodes of mass extinction
   (a) Two
   (b) Three
   (c) Four
   (d) Five

3. The Indian Rhinoceros is a natural inhabitant of which one of the Indian states?
   (a) Uttarakhand
   (b) Uttar Pradesh
   (c) Himachal Pradesh
   (d) Assam

4. Tropics account for greater biodiversity. Which one of the following points does not match with the tropical environment?
   (a) More solar energy available
   (b) Less seasonable and more predictable
   (c) Frequent climatic disturbances
   (d) Have long evolutionary time for speciation

5. Match items given in column I with those given in column II.

Column I		Column II
A. Rhinoceros	I.	Bharatpur
B. Tiger project in Karnataka	II.	Tropical evergreen forest
C. Assemblage protection	III.	Kaziranga
D. Silent valley	IV.	National park
	V.	Bandipur

   (a) A–V; B–III; C–I; D–IV
   (b) A–II; B–IV; C–III; D–II
   (c) A–IV; B–III; C–II; D–V
   (d) A–III; B–V; C–I; D–II

6. According to IUCN Red List, what is the status of Red Panda (*Ailurus fulgens*)?
   (a) Critically endangered species
   (b) Vulnerable species
   (c) Extinct species
   (d) Endangered species

7. Which one of the following is the correct matched pair of an endangered animal and National Park?
   (a) Rhinoceros – Kaziranga National Park
   (b) Wild ass – Dudhwa National Park
   (c) Great Indian bustard – Keoladeo National Park
   (d) Lion – Corbett National Park

8. Which of the following pairs of an animal and a plant represents endangered organisms in India?
   (a) Tamarind and Rhesus monkey
   (b) *Cinchona* and leopard
   (c) Banyan and black buck
   (d) *Bentinckia nicobarica* and Red Panda

9. Among various categories of threatened species the percentage of various angiosperms categorized as vulnerable is about
   - (a) 14 %
   - (b) 19 %
   - (c) 41 %
   - (d) 51 %

10. Endangered or threatened animals are protected from its extinction by *ex- situ* conservation in
    - (a) Wild life sanctuary
    - (b) Biosphere reserves
    - (c) National parks
    - (d) Zoological parks

11. Just as a person moving from Delhi to Shimla to escape the heat for the duration of hot summer, thousands of migratory birds from Siberia and other extremely cold northern region move to
    - (a) Western Ghat
    - (b) Meghalaya
    - (c) Corbett National Park
    - (d) Keolado National Park

12. Reserpine, an active alkaloid, is obtained from:
    - (1) Atropa belladona
    - (2) Catharanthus roscus
    - (3) Digitalis pupurea
    - (4) Rauwolfia serpentine

13. Read the statement regarding a stable community and choose the correct option:
    - A. Must be resistant to occasional disturbances
    - B. Should show much variation in productivity from year to year
    - C. Must be resistant to invasions by alien species
    - (a) A and B are correct
    - (b) A, B and C are correct
    - (c) Only A is correct
    - (d) A and C are correct

14. The region of Biosphere Reserve which is legally protected and where no human activity is allowed, is known as
    - (a) Core zone
    - (b) Buffer zone
    - (c) Transition zone
    - (d) Restoration zone

15. Which one of the following is related to *Ex-situ* conservation of threatened animals and plants?
    - (a) Wild life safari park
    - (b) Biodiversity hot spots
    - (c) Amazon rain forest
    - (d) Himalayan region

16. Match the column -I with column -II

	Column I		Column II
A.	Bihar	I.	Indian elephant
B.	Rajasthan	II.	Gazello
C.	Madhya Pradesh	III.	Leopard
D.	Uttar Pradesh	IV.	Barasingha
E.	Gujarat	V.	Sloth Bear
		VI.	Asiatic Lion

   - (a) A–I; B–III; C–V; D–II; E–IV
   - (b) A–V; B–II; C–IV; D–III; E–VI
   - (c) A–III; B–V; C–II; D–IV; E–I
   - (d) A–VI; B–V; C–IV D–III; E–II

17. The Siberian crane from Russia is a regular visitor to the bird sanctuary in one of the following place in India.
    - (a) Lallbagh, Bangalore
    - (b) Vendanthgol sanctuary, Tamil Nadu
    - (c) Ranganathittis sactuary, Karnataka
    - (d) Bharatpur sactuary, Rajasthan

18. Buffer zone, Core zone and the Transition zone are three subdivisions of the Biosphere reserves. The transition zone
    - (a) Covers the Buffer zone and lies in between Buffer zone and the Core zone
    - (b) Covers the Core zone and lies in between the Core zone and the Buffer zone
    - (c) Is the innermost zone of the Biosphere reserve
    - (d) Is the outermost zone of the Biosphere reserve

19. Dachigam Wildlife Sanctuary in Kashmir is associated with
    - (a) *Rhinoceros*
    - (b) *Macaca silenus*
    - (c) *Cervus elaphus hanglu*
    - (d) None above

ANSWER KEY

1	(d)	2	(d)	3	(d)	4	(c)	5	(d)	6	(d)	7	(a)	8	(d)	9	(d)	10	(d)
11	(d)	12	(d)	13	(d)	14	(a)	15	(a)	16	(b)	17	(d)	18	(d)	19	(c)		

1. The maximum biomagnification would be in which of the following in case aquatic ecosystem?
   - (a) Zooplanktons
   - (b) Phytoplanktons
   - (c) Fishes
   - (d) Birds

2. All automobiles and fuel (petrol and diesel) were to have met the Euro III emission specification in eleven Indian cities from `1 April 2005 and have to meet the Euro IV norms by
   - (a) 1 April 2007
   - (b) 1 April 2008
   - (c) 1 April 2009
   - (d) 1 April 2010

3. Bagassosis is
   - (a) hypersensitivity pneumonia due to exposure to fibrous cellulose part of crushed sugar cane
   - (b) is an asthma like condition produced due to exposure to flax or cotton fibres
   - (c) hypersensitivity pneumonitis due to exposure to damp hay or grain
   - (d) hypersensitivity pneumonitis due to exposure to paprika

4. The common refrigerant chlorofluoro-methane (freon) and NO_2 is a serious pollutant because
   - (a) it lowers atmospheric temperature
   - (b) it prevents cloud condensation
   - (c) it destroys haemoglobin
   - (d) it disrupts O_3 layer

5. 'Freon Gas' causing stratospheric ozone depletion is used mainly in
   - (a) refrigerator
   - (b) automobile
   - (c) thermal power plant
   - (d) steel industry

6. IRRI proposed one of the following for the prevention of fertilizers pollution in agriculture
   - (a) trickling filter method
   - (b) mud ball technique
   - (c) both (a) and (b)
   - (d) none

7. Match the sources of solid waste in Column A with the type of solid waste in column B.

	Column I		Column II
A.	Old newspapers	I.	Municipal solid wastes
B.	Construction site	II.	Industrial solid wastes
C.	Discarded medicines	III.	Hospital solid wastes and syringes

   - (a) A–II; B–III; C–I
   - (b) A–I; B–III; C–II
   - (c) A–I; B–II; C–III
   - (d) A–II; B–III; C–I

8. Match the following columns.

	Column I		Column II
A.	Suspended solids	I.	Nitrates ammonia, phosphate sodium calcium
B.	Colloidal materials	II.	Faecal matter, bacteria, paper and cloth fibres
C.	Dissolved materials	III.	Sand, silt and clay

(a) A–I; B–II; C–III   (b) A–II; B–III; C–I
(c) A–III; B–I; C–II   (d) A–III; B–II; C–I

9. Which of the following equipment is used to study thermal behaviour of water?
(a) MALDI-TOF
(b) real time PCR
(c) differential scanning calorimeter
(d) SEM

10. Global agreement in specific control strategies to reduce the release of ozone depleting substances, was adopted by
(a) The Montreal Protocol
(b) The Kyoto Protocol
(c) The Vienna Convention
(d) Rio de Janeiro Conference

11. Measuring Biochemical Oxygen Demand (BOD) is a method used for
(a) Measuring the activity of *Saccharomyces cervisae* in producing curd on a commercial scale
(b) Working out the efficiency of RBCs about their capacity to carry oxygen
(c) Estimating the amount of organic matter in sewage water
(d) Working out the efficiency of oil driven automobile engines

12. According to Kyoto Protocol the major nations abide to reduce concentration of green house gases by
(a) 2008   (b) 2010
(c) 2012   (d) 2018

13. Which one of the following is **not correct** as regards to the harmful effects of particulate matter of the size 2.5 micrometers or less?
(a) It can be inhaled into the lungs
(b) It can cause respiratory problems
(c) It can directly enter into our circulatory system
(d) It can cause inflammation and damage to the lungs

14. Rachel Carson's famous book, 'Silent Spring' is related to
(a) Pesticide pollution
(b) Noise pollution
(c) Population explosion
(d) Ecosystem management

15. Which of the following is not one of the prime health risks associated with greater UV radiation through the atmosphere due to depletion of stratospheric ozone?
(a) Increased skin cancer
(b) Reduced immune system
(c) Damage to eyes
(d) Increased liver cancer

16. Match the following items in column I with column II and choose the correct answer.

	Calumn I		Column II
A.	Arsenic	I.	Minamata disease
B.	Nitrate	II.	Itai-itai
C.	Mercury	III.	Blue-baby syndrome
D.	Cadmium	IV.	Skeletal fluorosis
E.	Fluoride	V.	Black-fool disease

(a) A–II; B–III; C–V; D–I; E–IV
(b) A–V; B–III; C–I; D–II; E–IV
(c) A–III; B–IV; C–V; D–I; E–II
(d) A–V; B–IV; C–III; D–II; E–I

17. Choose the correct sequence of air pollution and its components with the effect it produces.
(a) Chemical factory $\rightarrow NO_2 \rightarrow$ ozone hole
(b) Automobile exhausts $\rightarrow N_2O \rightarrow$ green house effect
(c) Heavy industry $\rightarrow CO_2 \rightarrow$ acid rain
(d) Nox gases $\rightarrow$ PAN $\rightarrow$ photochemical smog

ANSWER KEY

1	(a)	2	(d)	3	(a)	4	(d)	5	(a)	6	(c)	7	(c)	8	(d)	9	(c)	10	(a)
11	(c)	12	(c)	13	(c)	14	(a)	15	(d)	16	(b)	17	(d)						

The Living World

1. (d) 2. (b) 3. (a) 4. (d) 5. (b)
6. (c) 7. (c) 8. (a) 9. (d) 10. (c)
11. (d) 12. (a)

Biological Classification

1. (a)	2. (b)	3. (d)	4. (c)	5. (c)	15. (d)	16. (d)	17. (c)	18. (a)	19. (d)
6. (a)	7. (e)	8. (d)	9. (e)	10. (b)	20. (d)	21. (a)	22. (d)	23. (a)	24. (b)
11. (b)	12. (c)	13. (b)	14 (d)		25. (a)				

Plant Kingdom

1. (a)	2. (b)	3. (c)	4. (b)	5. (b)	16. (a)	17. (b)	18. (b)	19. (a)	20. (d)
6. (a)	7. (b)	8. (b)	9. (b)	10. (a)	21. (d)	22. (d)			
11. (a)	12. (a)	13. (b)	14. (a)	15. (b)					

Animal Kingdom

1. (b) 2. (a) 3. (c) 4. (c) 5. (d)

6. (d) 7. (b) 8. (b) 9. (b) 10. (c)

11. (b) 12. (b) 13. (c) 14. (c) 15. (d)

16. (d) 17. (c) 18. (d) 19. (a) 20. (b)

21. (a) All groups higher than Platyhelminthes have tube-within tube body plan.

22. (c) 23. (a) 24. (b) 25. (b)

5 Morphology of Flowering Plants

1. (c)	2. (a)	3. (d)	4. (c)	5. (a)
6. (b)	7. (a)	8. (a)	9. (a)	10. (a)
11. (b)	12. (c)	13. (c)	14. (d)	15. (b)
16. (b)	17. (c)	18. (b)	19. (a)	20. (b)
21. (d)	22. (b)	23. (d)	24. (a)	25. (c)
26. (d)	27. (c)	28. (d)		

29. (d) Stolons are special kind of runners, which initially grow upwards like ordinary branches and then arch down to develop new daughter plants on coming in contact with the soil. Sucker is a sub-aerial branch, that arise from the main stem. Initially, it grows horizontally below soil surface and later grows obliquely upward.

30. (a)	31. (a)	32. (a)	33. (b)	34. (a)
35. (a)	36. (a)	37. (b)	38. (d)	

Anatomy of Flowering Plants

1. (c) 2. (c) 3. (a) 4. (a) 5. (a)
6. (a) 7. (d) 8. (d) 9. (a) 10. (a)
11. (c) 12. (d) 13. (d) 14. (b) 15. (a)
16. (d) 17. (c) 18. (d) 19. (e) 20. (d)

21. (d) 22. (d) 23. (b) 24. (d) 25. (c)
26. (b) 27. (c) 28. (b) 29. (b) 30. (a)
31. (d)

Structural Organisation in Animals

1. (b) 2. (d) 3. (d) 4. (d) 5. (d)
6. (d) 7. (c) 8. (b) 9. (c) 10. (c)
11. (d) 12. (c) 13. (a) 14. (a) 15. (c)
16. (a) 17. (d) 18. (c)
19. (d) In cockroach three pairs of legs are substantially different in lengths and functions, but they have the same parts and move the same way. The upper portion of the leg called the coxa, attaches the leg to the thorax.

The trochanter acts like a kneef and lets the cockroach bend its leg. The femur and tibia resemble thigh and shin bones. The segmented tarsus acts like an ankle and foot. The look-like tarsus also helps cockroaches climb walls and walk upside down on cilings.

8   Cell : The Unit of Life

1. **(a)**   2. **(a)**   3. **(a)**   4. **(a)**   5. **(b)**

6. **(a)**   7. **(b)**   8. **(a)**   9. **(d)**   10. **(d)**

11. **(b)**   12. **(b)**   13. **(d)**   14. **(a)**   15. **(b)**

16. **(a)**   17. **(a)**

18. **(c)** The cell membrane consists of three classes of amphipathic lipids; phospholipids, glycolipids, and steroids. The relative composition of each depends upon the type of cell, but in the majority of cases phospholipids are the most abundant. In RBC, 30% of the plasma membrane is lipid. About 5% of the plasma membrane weight is carbohydrate, predominantly glycoprotein, but with some lipoprotein (cerebrosides and gangliosides).

19. **(b)** Homeostasis is the property of either an open system or a closed system, especially a living organism, that regulates its internal environment so as to maintain a stable, constant condition.

20. **(b)**   21. **(a)**

22. **(b)** The chemical substances found most abundantly in the middle lamella are released into the phragmoplast by Golgi complex. The Golgi complex synthesises polysaccharides which bring about formation of a cell plate between daughter nuclei during cytokinesis.

23. **(d)** Prokaryotes are generally smaller and differ from eukaryotic cells in terms of structural elements and genetic processes. Unlike eukaryotes, prokaryotes lack a true nucleus, a nuclear membrane and the membrane bound organelles (mitochondria, chloroplast, Golgi bodies, ER).

24. **(a)** The mechanism of ciliary movement is not completely understood. It is known that the microtubules behave as sliding filament that move over one another much like the sliding filaments of vertebrate skeletal muscle. The fluxes of Ca^{2+} across the membrane is not responsible for controlling the organised beating of cilia.

25. **(a)** Double membranes are absent in lysosomes. They are enclosed by single lipoproteinaceous unit membrane. Lysosome called 'suicidal bag' of the cell due to presence of hydrolytic enzymes.

26. **(b)** Because the membrane which surrounds the vacuoles is known as tonoplast.

Biomolecules

1. (c)	2. (c)	3. (a)	4. (d)	5. (a)	16. (c)	17. (d)	18. (a)	19. (a)	20. (a)
6. (a)	7. (c)	8. (a)	9. (d)	10. (d)	21. (b)	22. (a)	23. (b)	24. (a)	25. (a)
11. (b)	12. (a)	13. (b)	14. (b)	15. (a)	26. (c)	27. (b)			

Cell Cycle and Cell Division

1. (d)   2. (c)   3. (a)   4. (b)   5. (c)   16. (c)   17. (a)   18. (c)   19. (b)   20. (a)

6. (b)   7. (a)   8. (a)   9. (c)   10. (d)   21. (d)   22. (c)   23. (c)

11. (c)   12. (c)   13. (a)   14. (d)   15. (c)

Transport in Plants

1. **(b)** 2. **(a)** 3. **(b)** 4. **(c)** 5. **(d)**

6. **(d)** The casparian strips function in regulation of the flow of water between outer tissues and the vascular cylinder.

7. **(a)**

8. **(c)** Water is placed upwards through the plants due to transpiration. Transpiration is the loss of water in the form of water vapour through stomata. The model that explains this translocation of water is called cohesion-tension transpoiration pall model of water transport. Less than one pecent of water reaching the plant is used in photosynthesis and plant growth.

9. **(c)** 10. **(c)** 11. **(b)** 12. **(c)** 13. **(c)**

14. **(c)** 15. **(b)** 16. **(b)** 17. **(b)** 18. **(a)**

19. **(b)** 20. **(c)**

21. **(c)** Pure water has the highest water potential as zero. As water enters the cells, solute potential becomes less negative and the pressure potential is usually positive. As water enters the cell, the volume of protoplast increases, causing the pressure potential to rise from zero MPa.

22. **(b)** With increasing humidity, the rate of transpiration decreases linearly, because the high saturation of water vapour in the atmosphere prevents the evaporation of more water from the leaf interior to the exterior.

23. **(a)**

Mineral Nutrition

1.   (b)   2.   (b)   3.   (c)   4.   (a)   5.   (a)   11.   (d)   12.   (a)   13.   (b)   14.   (c)   15.   (a)

6.   (d)   7.   (b)   8.   (b)   9.   (c)   10.   (a)   16.   (c)   17.   (c)

Photosynthesis in Higher Plants

1. (d) 2. (d) 3. (b) 4. (b) 5. (b)

6. (c) 7. (c) 8. (a) 9. (a) 10. (a)

11. (c) 12. (c) 13. (a) 14. (c) 15. (d)

16. (a) 17. (a) 18. (a) 19. (d) 20. (b)

21. (c) 22. (c) 23. (b) 24. (c)

25. (d) Damage in thylakoids have direct effect on the synthesis of ATP.

26. (c) 27. (c)

28. (c) During the calvin cycle, the radioactive CO_2 is accepted by ribulose 1,5 bisphosphate (RuBP) in the formation of the first product, 3-phosphoglyceraldehyde (PGA), which will be the first compound to contain ^{14}C.

29. (c) 30. (a)

Respiration in Plants

1. **(b)** 2. **(d)** 3. **(d)** 4. **(a)** 5. **(a)**

6. **(c)** 7. **(b)** 8. **(d)** 9. **(c)** 10. **(b)**

11. **(d)** 12. **(b)** 13. **(d)** 14. **(a)** 15. **(d)**

16. **(a)** 17. **(a)** 18. **(a)**

19. **(b)** Because Kreb's cycle occurs in matrix of mitochondria.

20. **(b)**

21. **(b)** Without the electron transport system, there is the net production of only 2 ATP. With a fully functional electron transport system, an additional 36 ATP may be produced.

22. **(c)** The last step regenerates NAD^+ from NADH and H^+.

23. **(d)**

24. **(b)** One of the functions of the electron transport chain and the conversion of pyruvate to lactate is the regeneration of NAD from reduced NAD. NAD is needed in glycolysis.

25. **(a)** Glucose is converted to hexose phosphate, which is broken down to triose phosphate, which is subsequently converted to pyruvate. Pyruvate enters the Krebs cycle, producing carbon dioxide, reduced NAD and ATP. Reduced NAD enters the electron transport chain, where oxygen is reduced to water and ATP is produced.

Plant Growth and Development

1. (d) 2. (b) 3. (a) 4. (c) 5. (c)

6. (a) 7. (d) 8. (c) 9. (c) 10. (a)

11. (d) 12. (a) 13. (b) 14. (c) 15. (d)

16. (b) 17. (a) 18. (d) 19. (a) 20. (b)

21. (c)

22. (a) Abscisic acid (ABA) promotes closing of stomata under condition of water stress (wilting). ABA play a significant inhibitory role, notably during physiological stress, e.g., drought, water logging etc. Deficiency of ABA in plant cells cause wilting.

23. (b) Ethylene gas promotes senescence and is one of the by products of burning your gas grill. You should move your grill or your camellia bush.

24. (a) Short day plant generally require light period of less than 12 hours and continuous dark period of about 14-16 hours for subsequent flowering.

25. (d) Vivipary is the germination of seeds before they leave the parent plant and is caused by a deficit of abscisic acid.

16   Digestion and Absorption

1. (d) 2. (d) 3. (a) 4. (a) 5. (a)

6. (d) 7. (c) 8. (b) 9. (b) 10. (a)

11. (d) 12. (b) 13. (d) 14. (d) 15. (c)

16. (d) 17. (b) 18. (b) 19. (b)

20. **(c)** In ruminants the cellulose is fermented in stomach.

21. **(d)** Lactase digests milk sugar which will not be present in potato. However, enzymes for nucleic acid digestion are present in pancreatic juice.

22. **(c)** The level of glucose will not be effective because hormones do not pass through ducts.

Breathing and Exchange of Gases

1. (a)	2. (d)	3. (a)	4. (c)	5. (c)
6. (c)	7. (b)	8. (d)	9. (c)	10. (b)
11. (d)	12. (c)	13. (d)	14. (d)	15. (b)
16. (b)	17. (b)	18. (a)	19. (a)	20. (b)

21. **(a)** Oxygen diffuses two times faster than nitrogen, while carbon-di-oxide diffuses 20 times faster than oxygen.

Body Fluids and Circulation

1. (b)   2. (a)   3. (c)   4. (b)   9. (a)   10. (c)   11. (d)
5. (d)   6. (d)   7. (a)   8. (a)   12. (a)   13. (a)   14. (d)

Excretory Products and their Elimination

1. (c) 2. (b) 3. (b) 4. (a) 5. (d)
6. (c) 7. (c) 8. (a) 9. (d) 10. (a)
11. (a) 12. (a)

13. (a) ANF stimulates the loss of sodium in urine while aldosterone absorbs sodium from glomerular filtrate.

20   Locomotion and Movement

1. **(a)** 2. **(b)** 3. **(a)** 4. **(d)**

5. **(b)** 6. **(b)** 7. **(b)** 8. **(b)**

9. **(a)** 10. **(d)** 11. **(a)** 12. **(b)**

13. **(c)** 14. **(b)** 15. **(d)** 16. **(c)**

17. **(d)** 18. **(b)**

19. **(c)** In Gouty arthritis the uric acid salts are deposited in the synovial fluid.

20. **(a)**

21. **(a)** The epimysium is the outermost connective tissue sheath of the muscle.

22. **(c)** This joint is also known as cartilaginous joint.

23. **(a)** 24. **(a)** 25. **(d)** 26. **(a)**

27. **(c)** This membrane is also called as Z-band.

21 Neural Control and Coordination

1.	(d)	2.	(c)	3.	(d)	4.	(d)	5.	(c)	21.	(b)	22.	(d)	23.	(a)	24.	(b)	25. (b)
6.	(d)	7.	(a)	8.	(d)	9.	(a)	10.	(a)	26.	(b)	27.	(c)	28.	(b)	29.	(d)	30. (c)
11.	(d)	12.	(a)	13.	(b)	14.	(a)	15.	(d)	31.	(c)	32.	(d)	33.	(b)	34.	(c)	
16.	(c)	17.	(d)	18.	(c)	19.	(d)	20.	(c)									

22 Chemical Coordination and Integration

1. **(d)** 2. **(c)** 3. **(b)** 4. **(d)** 5. **(a)**

6. **(b)** 7. **(d)** 8. **(d)** 9. **(b)** 10. **(a)**

11. **(c)** 12. **(b)**

13. **(b)** Pheromones are also known as ectohormones.

14. **(b)** Adrenaline is secreted from adrenal medulla.

15. **(a)**

16. **(d)** Female intersexes have ovary as gonad and the secretion of male hormones can be from adrenal only.

17. **(d)**

18. **(b)** The secretion of milk in mammals also, is regulated by Prolactin.

19. **(a)** 20. **(c)** 21. **(a)** 22. **(c)** 23. **(b)**

24. **(b)** 25. **(d)** 26. **(b)** 27. **(b)** 28. **(c)**

Reproduction in Organisms

1. (d) 2. (d) 3. (b) 4. (b) 5. (c)
6. (b) 7. (b) 8. (c) 9. (d) 10. (b)
11. (b) 12. (d) 13. (b) 14. (a) 15. (c)

16. (b) 17. (d) 18. (b) 19. (a) 20. (a)
21. (a) 22. (b) 23. (a) 24. (b)

24. Sexual Reproduction in Flowering Plants

1. (c)	2. (a)	3. (a)	4. (b)	5. (b)	21. (c)	22. (d)	23. (b)	24. (d)	25. (b)
6. (b)	7. (d)	8. (b)	9. (a)	10. (b)	26. (b)	27. (b)	28. (c)	29. (c)	30. (c)
11. (b)	12. (a)	13. (b)	14. (a)	15. (d)	31. (c)	32. (b)	33. (a)	34. (c)	35. (c)
16. (b)	17. (b)	18. (c)	19. (c)	20. (a)	36. (a)	37. (d)	38. (d)	39. (c)	

25 Human Reproduction

1. (a)	2. (d)	3. (a)	4. (c)	5. (c)	16. (d)	17. (d)	18. (b)	19. (b)	20. (c)
6. (d)	7. (c)	8. (c)	9. (b)	10. (d)	21. (b)	22. (c)	23. (a)	24. (c)	25. (b)
11. (b)	12. (c)	13. (a)	14. (d)	15. (d)	26. (a) Eye lens is derived from ectoderm.				

26   Reproductive Health

1. (b)   2. (c)   3. (b)   4. (b)   5. (c)

6. (a)   7. (d)   8. (b)   9. (d)   10. (b)

11. (a)   12. (a)

13. **(a)** Foetal sex can be determined by examining cells from the amniotic fluid by looking for barr bodies and sex chromosome. The process is called amoniocentesis (amniotic fluid test).

14. **(a)** Depo-provera injections contain the active ingredient medroxy progesterone acetate, a synthetic form of naturally occurring female sex hormone 'progesterone.'

15. (c)   16. (b)   17. (a)   18. (c)   19. (b)

20. (d)

21. **(c)** Oral administration of the small dose of either progestogens or progestogen-oestrogen combinations is one of the contraceptive method used by the females. They are used in the form of tablets and hence, are popularly called 'pills'. Pills have to be consumed on a daily basis for 21 days, preferably beginning within the first five days of menstrual cycle.

It has to be stopped and after which within 7 days menstruation occurs and then the same routine must be continued till the female desires to prevent conception. They inhibit ovulation and implantation as well as after the quality of cervical mucus to prevent/retard entry of sperms. Pills are very effective with lesser side effects and are well accepted by the females. Saheli the new oral contraceptive for the females contains a non-steroidal preparation. It is a once a week pill with very few side effects and high contraceptive value.

22. **(c)** Reproductive health in society can be improved by creating awareness among people about various reproduction related aspects and providing facilities and support for building up a reproductively health society.

27 Principles of Inheritance and Variation

1. **(b)** 2. **(d)** 3. **(b)** 4. **(a)** 5. **(a)**

6. **(d)** 7. **(a)** 8. **(a)** 9. **(c)** 10. **(d)**

11. **(d)** 12. **(a)** 13. **(b)** 14. **(b)** 15. **(d)**

16. **(c)** 17. **(d)** 18. **(c)** 19. **(c)**

20. **(b)** Kappa particles are found in Paramecium and possess cytoplasmic inheritance, also called extra-chromosomal inheritance.

21. **(d)** 22. **(c)** 23. **(c)** 24. **(a)** 25. **(c)**

26. **(a)** 27. **(d)**

28. **(d)** This disease is the result of sex-linked recessive genes. As neither man nor woman shows signs of disease, woman could be the carrier for disease causing gene. In their children none of the daughter is suffereing from disease, while the sons are suffering, it means daughters are carriers, *i.e*, X-linked recessive.

Suppose, genotype of man = XY

Genotype of woman = X^dX

(d-disease causing gene)

The probability for each combination is 25%. So, among seven children, 2 normal daughter 3 diseased sons and 2 normal sons are possible.

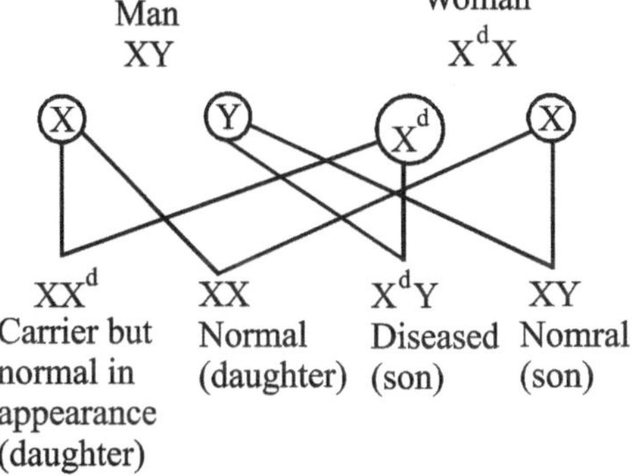

29. **(a)** 30. **(a)** 31. **(b)** 32. **(a)**

33. **(d)** Epistasis is the interaction between non-allelic genes in which one gene masks the expression of other gene. The gene that suppresses the other gene known as epistatic factor and the one, which is prevented from exhibiting itself, known as hypostatic.

34. **(a)**

35. **(a)** Persons having blood group O are universal donors as they lack both the antigens and Rh^- person can donate to Rh^+ person as well as Rh^- person but Rh^+ person cannot donate blood to Rh^- person.

36. **(a)** In the absence of 'B' allele, the B-antigen can not develop in the child.

37. **(d)** 38. **(a)**

39. **(b)** Mongoloid idiocy is due to trisomy of 21st chromosome.

40. **(c)** 41. **(a)** 42. **(c)** 43. **(b)**

28 Molecular Basis of Inheritance

1. (d)   2. (d)   3. (c)   4. (a)

5. (b) tRNA or transfer RNA is a single stranded molecule and takes the shape of a clover leaf. In the process of transcription tRNA brings amino acid and reads the genetic code and acts as an adapter molecule. In the given structure of tRNA, the labels A, B, C and D are respectively AA binding site (amino acid binding site), T C loop, anticodon loop (codon recognition site) and DHU loop (amino acid recognition site).

6. (d)   7. (a)   8. (b)   9. (c)   10. (d)

11. (d)   12. (c)   13. (c)   14. (d)   15. (a)

16. (d)   17. (d)   18. (c)

19. (a) The replication time for *E coli* is about 20 minute. That's way the DNA extracted after the interval of 20 minutes so that heavy N^{15} can be incorporated in its genetic material.

20. (b) Operons are segments of genetic material which function as regulated unit or units that can be switched on and switched off. An operon consists of one to several structural genes. (Three in lac operon)

    These are genes which produce mRNAs for forming polypeptides / proteins / enzymes. Z (produces enzyme β galactosidase for splitting lactose into glucose and galactose). Y (produces enzyme galactoside permease required in entry of lactose) A (produces enzyme thiogalactoside trans- acetylase).

    The three structural genes of the operon produce a single polycistronic mRNA.

21. (b)

22. (a) Neomycin is the antibiotic which inhibits the translation of bacterial cell so that it can not affect the host cell.

23. (b)

24. (c) Okazaki fragments in DNA are linked up by the enzyme DNA *ligase*. Replication always ocur in 5' - 3' direction. Okazaki fragments synthesized on 3' - 5' DNA template, join to form lagging strand which grows in 3' - 5' direction.

25. (d) The process of formation of protein sequence from DNA strand is called transcription which requires RNA polymerase chain. RNA polymerase chains are of 3-types in eukaryotes

    (i) RNA polymerase-I

    (ii) RNA polymerase II

    (iii) RNA polymerase-III

26. (c)

27. (b) The figure below is the replicating fork of DNA. The DNA replication takes place in 5′ to 3′ direction always. On the leading strand DNA replication is continuous while on lagging strand DNA replication is discontinuous. The polarity of lagging strand is incorrect in the given figure. The correct figure should be

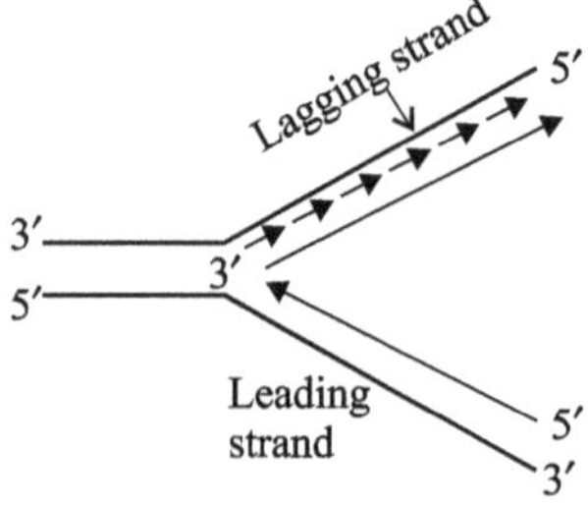

Both the strands are antiparallel. In one strand carbon of sugar are in 3′ – 5′ direction and in other the carbon of sugar are in 5′ – 3′ direction.

28. (d)   29. (d)   30. (b)

31. (b)

$$\text{DNA} \xrightarrow{\;A\;} \text{mRNA} \xrightarrow{\;B\;} \text{protein} \xrightarrow{\substack{\text{Proposed by} \\ C}}$$

In this question A is transcription, B - translation C - Francis Crick (central dogma) It is unidirectional flow of information DNA to mRNA (transcription) and then decoding the information present in mRNA in the formation of polypeptide chain or protein (translation).

32. (a)

33. (b) β-gal is primarily responsible for the hydrolysis of the disaccharide lactose into its monomeric units, galactose and glucose. It is coded by Z structural gene.

34. (a) The promoters are bacterial and viral genes usually containing a consensus sequence of 5'-TATAAT-3' that forms RNA polymerase binding site or the Pribnow box named after its discoverer. Pribnow box lies in within the promoter about 10 base pairs before the starting point of transcription.

35. (d) Erwin Chargaff (1950) made quantitiatve analysis of DNA and showed that the compositon of DNA molecules varies in ways that depend upon the source of DNA. He proposed the Base Equivalence rule or Chargaff's rule, which states that adenine is always equals to that of thymine and proportion of guanine always equals to that of cytosine,

i.e. $A = T$ and $G = C$.

It follows that, an equal proportion of purines and pyrimidines is always seen in a double-stranded DNA, i.e

$$A + G = T + C \text{ or } \frac{A+G}{T+C} = 1$$

36. (b) Bidirectional flow of information. In some viruses, formation of DNA occurs from RNA. This takes place by a special enzyme called reverse transcriptase or RNA dependent DNA polymerase. The following image is a representation of central dogma after the discovery of reverse transcriptase.

Evolution

1. (d)	2. (a)	3. (b)	4. (d)	5. (a)	16. (d)	17. (c)	18. (d)	19. (c)	20. (b)
6. (c)	7. (c)	8. (b)	9. (c)	10. (a)	21. (d)	22. (b)	23. (d)	24. (a)	25. (a)
11. (c)	12. (d)	13. (b)	14. (a)	15. (a)	26. (b)	27. (b)	28. (a)	29. (c)	30. (c)
					31. (c)				

Human Health and Disease

1. (b)	2. (c)	3. (c)	4. (a)	5. (c)	21. (d)	22. (c)	23. (a)	24. (d)	25. (c)
6. (a)	7. (c)	8. (a)	9. (a)	10. (c)	26. (b)	27. (d)	28. (b)	29. (d)	30. (d)
11. (c)	12. (a)	13. (a)	14. (a)	15. (b)	31. (a)	32. (c)	33. (a)	34. (c)	
16. (a)	17. (d)	18. (c)	19. (d)	20. (a)					

Strategies for Enhancement in Food Production

1. **(d)**   2. **(b)**   3 **(b)**   4 **(d)**   5. **(a)**

6. **(c)**   7. **(c)**   8. **(d)**   9. **(b)**   10. **(c)**

11. **(b)**

12. **(c)** Use of only disease free seeds and use of disease resistant varieties are the most important control measures that could be taken to successfully grow chickpea in an area where bacterial blight disease is common.

13. **(a)** The plant hormone, auxin is more distributed on the side away from the unilateral illumination causing cells to grow faster in the darkerside, which in turn, causes the plant to bend toward the light. If the distribution were equal, the plant would grow just upwards. Neuro-transmitters are chemicals secreted by multicellular animals and are used in transmitting impulses in the nervous system.

14. **(b)**   15. **(c)**   16. **(b)**

17. **(c)** A horse (Equus ferus caballus) and a donkey (Equus africanus asinus) can breed to produce mule, which is an infertile animal. The infertility is because horse and donkey belong to different species.

18. **(b)**   19. **(c)**   20. **(a)**   21. **(c)**   22. **(d)**

23. **(d)**   24. **(a)**

25. **(d)** Low nitrogen, sugar and high aspartic acid in maize stem borers.

26. **(c)** During somatic hybridization, naked protoplasts from different species are brought tugether and allowed to fuse in the presence of fusogens. This technique is used to overcome the incompatibility between unrelated plant species.

27. **(b)**   28. **(b)**   29. **(c)**   30. **(b)**

32 Microbes in Human Welfare

1. (a) 2. (a) 3. (d) 4. (c) 5. (a)

6. (a) A-heart, B-Streptococcus. Streptokinase is an enzyme obtained from the cultures of some haemolytic bacterium Streptococcus and modified genetically to function as clot buster.

7. (a) 8. (a) 9. (c)

10. (d) Trichoderma harzianum has proved a useful microorganism for biological control of soil borne plant pathogens. Trichoderma harzianum is a fungus that is also used as a fungicide. It is used for foliar application, seed treatment and soil treatment for suppression of various disease causing fungal pathogens. Commercial biotechnological products such as 3 Tac have been useful for treatment of *Botrytis, Fusarium, Penicillium sp.* It is also used for manufacturing enzymes.

11. (a) 12. (b) 13. (b) 14. (d) 15. (d)

16. (b) 17. (a) 18. (d)

19. (d) Clostridium butylicum is used for butyric acid production.

20. (d) 21. (b) 22. (c) 23. (b) 24. (d)

25. (d) 26. (d) 27. (a) 28. (a)

Biotechnology : Principles and Processes

1. (d) 2. (c) 3. (d) 4. (c) 5. (b)

6. (c) 7. (a) 8. (a) 9. (c) 10. (c)

11. (a) 12. (c) 13. (a) 14. (d)

15. (b) Plasmid Circular - extrachromosomal DNA

Bacteriophages - Virus infecting bacteria

Cosmids - Hybrid vector derived from plasmids

Agarose - Natural polymer of D - galactose

16. (c) Arber, Nathan and Hamilton Smith - Isolated first restriction endonuclease from bacteria

Paul berg - Father of genetic engineering

Herbert Boyer and Stanley Cohen - First recombinant DNA

Karl Erkey - Term biotechnology

17. (c)

18. (b) c DNA probes are copied from the mRNA molecules with the help of reverse transcriptase.

19. (c) 20. (c) 21. (c)

22. (d) Structural genes and their products in lac operon are as follow:

DNA	lac p / t	lac o	lac z	lac y	lac a	t
$-40-11$	1111	26	3063	800	800	
mRNA	lac i mRNA	mRNA for lac genes		(z, y, a)		
Polypetide	60 3800	1021 125,000		275 30,000	275 30,000	amino acids daltons
Active protein	tetramer 152,000	tetramer 5000,000		monomer 30,000	dimer 30,000	daltons
function	repressor	b-galactosidase		permease	transac-etylase	

Lac Z (3063bp): This gene codes for the enzyme β-galactosidase which breaks operon into glucose and galactose. Therefore, *E.coli* cells with a mutated Z genes of the lac operon cannot grow in a medium containing only lactose as the source of energy as they cannot synthesize functional β-galactosidase.

23. (a) 24. (d) 25. (a) 26. (d)

27. **(b)** Human Genome Project (HGP) is closely associated with the rapid development of a new area in biology called Bioinformatics which is used for storage and analysis of enormous amount of data.

28. **(c)** **29.** **(d)** **30.** **(a)** **31.** **(b)**

32. **(b)** **33.** **(d)** **34.** **(d)** **35.** **(a)**

36. **(a)** **37.** **(c)**

38. **(b)** Interferons are antiviral proteins which were produced by "Charles Weismann" (1980) by recombinant DNA technology in *E. coli*.

39. **(d)**

40. **(c)** *EcoRI* - *Escherichia coli RY13*

  HindII - *Haemophilus infulenzae*

  BamHI - *Bacillus amyloliquefaciens*

  EcoRII - *E. coli R 245*

41. **(a)** Sticky ends are also called cohesive ends. They easily form hydrogen bonds with their complementary counter parts.

42. **(b)** E - Name of genus

  co - Name of species

  R - Name of strain

  I - 1st in order of identification

34

Biotechnology and its Applications

1. (b) 2. (b) 3. (d) 4. (a) 5. (b)
6. (d) 7. (d) 8. (b) 9. (b)
10. (a) Gene therapy - Effort to fix functional gene
Humulin - Diabetes
Probe - A single stranded DNA of RNA tagged with a radioactive molecule
11. (b) 12. (a) 13. (b) 14. (d) 15. (a)
16. (c) 17. (a) 18. (d) 19. (c) 20. (a)
21. (c) 22. (c)
23. (a) Vitamin B_2 (Riboflavin) is an essential nutrient for humans and animals that must be obtained from the diet. Accordingly, it is usually included in fortified foods and multivitamin supplements The production of riboflavin by microbial fermentation is an example of biotechnology using different cell factories such as *Bacillus subtilis*, *Candida flareri* and, especially, *Ashbya gossypii* . About half the world production of riboflavin is obtained through the fermentation of *A. gossypii* strains.
24. (d) 25. (c) 26. (a) 27. (c) 28. (c)
29. (c) 30. (c) 31. (a) 32. (b) 33. (d)
34. (d) 35. (b)
36. (c) Patients suffering from SCID have defective genes for the enzyme Adenosine Deaminase (ADA). Functional T-lymphocytes are missing thus making them prone to infections.
37. (a)

Organisms and Populations

1. (1) 2. (1) 3. (3) 4. (1) 5. (1)

6. (4) 7. (3) 8. (1) 9. (4) 10. (1)

11. (4) 12. (2)

13. (a) Within biological communities, some species may be important in determining the ability of large number of other species to persist in the community. These crucial species are known as key stone species. Allopatric species are species having exclusive areas of geographic distribution. Sympatric species are species having overlapping area of geographical distribution.

14. (c) 15. (b) 16. (b) 17. (a) 18. (c)

19. (a) 20. (b) 21. (d) 22. (b)

Ecosystem

1. **(a)** 2. **(b)** 3. **(a)**
4. **(d)** Nitrogen and carbon cycle.
5. **(d)**
6. **(d)** Burning of wood, forest fire, volcanic activity and combustion of organic matter and fossil fuels area are some essential sources for releasing CO_2 in the atmosphere.
7. **(d)** 8. **(c)** 9. **(a)** 10. **(b)**
11. **(a)** Scavengers - Consumers of dead bodes
    Parasites - Consumers that feed on a small part of a living being
    Producers - Autotrophs
    Phagotrophs - Heterotrophs
12. **(c)** *Leaves → Aphids → Ladybird → Robin → Snake → Hawk*
    Leaves → Snail → Pigeon → Hawk
13. **(a)** There is some sort of relationship between the numbers, biomass and energy contents of the producers and consumers of different orders in any ecosystem. These relationship, when represented in diagrammatic ways, are called ecological pyramids. Ecological pyramids are of three types.
    (i) Pyramid of number
    (ii) Pyramid of biomass
    (iii) Pyramid of energy
    The concept of pyramid was proposed by Charles Elton (1927) so, they are also called as Eltonian pyramids.
14. **(c)** 15. **(a)** 16. **(b)**
17. **(b)** Inorganic substances - Carbon, nitrogen, oxygen and water.
    Organic compounds - Proteins, carbohydrates, lipids and nucleic acid.
    Climatic factors - Light, temperature and humidity.
    Edaphic factors - Soil, pH, minerals.
18. **(a)** 19. **(d)** 20. **(a)** 21. **(a)** 22. **(a)**

23. **(d)** Population consists of organisms of same species, community have organisms of different species and ecosystem include biotic and abiotic components. Ecosphere is part of the earth consisting of all the ecosystems of the world.
24. **(c)**
25. **(b)** Primary consumer : That eats autotrophs.
    Secondary consumer : A meat eater that eats primary consumers.
    Tertiary consumer : A meat eater that eats secondary consumers.
    Quaternary consumer : A meat eater that eats tertiary consumers.
26. **(a)** There is some sort of relationship between the number, biomass and energy contents of the producers and consumers of different orders in any ecosystem. These relationships, when represented in diagrammatic ways are called ecological pyramids. The concept of pyramid was proposed by Charles Elton (1927) so, they are also called as Eltonian pyramids.
27. **(c)** Primary succession – Colonisation of a new environment
    Climas community – Community that has completed succession
    Pioneer community – Crustose lichen on lithosphere
    Ecological – Ecosystem development succession
28. **(c)** First trophic level - Phytoplankton
    Decomposer – Bacteria
    Primary productivity – Producer
    Secondary productivity – Consumer
29. **(a)** 30. **(b)**
31. **(c)** Xeroseres: Ecological succession start on terrestrial habitat
    Hydroseres: Succession begins from open water
    Lithoseres: Succession starts on a bare rock.
    Psammoseres: Succession begins on sand.

Biodiversity and its Conservation

1. (d) 2. (d) 3. (d) 4. (c) 5. (d)
6. (d) 7. (a) 8. (d) 9. (d) 10. (d)
11. (d) 12. (d) 13. (d) 14. (a) 15. (a)
16. (b) 17. (d)

18. (d) The transition zone of biosphere reserve is also known as manipulation zone.

19. (c)

Environmental Issues

1. **(a)** According to Central Pollution Control Board (CPCB), particulate size 2.5 micrometres or less in diameter (PM 2.5) are responsible for causing the greatest harm to human health. These fine particulates can be inhaled deep into the lungs and can cause breathing and respiratory symptoms, irritation inflammations and damage to the lungs and premature deaths. Failure of testosterone secretion causes eunuchoidism.

2. **(d)** All automobiles and fuel were to have met the Euro III emission specification in eleven Indian cities from 1 April 2005 and have to meet the Euro IV norms by 1 April 2010.

3. **(a)**

4. **(d)** Chlorofluorocarbons and Freon cause depletion of ozone layers.

5. **(a)** 6. **(c)** 7. **(c)**

8. **(d)** Suspended Solid - Sand, silt and clay Colloidal Materials -Faecal matter, bacteria, paper and cloth fibres Dissolved Materials- Nitrates. ammonia phosphates, sodium and calcium

9. **(c)**

10. **(a)** Global agreement in specific control strategies to reduce the release of ozone depleting substances was adopted by the Montreal protocol. The treaty was originally signed in 1987 and substantially amended in 1990 and 1992. The Montreal protocol stipulates that the production and consumption of compounds that deplete ozone in the stratosphere-chlorofluoro-carbons (CFCs), halogens, carbon tetrachloride, and methyl chloroform– are to be phased out by 2000 (2005 for methyl chloroform).

11. **(c)** 12. **(c)**

13. **(c)** According to Centrol Pollution Control Board (CPCB) particulate size 2.5 micrometers or less in diameter are responsible for causing various breathing and respiratory problems. They can also cause irritation, inflammations, damage to the lungs and premature deaths. It cannot directly enter circulatory system but indirectly through respiratory system.

14. **(a)** 15. **(d)** 16. **(b)**

17. **(d)** The Major reason or source which depletes ozone hole is chlorofluorocarbon and aerosols. CO_2 is the major gas responsible for green house effect. Acid rain is caused due to oxides of sulphur and nitrogen.

www.ingramcontent.com/pod-product-compliance
Lightning Source LLC
LaVergne TN
LVHW072159150726
843469LV00056B/2248